D1398958

New Strategies for Educational Development

Fourteen of the seventeen papers in this volume were originally presented at three seminars on nonformal education held by the Education and Human Resource Development Panel of the Southeast Asia Development Advisory Group (SEADAG) of The Asia Society, New York. The first seminar met in Washington, D.C., the second in Penang, Malaysia, and the third in Seoul, Korea. The Penang seminar was jointly sponsored by SEADAG and the Southeast Asia Ministers of Education Organization (SEAMEO); the Seoul seminar by SEADAG and the Korean Central Education Research Institute.

The Asia Society, a nonprofit educational institution, was founded in 1956 to enhance American understanding of Asia and Asians and to stimulate meaningful intellectual exchange across the Pacific. Within this framework, SEADAG, which is at present funded by the United States Agency for International Development, seeks to promote and facilitate communication and collaboration among Asian and American scholars and policy makers concerned with development in Southeast Asia.

New Strategies For Educational Development

**The Cross-Cultural Search
For Nonformal Alternatives**

Cole S. Brembeck
Timothy J. Thompson

Institute for International Studies
College of Education
Michigan State University

Lexington Books
D.C. Heath and Company
Lexington, Massachusetts
Toronto   London

Library of Congress Cataloging in Publication Data

Main entry under title:

New strategies for educational development.

Selection of papers originally presented at 3 international seminars, sponsored by SEADAG, held in Washington, D.C., May 1971 and Penang, Malaysia and Seoul, Korea, October 1971.

1. Education — Aims and objectives. 2. Education and state. 3. Under-developed areas — Education. 4. Educational innovations. I. Brembeck, Cole Speicher, ed. II. Thompson, Timothy J., ed. III. Southeast Asia Development Advisory Group.

LB41.N43   370   72-14138
ISBN 0-660-86306-8

Contents

Lists of Figures and Tables   vii

Preface   xi

Introduction, *Cole S. Brembeck*   xiii

Part I   **The Character of Nonformal Education**

Chapter 1   Human Resources and Nonformal Education   5
                Frederick H. Harbison

Chapter 2   Frontiers of Out-of-School Education   13
                Archibald Callaway

Chapter 3   Fostering and Inhibiting Factors   25
                C. Arnold Anderson

Part 2   **Locating Educational Functions**

Chapter 4   Are Formal Schools the Best Place to Educate?   41
                Marvin Grandstaff

Chapter 5   The Strategic Uses of Formal and Nonformal Education   53
                Cole S. Brembeck

Chapter 6   Nonformal Educational Alternatives   65
                Rolland G. Paulston

Part 3   **Nonformal Education and Individual Change**

Chapter 7   The Role of Occupational Experience   87
                Alex Inkeles

Chapter 8   Individual Modernity and Nonformal Education   101
                F. B. Waisanen

Chapter 9   Designing Effective Learning in Nonformal Modes   111
                Ted Ward, Lois McKinney and *John Dettoni*

Part 4   **Issues in Planning Nonformal Education**

Chapter 10   Who Gets What When Education is Deformalized?   129
                James F. Guyot

Chapter 11   Elements of an Action Program   137
              John F. Hilliard

Chapter 12   How Shall We Plan Nonformal Education?   145
              Philip H. Coombs

Chapter 13   Economic Evaluations of Nonformal Education   159
              Einar Hardin

Part 5   **Comparative Programs**

Chapter 14   Nonformal Education in Korea: 175
              Programs and Prospects
              Hyun Ki Paik

Chapter 15   The "Shadow School System" in Peru   185
              Rolland G. Paulston

Chapter 16   National Training Schemes   195
              Frederick H. Harbison and *George Seltzer*

Chapter 17   A Land Grant University's Program in Appalachia   207
              Willis H. Griffin

              About the Contributors

List of Figures

8-1   A Two-Dimension Conceptualization of Individual   102
           Modernity

List of Tables

6-1 Some Modal-defining Characteristics of Nonformal
     and Formal Educational Programs   66

8-1 Impact of a Nonformal Educational Program upon
     Adoption of Some Recommended Practices in
     Agriculture, Health, and Social Education   104

8-2 Correlates of Knowledge and Adoption in Costa Rica   106

8-3 Prediction of Total Knowledge and Adoption in Costa
     Rica by StepWise Multiple Regression Analysis   107

15-1 Supply and Demand for Industrial Manpower in 1965   187

Preface

A word about the origin of these chapters may be in order. During 1971 the senior editor of this volume had the pleasure of assisting in planning and directing three international seminars on the subject of nonformal education in his capacity as chairman of the Panel on Education and Human Resource Development of the South East Asia Development Advisory Group (SEADAG), a program of the Asia Society of New York. The seminars were sponsored by SEADAG, with financing from the Agency for International Development. The meetings were held in Washington, D.C., in May and in Penang, Malaysia and Seoul, Korea in October. The Penang seminar was held in joint cooperation with the South East Asia Ministers of Education Organization (SEAMEO), whose Secretariat is in Bankok. The Korean seminar was held in cooperation with the Central Education Research Institute, Seoul.

All three seminars brought together leading American and Asian scholars and practitioners interested in nonformal education. Altogether over fifty papers were prepared for the three semianrs. Fourteen of the seventeen chapters of this volume were selected from this group. The other three were chosen because they fill particular gaps in the subject. We wish to acknowledge our gratitude to these three authors and their sponsors: Archibald Callaway and the International Institute for Educational Planning in Paris for chapter 2, Marvin Grandstaff and the Agency for International Development for chapter 4, and Rolland Paulston for chapter 15, reprinted with permission from his book *Education in Peru*.

We wish also to express our gratitude to Charles McVicker of SEADAG for his good counsel and to our secretaries, Debbie Ensign and Ruth Hefflebower, for their great assistance in the preparation of the manuscript.

Finally, we wish to thank the authors of these chapters for their permission to include them in this volume and their patience with us in bringing them to publishable form.

Cole S. Brembeck
Timothy Thompson

Introduction

The debunking of the schooling "myth" in our own society is at full throttle. Where it will end or how it will alter conventional schooling is not yet clear. The persistent calls for deschooling, the search for alternatives and cries for radical reform all have potential for changing educational institutions. Precisely how they will be changed is difficult to predict. This much does seem clear: the impression is widespread and growing that formal schools fall far short of our needs and expectations and that they are ripe for change. One change that seems to be taking place is to shift more learning experiences outside the formal schools to other settings of a less formal character — in short, to nonformal education, the concern of these chapters.

The new interest in nonformal education is an act of rediscovery. Historically, schools as we know them are relatively newcomers on the human scene. The act of learning, however, is as old as man himself. The human environment has always provided the stuff of learning, and the continuity of cultures testifies to the effectiveness with which men learn from one another.

Currently we are gaining a new awareness of just how much we do learn outside the formal schools and how important it is to our livelihood and well-being. The child's preschool years in the family set his basic attitudes and values. Even after he enters school his out-of-school hours in the home, with peer groups, and outside organizations are powerful teachers. Later, he enters the world of adult responsibilities and work. How he gets on in this world depends in no small measure upon his access to learning opportunities on the job and in the community and how he makes use of them. If we were able to quantify the relative impacts of school and out-of-school learning, it is quite likely that school-learning would fade into insignificance. Not that formal education isn't crucial, especially in its contribution to making men both literate and modern. It simply falls far short of making men whole, and whole men emerge from lifelong learning experiences, most of them in settings outside the formal schools. Our search for alternatives, not surprisingly, is hastening the rediscovery of the nonformal world of learning and how it may be utilized more effectively.

The intensity of the educational turmoil within our own country has left us largely unaware of what is happening elsewhere or what the comparative experience of others may do to help illuminate our own problems and our search for alternative futures for education. The chapters of this book take as their prime reference that portion of earth known sometimes as the developing world, where dedication to education is high, resources to support it low, and the demands to develop persistent. In this world there is growing recognition that conventional schooling is becoming too costly, frequently too ineffective, and that alternatives must be found which provide more effective learning opportunities for more people at less cost.

In short, the educational concerns of the developing nations are not unlike our own. And, as we hope the chapters of this book make clear, there is some profit for us in studying this experience. In doing so not uncommon responses are: "how like our own problems!" and "why didn't we think of that?" The result is an expanding view of educational development and change and an appreciation of the interlocking relationship of matters educational across national and cultural boundaries.

What are some of the conerns which have brought the nations of the Third World to think seriously about developing and expanding their programs of nonformal education? Here are some of them.

Decreasing Resources and Expanding School-Age Populations. Most developing nations have made gallant efforts to extend educational opportunity by the simple, linear expansion of their existing formal school systems. But the harder they try the farther they seem to fall behind. The reasons are manifold, but two stand out: (1) rampant population growth, and (2) rising costs, coupled frequently with diminishing resources. The result is that in many nations of the developing world the absolute numbers of school-age children out of school is actually increasing. New, less costly ways to educate must be found. One attractive area for exploration is nonformal education.

Equity. Formal education the world over tends to provide access to elite positions and power. Those who are denied educational opportunity tend also to be denied opportunities for upward mobility. The demands for equal educational opportunity are as loud and persistent in the developing societies as they are in our own. If formal education cannot be expanded rapidly enough to meet the demands, can nonformal education help to widen the narrow paths to learning? The possibility that it can has an understandable appeal.

The Need for Educational Innovation. Is establishment education capable of reforming itself? That question is being raised with increasing frequency by development planners. Bureaucratic encrustations tend to stifle change, and the record of ministries and departments of education in creating truly new educational programs and environments is on the dreary side.

Nonformal education programs tend not to be part of large bureaucratic arrangements, are typically smaller in scale, arise to meet a specific need, go out of existence when the need is filled, and have a variety of sponsoring organizations. It would seem that these qualities would enable nonformal education to be more flexible and innovative than formal education and to enable it to respond in more appropriate ways to new educational demands. The chapters of this book explore this possibility in a variety of ways.

Maximizing the Benefits of Formal Education. Formal education represents a very heavy investment in people development, not infrequently as much as 20 percent of national budgets. Much of this investment is used in the education of children in the early primary grades where droupout rates tend to be very high. This investment is lost unless other learning opportunities are made available to pick up where formal schools leave off. This applies also to high school and even college and university graduates. The need to create lifelong learning opportunities can partially be met by well thought-out plans of nonformal education which plan in terms of life spans rather than school years.

Newer Conceptions of Development. Traditionally, gross national product (GNP) has been used as the sole criterion for measuring the development of a country. If the GNP were on the rise, the country's economic future was bright — or so it was thought. If the BNP were stagnant or falling there was trouble ahead.

Now there is growing skepticism whether GNP, by itself, is an adequate measure of development, especially as it relates to human well-being and happiness. A high and rising GNP, experience in a number of countries suggests, does not necessarily guarantee a wider spread of economic benefits or greater human welfare. Nor does it necessarily lead to greater political stability, more employment, better health care, and stronger village communities.

Human measures like these are now coming to be seen as being equal in importance with GNP as indices of development. The spread of benefits throughout the population, the eradication of poverty, the improvement of health-care systems, and the opportunities to participate meaningfully in civic and community affairs are all now coming to be regarded as necessary measures of development.

The role of nonformal education in these newer aspects of development can be great. The capacity of nonformal education to meet specific needs, as for example in public health education, population control, agriculture production, and village improvement makes it a useful tool of people development.

Doubts About Certification. The certifying functions of schools is widely accepted and practiced. Holders of school certificates, diplomas, and degrees are presumed to be qualified to undertake the nation's work. Now the questions are being asked: "Are they?" and, "for what are their holders really certified?" In many cases, it turns out, school graduates are certified only to undertake more schooling. Whether they are prepared to undertake the development work which the nation urgently needs is too frequently a matter left to chance.

Nonformal education programs suggest the possibility of shifting certification to the arena of performance and as a reward for learning to do important developmental tasks. Such certification would be work, employment, and service-oriented and would be given not as preparation *for* something but as a reward for actual accomplishment. Nonformal education programs are admirably suited to this purpose.

Perhaps a word about our use of the term *nonformal education* in this book would be in order. Such a broad, amorphous term obviously needs some parameters placed around it. Even then it is hard to get hold of. As Harbison comments, "getting hold of nonformal education is a little like trying to get hold of apple sauce. Put your hand in the bowl and you don't come up with much."

The chapters of this volume do impose certain conditions on the term. The largest, loosest parameter is that nonformal education deals with those learning activities that take place outside the formally organized educational system with its hierarchy of grades leading all the way from preschool to graduate and professional school. Included, however, are nonformal programs which are sponsored by formal educational institutions. Second, these chapters deal with purposeful attempts to educate toward some *specific goals*, under the sponsorship of an *identifiable person, group,* or *organization.* Thus excluded are the powerful educational influences of family and other informal groups such as street corner gangs. The thrust of these chapters, further, is toward the use of nonformal education in some aspects of employment. In some cases that means preparation for employment, in others skill improvement through on-the-job training.

In respect to its relationship with formal education, nonformal education is assumed to act in several ways. First, it may substitute for formal education for those who are denied it. Second, it may complement formal education, performing other tasks not performed by formal education. Third, nonformal education may extend formal education and, as we said earlier, maximize its usefulness.

The movement of the book through its various parts is intended to be an orderly presentation of important themes pervading the consideration of nonformal education. The parts begin with a consideration of the character of nonformal education and end with examples of programs in selected countries, including one from our own. Part 1 delineates the character of nonformal education by examing its gifts for dealing with human resource development in ways beyond the capability of formal schools. The impression that emerges is that of a huge resource for educating people which is probably grossly underutilized. In order to keep nonformal education in balanced perspective, Part 1 also offers an essay of caution dealing with fostering the inhibiting factors in nonformal education.

Part 2 raises two questions of great importance, which surprisingly are frequently ignored: "Why do we usually end up placing educational functions in school?"; and "Why do we tend not to assign some of them elsewhere?" The chapters come at the question from several perspectives. One is historical. It is important to know how it is that formal schools came to be overloaded with all kinds of responsibilities when other reasonable options for educating people were available but went unexplored and unused.

Another way to come at the matter is to ask: given the two modes of education, formal and informal, what are the unique capabilities of each? Is formal education, by its very nature, better at performing certain functions that others? What are the unique capabilities of nonformal education? Raising questions like these permits us to venture some points of view about the strategic uses of formal and nonformal education.

The question remains, of course, about the actual experience of nations that have assigned educational functions to agencies outside the formal schools. This question is examined in the concluding chapter of Part 2.

There is a great temptation in discussing nonformal education to stay at the abstract level and neglect individual human change. How do nonformal educational experiences influence individual behavior? Considerable thought has been given to the influence of formal education on persons, but how about nonformal education? This important issue is explored in three different ways in Part 3. First, we examine the role of work as nonformal teacher, especially work in a modern-oriented institution such as a factory. The modernizing influences of this experience are reported to be almost equal to those of attendance in school. Second, we examine the influence on individuals of nonformal education programs, in this case radio forums. The results of an experiment are reported. Finally, the ultimate influence of nonformal education on individual change depends upon the effectiveness of the learning environment. This matter is carefully explored in the concluding chapter of Part 3.

Part 4 enters the arena of issues in planning nonformal education. The first issue tackled is that of "who gets what?" when education is deformalized. The politics of nonformal education is as urgent an issue as it is in formal education. Some seminal questions about it are raised by the first chapter of Part 4.

Programmatically, the test of a nonformal education program comes in action and implementation. Designing the action to achieve the educational goal is a topic of deep interest, and it is perceptively explored in the second chapter of Part 4. A discussion of the whole range of planning problems associated with nonformal education follows, with special emphasis upon linking nonformal education into a reinforcing system of learning. The final chapter of this part raises an unavoidable question: economically, is nonformal education worth it? Does it pay off? Do its benefits exceed its costs? These questions come under review in the concluding chapter of Part 4.

Part 5 is intended to round out the book with actual cases describing nonformal education programs. They span a number of countries and are of quite different types. In them nonformal education comes alive, not in one form, but many, and its real potential for lifting educational perspectives and practice begin to become apparent.

Education in the future is less likely to be thought of as being the exclusive franchise of public schools and will more likely find free expression in "schools of the public," open, available upon demand, accessible at any stage in life. both work and happiness oriented, and dedicated to releasing the natural joy of learning so widespread among human beings. The chapters of this volume explore but one path to this exciting educational future. We think it is an important path. It will likely lead somewhere.

Cole S. Brembeck

Part 1
The Character of Nonformal Education

Introduction to Part 1

In developing countries the search for alternatives to schools has been precipitated by a growing awareness of the immensity of the educational task facing them and by a realization that schools alone are not an adequate means of meeting their educational needs. Attempts by these countries to expand school enrollments cannot keep up with exploding populations and the resulting increasing press for schooling. They have neither the financial nor the human resources to meet the demands. Moreover, the output of the schools is frequently not congruent with the human resource needs of developing societies. Rigid social structures, set attitudes toward schooling, and the inertia of the schools themselves make it difficult to change education in order to meet these needs.

And even if schools could be changed, the assumption that most education should take place in them is being challenged by those who are searching for nonformal alternatives to schools. Their search may have as its immediate goal finding an alternative to some existing school program, but as more nonformal programs are discovered and developed, and as their importance is realized, some persons are trying to stand back and gain some perspective on the "heterogenous conglomeration of unstandardized and seemingly unrelated activities" which make up nonformal education. They are trying to recognize instances of nonformal education and to classify them according to some scheme. But more than mere classification is aimed at. Any characterization of nonformal education should help identify links between formal and nonformal education and links between nonformal education and the total environment.

The three chapters that follow represent attempts to survey the scene of nonformal education in cross-cultural perspective. They cite examples of nonformal education; they examine, characterize, and classify it from different vantage points, and while the authors overlap in their considerations, they also diverge and even disagree in their conclusions.

National youth service programs, rural adult education centers, and mobile trade training units are some of the programs discussed. They illustrate a diversity in both scope and structure characteristic of nonformal education. Such programs also raise questions about organization, effectiveness, and cost.

In chapter 1 Harbison defines nonformal education as a residual — all the skill and knowledge generation that has been accomplished apart from the schools; he approaches the subject with the perspective of a national planner and sees the task as one of providing a more rational structure for the diverse activities which make up nonformal education. In the second chapter Callaway describes the array of learning activities going on outside formal schools and their many links with formal education through common goals and shared resources. His description also indicates some of the purposes of out-of-school education, as well as problems faced in planning nonformal education. It is the educational planner's perspective that dominates Anderson's chapter. To speak of planning nonformal education, from Anderson's perspective, is misleading; he asserts that we simply do not know how to produce an integrated system of education and development. The best that can be done is to expedite, especially by economic incentives, the provision of training, and to coordinate the supply and demand for skills by the same means.

Many typologies of nonformal education can be constructed. Callaway suggests several possibilities and presents a typology whose first division is by the age of the target group — young people and adults; these two are further divided according to the relation between learning and work — prejob learning, on-the-job learning, and learning not directly related to work and according to the subjects' previous education — those with formal schooling and those without. Harbison's typology is similar to this, but Anderson finds no need for presenting a breakdown of nonformal programs. He is concerned with expediting existing programs by seeing that they function in a more open and free skill market.

No educational program can be adequately understood apart from its milieu; this is especially true for systems as complex and diffuse as nonformal education programs. And no planning of such programs, if indeed such planning is possible, can take place in isolation, for some of the most important aspects of an educational program are its links with other institutions of society. From the vantage point of nonformal education, the most important of these links are those with the formal educational system and with the world of work. All the authors agree on the importance of integrating the educational system; nonformal education is not intended to replace formal schools, but, as Harbison points out, it has some unique functions, such as adult literacy programs, that formal education cannot properly discharge.

1

Human Resources and Nonformal Education

FREDERICK H. HARBISON

Human resource development is concerned with two systems of skill and knowlege generation: formal schooling and nonformal education and training. In most countries formal education connotes age-specific, full-time classroom attendance in a linear graded system geared to certificates, diplomas, degrees, or other formal credentials. Formal education is thus easily defined — its administration and control in most developing countries is lodged in a ministry of education; its costs are measurable; and its outputs are easily identified.

In contrast, nonformal education, which is probably best defined as skill and knowledge generation taking place outside the formal schooling system is a heterogeneous conglomeration of unstandardized and seemingly unrelated activities aimed at a wide variety of goals. Nonformal education is the responsibility of no single ministry; its administration and control are widely diffused throughout the private as well as the public sectors; and its costs, inputs, and outputs are not readily measurable. Nonformal education is perhaps one of the most "unsystematic" of all systems, yet in most developing countries its role in generating skills, influencing attitudes, and molding values is of equal, if not greater, importance than formal schooling. Indeed, perhaps most of man's development takes place routinely and often unconsciously through learning-by-doing, being instructed or inspired by others to perform specific tasks through association and communication with others or simply by participation in a community or in a working environment.

Nonformal education may be classified under three broad categories: (1) activities oriented primarily to development of the skill and knowledge of members of the labor force who are already employed; (2) activities designed primarily to prepare persons, mostly youth, for entry into employment; and (3) activities designed to develop skill, knowledge, and understanding that transcend the work world. These three categories may be illustrated by examples:

1. The category of programs for development of employed manpower would include such activities as these: agricultural extension, farmer training centers, rural community development services, on-the-job training of craftsmen in all kinds of construction, in-service training in manufacturing and commercial enterprises as well as government agencies, labor education conducted by trade unions, apprenticeship arrangements, and most "learning-by-doing" activity in trade, marketing, cooperatives, and social and political organiza-

tions. Here the training may take the form of learning by trial and error, acquiring experience by intermittent or casual instruction, organized training classes, or systematic task rotation.

2. Activities designed to facilitate access to employment would include youth brigades, village polytechnics, mobile training units, counseling, vocational training in the military, and other programs to build skills for entry-level jobs. These activities may be alternatives for, or extensions of, formal education in primary, secondary, or vocational schools.

3. Activities not specifically related to labor force participation would include adult literacy programs, nutrition and health clinics, homemaking classes, family planning, and a wide range of political education schemes. In this category we would also include radio programs, newspapers, speeches, discussions, and day-to-day palaver from which we learn and acquire information.

The activities listed above are illustrative rather than definitive. Some are obviously relevant for all three functions of preparation for employment, development-in-employment, and building of skills and knowledge not directly connected with the working world. Farmer training centers, village polytechnics, and adult literacy programs are perhaps cases in point. But in the aggregate the skill and knowledge generating capacity of nonformal education is enormous. Without such activities, the production of goods and services would grind to a halt and the resources devoted to nonformal education, in time, energy, and other outlays are extensive.

The arguments for greater emphasis on nonformal education in development policy are cogent and compelling. First, the formal schooling system is becoming prohibitively expensive. High rates of population increase are swelling the school-age population. The laudable desire to upgrade the qualifications of teachers and to improve the quality of education by lowering student-to-teacher ratios leads to sharp increases in per-pupil expenditures. The pressure for expansion of the more expensive formal education at the secondary, vocational, and higher levels magnifies further increases in costs. Nonformal education may offer, in many areas, a less costly and more attainable alternative.

Second, at least for the next two or three decades, very large proportions of the school-age population in many countries will have little or no access to any kind of formal schooling. This is, of course, in addition to the vast majority of adults presently without schooling. If one of the goals of modernization is to make every individual a "learning-station," then nonformal education may be the only means of filling the gap between the "schooled" and "unschooled" population.

Third, nonformal education may be one means of counterbalancing some of the distortion created by formal education. To a considerable extent, formal education establishes the gateways to positions of wealth, status, and power. It issues entry passes in the form of certificates, diplomas, and degrees to a privileged minority; it blocks access to those without the proper credentials. But competence and learning are very often poorly measured by credentials. Achievement-oriented, nonformal education may provide the means for growing numbers of competent but "uncredentialed" people to reform the requirements for entry.

Fourth, in part because of its heterogeneity, disorganization, and lack of central direction and control, nonformal education affords greater opportunity for innovation than the often encrusted formal education establishment. This may have strong appeal both to the dispensers of external aid as well as to local statesmen who become impatient in their attempt to reform educational systems.

Finally, one may argue that without nonformal education the benefits of formal schooling will not be fully realized. Education, indeed, is a continous lifetime process. Skills and knowledge generated in the formal schooling process may atrophy without the stimulation, extension, and enrichment provided by postschool, nonformal educational activity. In short, the continuation of human skill and knowledge generation over a lifetime may be one of the best ways of maximizing the returns on initial investment in formal schooling.

In theory it would be desirable for every country to make a complete inventory of all nonformal education, to evaluate the usefulness of each separate activity, to plan extension and improvement of the most promising programs, to estimate their costs and benefits, and above all to build a strategy for integration into a more logically consistent and better functioning system of the motley assortment of unrelated activities. Such a master plan of nonformal education would be ideal. But few countries are able to undertake so comprehensive and time-consuming a task.

The more realistic approach is probaly a sector-by-sector analysis, concentrating selectively on a relatively small number of clearly defined but strategic leverage points for investigation and effort. The possible leverage points are many, and they would differ from country to country. Here, a framework for analysis may be useful, and a few examples may clarify possible approaches.

In some cases nonformal education performs unique functions that lie completely beyond the reach of formal schooling. In others, the nonformal activities may be an alternative to, or substitute for, learning in the graded school curricula. In most cases, perhaps, nonformal and formal education may be complementary and reinforcing. Here, the benefits accruing from effective integration of the nonformal systems may be greater than the sum of the individual returns to each.

In examining nonformal education, planners should pose central questions such as these:

1. Can nonformal education activities satisfy educational needs that cannot be met by the formal education system?

2. Are nonformal education projects, because of their flexibility in comparison

with the rigidities of formal education, more susceptible to innovation?

3. Do successful innovations in nonformal education induce desirable innovations in the formal education system?

4. To what extent, if any, do nonformal education activities have better ratios of cost-effectiveness than formal education?

It is very difficult to answer such questions. However, they do show clearly the need for incorporation of evaluation mechanisms in present and future programs. The "tracing" of the participants in all programs would, in itself, help to provide at least partial answers.

Unique Functions of Nonformal Education

Unskilled and semiskilled workers in factories or construction are most easily trained on the job. The skill and knowledge of farmers are best generated through extension and/or farmer training centers. Almost by definition, adult literacy programs are beyond the range of age-specific, graded schooling. The same is true of nutrition, health, or family-planning education. In this general area, the leverage points are to be found in better organization, coordination, and direction of related activities.

A plan for development of rural adult education centers in Kenya is a good example. Here the Board of Adult Education, in collaboration with the Ministries of Cooperatives, Social Services, Agriculture, Health, Commerce and Industry, Information and Broadcasting, Local Government, and Economic Planning and Development, has evolved a concrete blueprint for multipurpose training centers at the district level which will provide facilities to both government and voluntary agencies to plan, integrate, and implement a number of related adult education activities. The centers, each with a resident director and staff, will determine priorities, coordinate rural educational activities at the district and subdistrict levels, and facilitate the execution of programs. They would provide for maximum involvement of the local community in building programs directly related to the special Rural Development Projects which are being established as an outgrowth of the Kericho Conference. They would thus constitute the apex of all rural extension and nonformal educational activity. This plan, essentially an extension of the farmer training center concept, raises many practical problems of interagency cooperation. But at least it is an attempt to rationalize the delivery of much needed rural services.

Nonformal Education as an Alternative to Formal Schooling

The training of craftsmen for modern sector activity poses another set of problems. For the most part, electricians, carpenters, masons, fitters, and automobile mechanics are trained in employment, either through apprenticeship arrangements or by some less formal means of learning on the job. But they can also be produced under a graded curriculum in formal vocational schools. Many ministries of education have attempted to "vocationalize" their secondary school systems either by building more technical schools or by establishing "comprehensive" secondary schools with vocational streams. Here the assumption is that craftsmen, foremen, and even technicians are best produced in a formal system. The area of greatest leverage for development planners lies in a careful analysis of the trade-offs and the optimal mixes between the two systems.

The training of automible mechanics, as a typical case, illustrates the range of possible choices. In all developing countries there is a shortage of automobile mechanics in the sense that there are unfilled jobs at prevailing wage levels. Most young people learn the trade as apprentices in small garages and shops as described by Callaway.[1] The indigenous apprencticeship system could be improved by organizing training extension services to the garage owners, as well as by organized off-duty training classes in the principal towns or cities. The major distributors of automobiles and trucks are better producers of mechanics. They could be required, or encouraged by subsidies, to train a surplus beyond their immediate need in their own service department. Preemployment formal training in vocational schools is another, and probably the most expensive, alternative. Combinations of all three avenues of training might in the end provide the most effective solution.

The training of building craftsmen presents a similar range of alternatives. The central problem is not what should be learned, nor even the techniques of teaching. The critical issue is the organization of training activity and allocation of responsibílity for carrying it out. In most developing countries, the ministries of education, the labor departments, and the employing institutions pursue their independent courses, often at cross-purposes. Perhaps only in the ministries of planning is there hope of building a strategy for a rational allocation or resources.

The organization of "training pools" has great potential as a leverage device. Here groups of employers may pool resources to provide common training services to meet their common needs. In the Latin American countries a tax levy on payrolls of all employers above a specified size provides ample funds to support central training organizations which provide both institutional and on-the-job training services. Many African and Asian countries are now considering various kinds of employer tax levy schemes as means of financing and organizing nonformal training activities for modern sector industrial and commercial enterprises. Training pools have very important advantages: (1) they are extremely effective in tapping funds for training beyond the resources allocated by governments for formal education; (2) they provide services more closely related to employer needs than formal vocational schools; (3) they place responsibility on employing institutions for the training function. And in many, though not all, cases they can provide services at relatively low costs. It is quite possible, indeed, that training pool systems, as an alternative to formal vocational schools, may become the centerpieces for training semiskilled and skilled craftsmen in many developing countries.

There are, of course, other possibilities in most countries. The Mobile Trade Training Unit System in Thailand is one example.[2] Another is to force, or to induce by subsidy, large corporations to train craftsmen beyond their own needs. Our argument is that in nearly every developing country there are alternatives to formal education which should be carefully investigated.

Nonformal Education as an Improvement-Factor in Formal Education

Nonformal education has great potential for improving the formal education system. It can magnify those benefits which accrue from formal schooling, and in many cases it may lead to changes in the orientation of schools, technical institutions, and universities. The closer integration of nonformal and formal education may in the long run win the highest returns of all programs for human resource development. The list of possible leverage points is almost endless, but a few of the more obvious are mentioned here.

Technician training requires both theoretical education and practical experience. Shared-time arrangements between working on-the-job training and formal instruction in technical institutions are proving to be effective in many countries. An outstanding example is the Kenya Polytechnic Institute where all students are sponsored by their employers. At the Haile Selassie I University in Ethiopia all students are required to spend one university service year doing practical work in government offices, schools, or business enterprises. In other cases, university students may serve internships as research workers on development programs. Many countries require secondary school or university graduates to serve time in national service. In others, youth brigades are set up to provide practical retraining for school dropouts. Most of these programs, to be sure, have shortcomings both in orientation and practical organization, but with better planning and implementation they may have great potential for the generation of more development-oriented, high-level manpower.

Perhaps the most productive area of all for better integration of formal and nonformal education is development of more effective cadres of rural service workers. Agricultural extension assistants, suppliers of rural inputs (fertilizer, seeds, tools, etc.), cooperative managers, and marketing experts all require considerable preemployment formal education. At the same time, they need refresher training, information about changing technologies and markets, exchange of experience in "teaching" farmers, and other kinds of continuing skill and knowledge development. Here, nonformal education, which can build upon the formal, may have the highest payoff of any program of rural development. Yet, by and large, the universities have neglected this function. Ministries may have inadequate resources to perform it. Thus new organizations or the revitalization of old ones are worth serious consideration.

Summary

In summary, the range of activities in nonformal education is vast. The resources already invested in them are very considerable in the aggregate. Their contribution to national development is far-reaching. In some cases, nonformal education is the only practical means of skill and knowledge development; in others, it offers an alternative, and often a more effective one, to education and training in formal schooling; in most cases, it can supplement, extend, and improve the processes of formal education. The formulation of a strategy for development of nonformal education is no easy task. An initial step would be to identify the principal target groups, to specify the actual and possible roles of both formal and nonformal education in their development, to evaluate alternatives, and to select "leverage points" where more concentrated efforts would have the highest payoffs. The cost-effectiveness of these efforts should be objectively analyzed by systematic tracing of the employment and career pathways of persons who have participated in the various programs.

Notes

1. Archibald Callaway, "Nigeria's Indigenous Education: The Apprenticeship System," *ODU, 1, No. 1* (July 1964) :67-69.

2. Vocational Education Department, Ministry of Education, *Mobile Trade Training Units,* 1969 Report, Bangkok, Thailand.

2 Frontiers of Out-of-School Education

ARCHIBALD CALLAWAY

Broadening the Field of Educational Planning

Planning for Nationwide Learning

Much progress has been made, particularly in recent years, in research on systems of formal education and their development. The more urgent problems have been identified. Methodologies for analyzing these problems have been created. Substantial results are now on hand and are being applied in many countries within the process of educational planning.

An area of research for educational planning that has been relatively neglected, however, is out-of-school education — that is, the array of learning activities going on outside schools and universities. These include programs of literacy for youth and adults who have had little or no formal schooling; apprenticing and on-the-job training; in-service training and continuing education for those with professional qualifications; extension programs for agriculture and small-scale industries; and a wide range of educative services designed to encourage community development, improved health, and better living.

To some extent, research on formal education itself has revealed the significance of out-of-school learning processes. For example, efficient performance in specific occupations requires differing proportions not only of formal education but also of specialized training and experience. The contribution to this long-term educational process by schools and universities, on the one hand, and by programs of out-of-school education, on the other, needs to be more closely examined. New priorities may well emerge.

Again, investment in out-of-school education is a substitute for, or an extension of, investment in conventional schooling. Thus certain problems in the use of resources and of curriculum within formal education cannot be adequately dealt with unless there is a more systematic understanding of the objectives, the content, as well as the costs and returns, of out-of-school education.

Research on out-of-school education is particularly vital for educational planning in developing countries. Here rising populations against backgrounds of low average economic productivity, poor general health, ineffective communica-

13

tions, often marked ethnic differences, present special problems. Out-of-school educational arrangements have often arisen in piecemeal fashion to meet special problems, such as to provide literacy courses for those who have had little or no classroom experience. Organizers of community development have set up educative services as a means of awakening groups of people to the possibilities of self-help. Since developing nations have scarce resources of finance and of teaching and administrative abilities, research is urgently required that can lead to improved balances among public and private investments in education of all kinds, geared to national objectives for development.

While some attention has been given to specific types of out-of-school education (including the efforts of the United Nations specialized agencies), little attempt has been made to look at out-of-school education as a whole to discern its dynamics in meeting the needs of changing societies and to see its complementary links with formal schooling at all levels, thus bringing it within a comprehensive strategy of educational planning. Such planning for nationwide learning is the opposite of exclusive; its premise is to involve everyone — farmers, herdsmen, artisans, women traders, families, entire villages.

It is the purpose of this chapter to map the frontiers of out-of-school education in developing countries, to indicate its purposes, to suggest lines of research, and to draw attention to problems of planning and coordinating individual and overall programs.

Lessons from the 1960s.

The present determination to explore the processes of out-of-school education derives mainly from experiences during the 1960s in expanding systems of formal education. Although substantial progress was made, difficulties — some foreseen, others not adequately predicted — were encountered.

During the period of 1950 through 1965 enrollments at the three main levels of formal education in developing countries nearly tripled. The push began at the primary level where enrollments grew from 57 million to 137 million during the fifteen years. Then, with increasing numbers coming to the secondary level, the demand for expansion there raised enrollments from 1.5 million pupils in 1960 to 5.8 million in 1965. During the same period students in postsecondary schools and universities increased from 1 million to 3.5 million.

These achievements should be noted. Millions of children throughout the less-developed nations have entered schools as the first representatives of their families. At the same time, universities in Africa, Asia, and Latin America have turned out doctors, scientists, engineers, lawyers, social scientists. Vast numbers of teachers have been trained. In general, the greater number of educated people now permeate whole societies with a heightened readiness to take on development tasks.

Even so, there is still a long way to go toward universal primary education.

Today in Africa only some 40 percent of school-age children attend schools; in Asia, 50 to 60 percent; in Latin America, 50 to 60 percent. This means that about half the children in these areas do not have the opportunities to enter classrooms and are not likely to get any formal schooling.

It is well known that this period of unprecedented educational expansion brought with it many problems. In many countries the sharp rise in educational costs went far beyond the figures estimated. On the average, the share of national budgets now being devoted to formal education amounts to 16 percent. Over a dozen countries allocate as high as 25 percent of their government expenditure to education. Between 1960 and 1965 the annual rate of growth of educational expenditures was 13 percent in Asia, 16 percent in Africa, and over 20 percent in Latin America. When private and local government expenditures are added to central government outlays, then the amount developing countries are spending on formal education comes to around 4 percent of their national incomes.

Another serious result of such rapid expansion was a drastic fall in quality in many countries. There are substantial inequalities among regions within countries and between rural and urban areas not only in school facilities available but also in the quality of education imparted in classrooms. Now a period of consolidation is taking place with emphasis on upgrading the abilities of teachers, improving school administrations, and providing better teaching materials.

Inefficiencies have been revealed. Perhaps the most awkward one is the high number of dropouts. Children start school and then after a few years fade away. In developing countries as a whole, only 30 children out of an initial 100 stay the course and complete primary schooling. Clearly, resources are not being well utilized.

By far the most serious problem, however, is the emergence of widespread unemployment among school leavers. This employment problem of the young educated appears to run the whole length of the outputs of formal education systems with clusters at different levels and of varying types for different countries. Educational systems are not sufficiently in harmony with the difficulties of developing economies in absorbing educated youth into productive work. Given that such a small proportion, usually between 10 and 20 percent, of primary school leavers go to secondary schools, the problem of lack of jobs is especially critical among younger people. The result is teenage idleness and discontent.

With populations rising at between 2 and 3 percent each year, nations are finding difficulty in providing the school places for the increasing numbers of children coming forward. This situation is made more acute by rising unit costs of education. As a consequence, the goal of universal primary education, along with higher proportions of children in secondary schools, is still far off. In fact, for many countries, it is hard to imagine how all school-age children can be in schools by the end of the century.

Fresh solutions are being called for. Unless these solutions can be decided upon and put into effect, most of the next generation of adults, like the present generation, will not gain the modern knowledge and the specific skills required to create healthier family lives, transform the economies, and cure the malaise of rural societies.

The first approach is that formal education be more closely related to national objectives and to the urgencies of local communites. The quality of the learning needs to be improved, and the wastage of the high number of dropouts reduced. But whatever modifications are made within formal education, the problem still remains of the vast numbers who will grow up without attending schools at all.

What more can be done? What is now required is the strengthening of existing out-of-school programs and the introduction of well-designed new — and, if need be, radical — programs. These programs complement formal school and university classes either by substituting for them or by extending them. They should be designed to bring new knowledge and skills to masses of young people and adults and make a direct and low-cost contribution to development — especially in the rural areas, where most people in developing countries live.

Such emphasis on out-of-school education does not mean reducing the importance attached to formal education. It simply asserts that learning experiences should be expanded and made available to a much larger proportion of the population. And, as far as possible, this buildup of out-of-school programs should be supported by national and local financial resources not available to formal education.

Characteristics of Out-of-School Education

Main Features

Each developing nation has a large number of out-of-school learning activities. These have arisen from special historical and cultural circumstances as well as from contemporary social and economic organization. Certain common characteristics of these activities account for special problems in planning out-of-school education.

1. The diverse types of out-of-school education are designed to accomplish many purposes. They do not comprise a "system" but rather unrelated and uncoordinated "sub-systems" which coexist with and compliment the system of formal education.

2. The boundary is a shifting one between what may be considered as formal education and these many complementary types of education. (For example, vocational training centers, started by voluntary agencies or individuals, have later been brought under public direction within the system of formal education.)

3. Responsibility for the running of out-of-school educational institutions is diffuse, consisting of public control (by a variety of ministries or departments of central and local government, statutory corporations, military establishments), private control (by firms, voluntary associations, individuals), or combinations of these.

4. Some out-of-school educational institutions are closely disciplined with regular timings for instruction and with modern technology, equipment, and texts. Others are less well disciplined, irregular, and have less modern instructional materials.

5. Methods of instruction also vary: from personal confrontation between the teacher and learning group to the use of radio and television, mobile training units, demonstrations, correspondence courses, visual aids.

6. The relative emphasis on theory and practice differs in the varied programs of out-of-school education. So, too, the ages at which people are involved as learners, the prerequisites for the courses, the length of courses, the timing (many, but not all, are part-time), and whether classrooms are used. Almost all are based on voluntary attendance (an exception perhaps being military technical training).

7. Unlike the formal, graded system of education (with its diplomas, certificates, degrees), out-of-school education has fewer programs leading to such widely-recognized credentials.

8. Teachers may be specifically trained for their tasks (as, for example, of functional literacy) or have only professional qualifications that do not include training as teachers (field officers of agricultural extension).

9. Documentation — on enrollments, teachers' and leaders' credentials, successes of those involved in learning, their consequent increased economic productivity or improved well-being, and the costs to the learners and the sponsors — is rare.

10. Investment in particular types of out-of-school education may have more pronounced effects on economic productivity and social change in the short run (for example, courses of learning while working) than is the case with formal schooling. Opportunities for such out-of-school education, however, may fluctuate (for example, with industrial or commercial firms where on-the-job training may depend on the state of business activities).

11. The greater number of programs for out-of-school education are conducted close to where young people and adults live and work. Such programs thus integrate well with specific educational deficiencies within the local community. They are also likely to be flexible, beginning when most required and ending when no longer needed, as indicated by the demands of the work process.

12. Because of nearness to the points of use, out-of-school education makes a vigorous contribution to national development. Its role in passing on

knowledge, creating skills, and influencing personal values is considerable.

Links with Formal Education

1. By providing opportunities for continued learning, out-of-school education enlarges the benefits derived from formal education. It preserves literacy and extends other disciplines of schools and universities. It may also provide practical experience after theoretical knowledge gained in formal schooling.

2. Out-of-school education makes it possible for some pupils (early dropouts, for example) to reenter formal schools or, at least, promotes a higher payoff from the formal education they have received.

3. Successful innovations within out-of-school education processes could be taken up within formal schooling.

4. Out-of-school education can share facilities of schools (for example, literacy classes for adults using buildings and equipment during off-school hours).

5. Out-of-school education may contribute directly to school lessons (for example, agricultural extension officers giving instruction on local farming practices; health officers giving talks on special topics).

6. As part of their degree requirements, university students may participate with government field officers in bringing extension services to rural producers.

7. Especially in rural areas, there is considerable potential for mobilizing educated persons (voluntary or paid, part-time) to bring out-of-school education to large numbers of people at low cost (for example, literacy campaigns).

These and other links between education in schools and universities, on the one hand, and out-of-school education, on the other, serve to blur the edge of the overly severe separation usually made (or implied) between these two main educational processes.

Types of Out-of-school Education

Basis for Classification

Meaningful typologies of different kinds of out-of-school education can be achieved. They depend, however, on the purpose in mind and may be constructed by alternative procedures.

Categories could be created, for example, according to the following criteria, or combinations of them: (1) occupational groupings of those who receive the instruction (administrators, teachers, other professionals, craftsmen, farmers, etc.); (2) succession of learning experiences (general education, prevocational, on-the-job, in-service career advancement); (3) institutions which provide the education (how controlled, i.e., by government, voluntary organization, other private initiatives; or by description, i.e., rural training centers, home economics institutes, industrial in-service training etc.); (4) length of out-of-school education processes (short or long courses, continuous); (5) material taught (general, technical, civic); and (6) whether programs are directly or indirectly related to employment creation and to immediate prospects of enhancing economic productivity.

For present purposes, two main categories are used: "Out-of-School Education for Young People" and "Out-of-School Education for Adults." These groupings have the virtue of being broadly consistent with the focus of major problems in developing countries and also with current practice within UNESCO.

Out-of-School Education for Young People

More than half of today's school-age children in poor countries receive no sustained formal schooling. They gain education in the traditional manner. While growing up, they learn the values and responsible behavior sanctioned by their communities and they receive specialized vocational training through customary apprenticeship patterns. But this may not be an education leading to pronounced social and economic improvement. What types of modern out-of-school education can best supplement the traditional learning these children receive in their homes and villages?

Where formal education has been established, new problems emerge: the impact of modern schooling within the setting of customary work and social life in villages, stepped-up migration of youth from rural areas to towns and cities, the aspirations of these job-seeking school leavers. The populations of many cities in the developing nations are rising at 6, 8, or 10 percent a year; the consequent problem in human and financial terms is added to this by infusion of jobless educated youth from the countryside. What part can out-of-school educative activities take in providing skills to enable jobless school leavers to take up existing jobs or self-create new ones?

Both in rural and urban areas, group activities (such as youth clubs, young farmers' clubs, apprentice guilds) promote leadership, awareness of civic responsibilities, and may be slanted towards vocational improvement. How can these group activities be spread more widely? And, in the last decade, to meet the problems of large numbers of unemployed and relatively untrained youth, programs for national youth service have been started in countries of Africa, Asia, and Latin America. These provide general, civic, and technical education while allowing for organized, disciplined contributions by youth to national development through community service, chiefly in the rural areas. What are the costs and returns of these programs compared with alternative ways of achieving the same, or better, results?

Out-of-School Education for Adults

Both those who have substantial formal education and those who have little or none are served by their programs. For adults engaged in professional work and in other skilled occupations, there are types of continuing education given by short courses, in-service training, and correspondence which help to keep them in touch with contemporary advances in their fields. Such courses for teachers have a strategic importance in heightening the quality of formal education.

In the developing countries, the majority of programs for adults are devoted, necessarily, to those with little or no schooling in the belief that economic productivity in the short run can be raised by such education — particularly when directed to improving work performances of farmers and small-scale entrepreneurs. These programs include literacy instruction and, following the direction of UNESCO in recent years, functional literacy courses, which combine learning to read with acquiring improved techniques in specific occupations. There are also courses, usually short-term, for farmers and artisans as well as extension services which reach them at their places of work.

Finally, there are the educative services in rural and urban areas devoted to the creation and improvement of community programs for social and economic development. These may be run by the participants themselves, by local or central governments, voluntary organizations, or by combinations of these. They include training in planning and carrying out projects such as building market stalls, community meeting halls, access roads, maternity clinics. For women, there may be instruction in health, sanitation, nutrition, and childcare.

This out-of-school education for community improvement has evolved from the obvious fact that since no government can provide the amenities so sorely needed by local communities, economies in the spread of available resources can be achieved through programs which step up local enthusaism and organization for self-help and which permit a closer, creative alliance between local communities and governments.

Relations among These Programs

The categories, Out-of-School Education for Young People and Out-of-School Education for Adults, obviously are not exclusive. There are numerous interactions among the varied programs.

For example, the rise in economic productivity — as well as the possibilities of job creation — arising from a program of out-of-school education that lifts the abilities of young workers will depend, in part, on the presence of other factors of production, such as on the skills of adult workers (along with physical capital available to work with).

Again, programs for adults in health, nutrition, and civic education would be expected to improve the well-being of youthful members of their families, including attitudes to work and society.

Similarly, programs that raise the competence of family farmers and small-scale businessmen will improve the performances of young people dependent upon them (whether on the farm, on local building site, transport, in markets), through instruction, by imitation, "learning by doing."

Out-of-School Education: Planning and Research

By broadening the field of educational planning to include out-of-school education, a new set of tasks makes its appearance. This concluding section sets out some of these tasks and indicates research objectives that must be taken up if the tasks are to be accomplished.

Identifying and Classifying Programs that Exist

The main programs of out-of-school education should be identified and classified so as to reveal patterns within their diversity. The target groups ought to be identified by age, occupation, and place or residence. Planning procedures can then be developed to analyze the interrelations among programs of formal and out-of-school education. All this has to be done to better achieve social and economic goals, but it is still subject to the constraints imposed by limited resources. The 'systems analysis' approach may be helpful in performing these complex tasks.

Establishing Priorities

The contributions of existing programs and their crucial areas of impact in accomplishing the nation's development objectives must be determined along with the dimensions of the nation's education gap. Strategies to overcome these educational deficiencies among both young persons and adults, at the work place, in the home, and in local society must be devised so that some out-of-school programs can be selected for priority attention.

Evaluating Present and the New Programs

Given limited time and data, suitable methods for appraising the efficiency and productivity of out-of-school education must be selected and careful attention given to their application so as to achieve correct program design and proper use. Tracing the subsequent performances of participants at the work place and within local society is one example of such methods. Particular programs may warrant fuller case studies using cost-benefit analyses to reap detailed lessons from their experiences. In light of the results from these evaluations, some experiments should be undertaken and innovations applied to modify and transform out-of-school education so as to achieve better results from public and private expenditures. Alternative models of teacher-learning situations to bring better results should be tried, and the educational potential of various media should be exploited. The benefits of programs presently provided for "the few" must be widely diffused so as to reach "the many" whose needs are equally great.

Administering and Coordinating

Having determined how out-of-school programs are being administered at present, the coordination of these should be improved by such strategies as shifting responsibility for administration from one agency to another and by improved coordination of educational activities at the local level. Existing weaknesses in administrative procedures and methods and in planning must be identified. And since the productivity of each particular program of out-of-school education depends on complementary investments, planning and administering projects specific to local areas must be improved so as to better integrate local development plans, especially in rural areas.

Voluntary participation in out-of-school education must be encouraged. This will require some changes in the structure of wages and incomes to give participants opportunities and incentives to put into practice the benefits of their learning.

If prices are to reflect priorities of national and local development, subsidies and changes in tariffs may be necessary to reduce the costs of inputs to high-priority programs of out-of-school education. Full administrative opportunities must be taken to ensure that successful innovations in out-of-school education induce desirable changes in schools and universities.

Sources of Finance

Present sources (public and private) of finance for formal and out-of-school education must be determined and additional sources of finance made available for expanding out-of-school education so as not to deplete funds for formal education. The division of future responsibilities between public and private sources in financing out-of-school education may differ from the division within

formal education. Self-generating finance made possible by heightened productivity consequent upon out-of-school education should be considered, and
points where external assistance would be most helpful and productive — bearing
in mind the desire for encouraging local capacity and self-reliance — should be
identified.

3

Fostering and Inhibiting Factors

C. ARNOLD ANDERSON

Whenever we attempt to assess the worthwhileness of any kind of education, especially if it is one of the less conventional sorts, we have to ask how schooling or training fits into or contributes to growth, however growth be defined.[1] Even after we have surveyed the main variants of nonformal education, we must go on to demonstrate our appreciation of the fact that it is not the content of education but the use made of it by the recipients that determines how much the training will contribute to development. The data supplied by Harbison and Myers[2] indicate that while GNP is unrelated to the proportion of college students who study science or technology, income levels are fairly closely associated with the proportions of employed workers who possess such skills; in short, an economy finds the supply of the kinds of technicians that it is prepared to utilize productively. Many efforts have been made recently in this country to compare the "rate of return" to technical training (at secondary or junior-college level) with that from academic education; some vocational programs do pay off better, but these are exceptions and the basis of their superiority usually eludes the investigator. Meanwhile, for generations, as we all know, employers have been operating varied and extensive training programs that enhance the earning power of workers who have received only a conventional "common schooling"[3] Recurring in the controversies on this topic is a yearning for someone to show us how to provide the appropriate balance in dual education (academic and specialized) while making sure that tax-supported schooling for most individuals will be terminal. Nevertheless, we face the possiblity that going to school will become our largest occupation, while employers also will be forced to expand their on-the-job education as rapidly as costs for the conventional system of schools rise.

I come now to a working definition of nonformal education. I qualify the predominant notion that nonformal education is what goes on outside of the regular school system by classifying formal vocational programs or schools in the nonformal category — thinking of course of the preuniversity schools. Just because they are formalized, often cut off from the world of work, and extraordinarily expensive for the public fisc, whether to have in-school practical courses has to be reasoned out by the same logic and evidence that is used in assessing on-the-job training or agricultural extension programs. Accordingly, I construe nonformal instruction[4] as that which is conducted outside the conventional "academic" or "college-bound" courses.

The Demography of Primary-School Leavers

Conviction that we can devise more appropriate forms of education arises not solely from a desire to obtain economic growth; nor is it an expression only of our reputed gadget-mindedness. Due to spread of mortality-reducing technology,[5] vast armies of youth flow out of the schools and only a minor part of each cohort in most countries can count on finding a regular job that will pay in hard cash.[6] The large proportions of each age cohort who receive very little or no schooling are in an even worse situation.

The oft-quoted figures for Tanzania illustrate the cruel impasse that in many countries has resulted from sluggish economic growth combined with buoyant school enrollments. Less than 50% of the cohort enter any school; a 20% finish elementary school; and less than 3 percent enter a secondary school. Even though the proportions do vary among countries, nevertheless over much of the world, while the percentage of the population who are literate or are attending school rises, the *numbers* remaining illiterate or unschooled do not shrink. If the government is unusually compliant in expanding postelementary places in schools or tolerates "voluntary" schools, the situation is not improved.[7] The entrants to secondary school may multiply, but this is only to present the nation with demands a few years hence for some kind of college places for the expanded army of applicants. Yet the always better-trained graduates can only slowly count on much if any improvement in employment outlook, even if the untrained graduates are disregarded in the calculations.

Unfortunately, the "Western" prejudice that academic education should be given the most prestige is one of the most dramatic "demostration effects" in countries striving to launch into development.[8] The schooling that leads to elite positions preoccupies the attention of those who manage the educational system. These managers are likely also to spend much energy in making sure that "irregular" schools do not become back entries to the higher levels of the most prestigious sector of education. Yet the goal is to supply training that is aligned with the opportunities to contribute to a rising level of living in a society.[9] That goal is most likely to be reached if there is a diversified system of openings for unconventional training and particularly if venturesome educational entrepreneurs are allowed to respond to the hard-cash demands for many new varieties of training.

How Education Fits into Development

The usefulness of any educational agency depends upon the milieu of supporting or countervailing influences amid which the schools are operating. In the same manner, a skill is more productive when combined with other skills or nonhuman factors of production in the best available manner. Correspondingly, there is substitutability among the various educational influences in a given situation.[10]

I identify six main functions of schools in a society; their relative weight varies with time and place and with the aspect of society with which we are concerned: (1) schools always help to prepare individuals to do part of the work on which the society subsists; (2) schools instruct in nonoccupational "specialties" (such as organizational leadership); (3) while extending and perpetuating the educational system itself, "modernization" presupposes that many kinds of both old and new intellectual systems become incorporated into a society's culture; (4) schools enable children to develop new conceptions of their own identity and of their potentialities while at the same time redefining traditional loyalties and fostering loyalties to new kinds of groups and to new kinds of activities; (5) those especially capable individuals who become members of the "elite" are in part identified and selected by the schools, and (since "modernization" is also in part "westernization") the schools form part of the media by which whole new systems of thought and action come to be exemplified by a nation's leaders; (6) everywhere schools continue the primordial function of indoctrinating youth with values appropriate to the future that the society's leaders are striving to bring to birth.[11]

Few of the "new nations" have been so fortunate as to possess that extra-school world of technological stimuli and other incentives for "achievement" that were so pervasive in the now-developed socities. Though expectations of what schools can do are heightened by the many media that today are purveying the message of "development," few of the societies now striving to develop are pervaded by either in-school or auxiliary facilities for implementing those hopes for rising popular welfare. Most societies, then, must avoid putting too many burdens upon their schools, even if no financial ceilings constrain their efforts.

Any attempt to explain in a few pages how education contributes to development would produce an overly dense exposition. It may be more lucid therefore to organize the discussion around a commentary on the fallacies that pervade this area than to try to work out a neat set of positive generalizations. For example, a country need not strive to abolish social-status disparities in opportunities for schooling in order to obtain economic advance. All of the most prosperous nations reached that state of affairs with assistance from educational systems that embodied large inequalities in educational opportunities between the sexes, among social strata, or between rural-urban and ethnic groups.[12]

Officials in most countries today have more opportunity to put ingenious programs of nonformal education into effect precisely because there is no simple relationship between national income levels and relative expenditures upon conventional schooling of any sort or level. The widespread tendency to neglect elementary schooling compared to other kinds offers abundant scope and resources for nonformal programs designed for the less-educated populace. Scope for innovation exists also because education has so many functions and is connected so diversely with other influences moving a society ahead or holding it back. While percentages of literacy can be raised without commensurate gains in aggregate productivity, I see no reason for altering an earlier conclusion that

40 percent male literacy will support, though not guarantee, an economic take-off.[13] Literacy does foster awareness of nonconventional possibilities and of new ways to do things within every sector of life. It opens men's eyes to a wider range of possible jobs, even though not itself required in many particular jobs. But a worker's innovativeness is favored by literacy, and he becomes more amenable to changes sponsored by employers or introduced by fellow workers. Literacy can also make men accessible to demagogues and to economic charlatans, and it can open to them a literature of dissent.

Whether nonformal education be devoted largely to disseminating literacy or not, offering an assortment of changes for nonformal training increases the yield from adult literacy more quickly than could accrue by just waiting for pupils to come into the labor force. Each additional kind of nonformal education injects a more than proportionate boost to modernization until we reach a rather high level at which redundancy or duplication of influences brings diminishing returns into play.

The Tenuous Association between Education and Occupation

To aim, as Dumont proposes,[14] that each man should be trained for his place in society, would almost certainly retard more than speed development. It is equally silly to talk about insuring that each developing society should strive to bring its engineers up to international quality. What counts is not the certificates workers carry but the cost of producing goods and services, and this cost always depends upon an idiosyncratic organization of production activities wherein an entrepreneur balances kinds and qualities of materials with assorted human skills. That school certificates and productivity are only modestly correlated is made possible largely by the fact that innumerable men have learned to operate a more complex economy and technology than the planners of the society imagined anyone could supply instruction for. In short, nonformal or irregular training turned out the requisite skills without waiting for some agency to figure out the country's supposed "needs" for a particular assortment of manpower.

The appropriate focus for attention is more how workers are being utilized and upon ways to improve that utilization than upon designing new educational plans to turn out the "right kinds" of workers. Indeed, the mechanisms for improving utilization of workers are in large measure themselves procedures for improving the training of the workers — needless to add, in nonformal ways. In most societies, given reasonable incentives, there usually are many profit-minded men eager to use and to improve the skills of the workers through whose labor they or some other employer can profit. It is conducive to better use of skills if both the jobs and the skills to perform them come in small "blocks" in order to permit a more precise match between what needs to be done and men who know how to do it. Incidentally, the fit between skills and jobs is likely to be more nearly optimum if there is a reasonably large volume of interjob and interoccupational shifts. Those who design or operate conventional schools all too seldom think in terms of skills or of production activities; they are more familiar with the language of certificates and with broad categories of workers: high-level, middle-level, and so on. So, while certificates of formal schooling are only weakly associated with performance on the job, the latter becomes closely associated with nonformal training almost unobserved. After all, workers can use only the skills they possess. Moreover, preoccupation with certificates encourages officials to guide the economy in ways that distort the prices of skills and thereby diminishes the amount of skill that can be employed.

Nonformal education has the additional advantage that it is especially suited for the passing on of know-how rather than of book-learning. After all, most occupational socialization has to be done after employment; i.e., nonformal education encourages putting training near the point of use. It also capitalizes on trainees' individual profiles of ability and motivation, thus brining training more in line with career patterns and with the most traveled routes of occupational mobility. Not least, the cost of nonformal training can often be put to the account of the worker himself (or to that of employers). Being less set into fixed streams and curricula, nonformal training encourages flexible shifting from one to another sort of it as opportunities take on new patterns. Almost certainly nonformal training is less encouraging than is conventional training to what we call "brain drain." But when foreign production units are imported it is easier to transmit the expatriate's know-how to his local counterparts because instructor and pupil are mainly interested in getting the job done, not in preparing to undertake another cycle of instruction. Finally, one should never forget that in developing countries most of the GNP comes from tiny firms, and those are the units most suited to the use of apprenticeship and of most other kinds of nonformal training.

I hope the foregoing dicta are persuasive, but until abundant data are procured and published regularly for nonformal education as already they are for academic schooling, empirical testing of assertions like these will be spotty and equivocal.

Regulating the Flow of Nonformal Education through Use of Economic Signals

In the foregoing pages propositions about development-oriented education have been organized to emphasize the special potentialities of nonformal education; for example, placing training near the point of use, giving priority to utilization of skills over formalized procedures for producing skilled men, and so on. In this section the theme will be that nonformal education particularly is likely to facilitate development if a society possesses a mechanism for coordinating the supplying of training and the accepting and using of it. That is, there should be some device to encourage expansion or induce contraction of different kinds of training "at the margin:" in experimental programs, on-the-job training in the more buoyant sectors, and so on. Under such conditions, I contend along with my economist colleagues, programs of training are more likely to have a useful wholeness and appropriateness than where education is guided by abstract and aggregate plans made by men possessing little concrete knowledge of economic activities. That a government can only weakly control the training that is made available may actually bring about a better alignment of training programs with the broad education aims of the country. This is true especially, I would assume, if the government is unable to manipulate the wage structure of the society and is not itself the main employer. Such conditions also encourage working out appropriate "age cycles" for different kinds of education and training, and — once more — they encourage keeping training near the point of use. Such a comparatively non-authoritative arrangement, one suspects, is more likely to raise the probability that present decisions about training will leave future decisions open rather than foreclosing them.

In most countries in which development has begun to "take hold" and to be a widely shared aspiration among citizens, one abserves a high elasticity in the demand for many kinds of education. Ordinary people reveal themselves to be progressively more willing to invest their hard cash or other resources in procuring those kinds of education, that they judge will pay off. The more widespread is nonformal education, the smaller the share of resources for education to be found in the hands of any one agency or supplier of training.[15] I have implied that nonformal arrangements reduce the normal tendency for educational finance to be regressive inasmuch as in most developing countries public educational funds come mainly from excise and other regressive taxes. Moving the costs toward the user (or his employer) may not democratize costs, but it does encourage letting the concerned individuals work out the relative benefits and sacrifices to them of alternative sorts of training.

These rather casual remarks about educational finance must be seen in the light of the gigantic disparities in annual costs per pupil between universities and village elementary schools. The ratio is sometimes over 200:1, not rarely it is 100:1, and rather commonly it is 40 or 50:1.[16] In developed countries by contrast, the ratio tends to be 5:1 or 10:1. These wide spreads are attributable partially to the heavy start-up costs of universities, magnified often by a nation's urge to displace expatriates over night. But the high ratios in costs reflect also "demonstration effects," and universities have spokesmen in key government positions while few people speak up for the interests of the village child when the money is being shared out. I therefore do regard it as constructive when more nonformal kinds of secondary and higher education are inaugurated and when beneficiaries of the more expensive schooling are expected to pay its costs. These fiscal rearrangements do tend to encourage the use of what I call "signals" for guiding the matching of supply to demand for different kinds of schooling.[17]

In most respects, then, if the supply and demand for various sorts of training are left comparatively free from stereotyped bureaucratic control, a balance between what is wanted and what will be supplied tends to emerge. Moreover, such an arrangement has some built-in controls against a runaway inflation of enrollments.

It is no reply to my argument to say that individual families cannot bear the costs of educating their children, for in most developing countries it is the ordinary and poor families who will have to pay the costs — though of course a means test can remove the grossest inequities. The Philippines, as we all know, is a dramatic example of how much money a society is willing to spend on buying education through direct private purchase from private suppliers. It is constructive, even in the absence of actual figures, to make use of the "rate of return" way of looking at costs, if only to discourage the flabby reasoning that "education is good, so let's have more of it." Combining the rate-of-return logic, the 100:1 ratio of university to elementary costs, and the common finding that elementary schools yield a better return on a society's investment than do higher schools, public opinion is encouraged to concern itself with a few basic questions about educational policy. Clearly, these beneficial outcomes will be more assured if parents and youth are supplied abundantly with dependable information about jobs and the related training. In comparison with the yield from a generous supply of such kinds of information, installing an expensive system for "educational and vocational guidance" must be viewed as pedagogic and fiscal irresponsibility.

Despite the many affirmations at international conferences of the importance of elementary education, university enrollments in many countries have proved to be the most expansive. One reason certainly is that decisions about university (or secondary) attendance do not require the prospective student or his parent to face payment of anything like the actual costs of staying in school. Respect for the ideology of "free education" (even where it cannot be implemented fully) discourages the setting up of nonformal training and encourages the linking of salaries to certificates rather than to demonstrated preparation for the job.

Nonformal Education Offers the Best Linkage with Local Traditions

In almost every new nation leaders strive to maintain continuity with local traditions while preparing their citizens to live in a new society.[18] While this effort may be a hopeless one, reliance upon nonformal modes of training wherever possible will increase chances of making this transition. Because it is more likely to insure that the people who are most ready to use a given kind of training are those who receive it, differentiation of training programs is less likely to be turned into a form of selection on some "elite" principles when nonformal procedures are used and less likely to perpetuate the present vast disparities among a nation's subpopulations in levels of expenditure of schools.

In a viable society there are communication bridges from elites to common men, and half-educated men and women can play key roles as those intermediaries. Moreover, almost by definition, nonformal education gives respectability to the nonliterary sorts of brains; certainly nonformal education does make use of a wider part of the spectrum of human abilities. Nonformal programs enhance the skills in leadership of local men, although not, to be sure, always in the manner that national leaders might prefer. Recalling the importance of small firms and of apprenticeship, one may credit nonformal training with arousing fewer clashes with local traditions. All in all, training is less likely than schooling to remain separate from, and hostile to, traditional ways; indeed, much of the content of nonformal education is itself traditional. Much of what has come to be called the "unstated curriculum" is moral education; while it may be difficult to modify that component, the emerging syncretisms will embody genuine local traditions and will contain relatively small admixtures of alien content.[19]

Nonformal Education Favors an Unpoliticized Teaching Corps

The disdain with which nonformal schooling is viewed in many quarters offers its dispensers considerable protection from the common busybody interference of governments. By the same token more scope is given for venturesome trial of new procedures for instruction. Teachers in nonformal arrangements are less likely to develop an inferiority attitude toward outside authorities, and they are much less likely to be teaching what they have never seen practiced. The nonformal teacher may feel more authoritative and may receive more authority in the eyes of his pupils; indeed, the teacher commonly is a superior practitioner.[20] On the other hand, improvement of his skill less often leads the nonformal teacher to forsake the occupation. Using expatriates and experts as instructors discourages the wasting of funds or energy on unproductive fads,[21] if only because a nonformal teacher is less likely to be tied into the networks that disseminate educational fads. By the same token, diffusion of what has been proved practical is speeded up.

In the formal school systems, pressure to raise enrollments leads to pressures to politicize education. Fortunately the management of nonformal schemes is likely to lie outside the capital, and much of nonformal training goes on almost out of sight of the educational or party officials. There is less anxiety to make sure that "the educational plan" works out. Because officials assume that nonformal instruction is more free of ideological bias, they less often look over the instructor's shoulder to see how he is running his classes.

Sets of general objectives for an all-embracing system of rural education have been written out by many persons. Thus Mongomery stipulates four objectives: (1) improvement of the total life of the village, (2) increasing productivity of individuals through the development of skills, (3) development of citizenship and leadership, and (4) inspiring and motivating rural youth. Many officials in new nations and many experts in multilateral organizations reorder these aims so as to focus the whole educational program within rural areas toward the goal of motivating rural youth to remain rural, seeming to believe (as someone said) that rural slums are more wholesome than urban slums. But development, as nearly everyone concedes in other contexts, has a quality of wholeness as well as being diversified. And while this wholeness means that forward movements can be cumulative, it means also that we can never set up one kind of school for youth in villages and a different kind for youth who happen to live at one of the "poles of development." And so I come to a scrutiny of the reasons why rural schools cannot by themselves bear much of the burden of development beyond laying the foundation for acquisition of practical skills. By the same token, as I hope will become clear, each of the obstacles to a ruralized formal school system points to an opening for a productive variety of nonformal education.

Drawbacks to Ruralized Schools

In agriculture as elsewhere a seductive line of reasoning has led to imprudent and premature inauguration of whole systems of education that in actuality have proved to have little attractiveness to peasants. For development, the argument goes, we need human capital; training of human capital calls for education; a technological economy requires technical education and technical education should be taught in trade or vocational schools. Some writers would go further and insist that past experience of the West is irrelevant; yet in reality the Western past was not laissez faire but mercantilist and paternalistic, while open markets for skills came comparatively late. What usually is overlooked is the vast array of nonformal or extra-school arrangements for the provision of skills. Apart from any other considerations, the now-developing countries have the advantage that we know of many ways to protect peasants against risks while they are venturing into new forms of production. Moreover, we now know also that an elaborate system of extension agents will bring few benefits unless they possess and can demonstrate new crops and procedures of proven effectiveness.

It is easier today than even a few years ago to see that Nyerere is more interested in equality than he is in growth, and that his constraints on inequality diminish the number of jobs available to the least-educated seekers of jobs. Today we can see more clearly that the desired production gains from redistribution of titles to land will appear only under rather special conditions. Regrettably, pupils will continue to go without textbooks in countries that deny royalties to teachers who are expected to produce inspiring new "localized" books solely from a sense of duty. In nonformal as in formal varieties of instruction, wastage of enrollment is less a sign of poor quality in what is taught or in the manner of teaching than it is a sign that education has been offered before people have come to see that it can bring them a solid payoff. In education, as in economic production, men's interests do not always run parallel, and they tend to diversify people; in political affairs, activities and sentiments are more often convergent, but they may bring results that mainly offset the potentials for gains in levels of living or in innovative ways of production. To propose, then, that children should be admitted to intermediate, secondary, or higher schools partially on the basis of some party official's judgment of how much each has contributed to "the community" is neither to motivate individuals to use their general education for raising incomes, nor does it arouse men either to supply or to ask for extra-school instruction in practical things. As more and more observers now concede, peasants wish their children to be prepared to a better life, which almost always means one outside farming itself. That education under colonial rule was slanted definitely toward preparation of individuals for clerkly tasks does not prove that installation under independence of an array of vocational schools will bring any more rapid rise of average incomes.

Nor can any society, in contemporary conditions of virtually universal suffrage, establish and preserve a dual system of education: one kind of lessons for the village child — except when belatedly it is discovered that he has the "talent" to be guided into "higher" occupations — and another kind for town children that makes the path to higher schools especially smooth.

It is distracting where not destructive to set up an ideal, as does UNESCO,[22] "of a true integration of knowledge and skills in the light of local and national necessity." It is misleading to encourage people "to produce a cogently integrated mechanism of education and development."[23] We do not know how to produce that kind of harmony amid the rushing tides of social change. Just for that reason, as has been asserted at so many points in this chapter, it is desirable to set modest bounds to our expectations from formal schools and give up vain efforts to "plan" a neat congruence between school and the "social needs" that arise from and also constitute development. By the same line of reasoning, a due modesty on these aspirations for formal school encourages a much more modest proliferation of nonformal ways of learning how to produce more and cheaper, how to bring one's neighbors into programs for the common benefit, or how to allocate individuals with varying capabilities among the many tasks of a changing society without recourse to the whip.

Undeniably, an educational system should be "downward looking" to the problems of peasants.[24] But if this viewpoint means also that those who must make choices for others come to regard peasants and ex-peasant laborers in towns mainly as sources of "labor capital" to be disposed of by officials with little experience in any kind of production subject to hard tests of profit and loss, then it were better to let the peasants find their own marketable lines of production and to follow their immemorial penchant to invest heavily in their own business.

There are yet many untried experiments to see whether transfer of learning from lessons in agriculture to science is easier or more difficult than turning science into farm practice. But in all these ventures, despite the many local circumstances, it remains a sound principle to use schools mainly to get individuals ready to be taught how to become effective producers. Meanwhile we can encourage varied and innovative enterprise in the supplying of knowledge, fanciful enlargement of horizons, and drill in the dirty work that builds tunnels or that lays out an irrigation system so that water flows where it will be used. Like that irrigation water, present skills and training for new skills need to be encouraged to flow where they will fructify zeal and ambition. The schoolmaster has enough to do if he makes men literate; let the tradesmaster lead his apprentices into the ventures that produce what people need, want, and for which they will pay from their slowly increasing hoard of goods, energy, and coins.

Notes

1. C. A. Anderson, "Technical and Vocational Education in the New Nations," in A. M. Kazamias and E. H. Epstein (eds.), *Schools in Transition* (Boston: Allyn and Bacon, 1968), pp. 174-89.

2. F. Harbison and C. A. Myers, *Education, Manpower, and Economic Growth* (New York: McGraw-Hill, 1964). See correlation matrix on p. 39 and related discussion.

3. Hong-Woo Lee, "A Multivariate Analysis of Education and Unemployment" (Ph.D. dissertation, Teachers College of College of Columbia University, 1971, sponsor: Walter I. Garms).

4. I refer specifically to instruction; if one were to think only of learning, there would be less point in talking about definite programs.

5. K. Mwendwa, "Constraint and Strategy in Planning Education," in J. R. Sheffield (ed.), *Education, Employment and Rural Development* (Kericho conference of September, 1966, Nairobi: East Africa Publishing House, 1967), p. 272.

6. G. Hunter, "Manpower, Employment and Education in Rural Economy of Tanzania," Paris: International Institute of Educational Planning, in *African Research Monographs, No. 9*, 1966, p. 15.

7. Mwendwa, "Planning Education," p. 278.

8. But in the absence of the Western irony among employers about the informative value of certificates.

9. J. Silvey, "Unwillingly from School: The Occupational Attitudes of Secondary School Leavers in Uganda," in R. Jolly (ed.) *Education in Africa* (Nairobi: East African Publishing House, 1969), p. 144.

10. See the many publications by I. de Pool about mass media.

11. I assume there will not be a major educational "breakthrough" (as in the use of television), despite the frequent view that nonformal education itself is a breakthrough.

12. For example, the "index of dissimilarity" between the distribution of paternal occupations of students and that of the employed population ranges among advanced countries from a high of about 75 to a low of about 20; for the secondary schools in the greater-Santiago (Chile) area the range is 75 to 15.

13. M. J. Bowman and C. A. Anderson, "Concerning the Role of Education in Development," in C. Geertz (ed.), *Old Societies and New States* (Glencoe: Free Press, 1963), pp. 247-79.

14. R. Dumont, "Agricultural Development, Particularly in Tropical Regions, Neccessitates a Completely Revised System of Education," prepared for a June 1963, UNESCO conference at Frascati, p. 7.

15. If resources for nonformal education are merely piled on top of those for an unrestrained formal school system, educational expenditures rapidly become unbearable for the public fisc, considering other investment needs. There has to be a mechanism to induce people to want a share of investment put into nonformal teaching, since otherwise the political pressures for endless expansion of the formal system will be irresistable.

16. Most computations, rough as they are, show elementary education to have at least as high a social rate of return as that to any other level of education.

17. Moreover, because nonformal education tends to be carried out by other than the conventional school system, the familiar squabbles over quotas of pupils by areas or tribes tend to be muted. An uncontrolled expansion of voluntary schools may also sap resources, and such schools often are far too imitative of the usual "academic" programs.

18. G. E. F. Urch, "The Africanization of the Curriculum in Kenya," *University of Michigan Comparative Education Dissertation Series, No. 12,* 1968, p. 69.

19. Obviously "the language issue" is entangled in many of these topics, but space does not permit discussion of its ramifications here.

20. One should not forget the steady refrain in nearly every country that the "vocational education" teachers are out of date and cannot keep up with the technique on which their instruction centers.

21. I would say, such as educational television.

22. UNESCO, "Adaptation of Education to the Needs of the Modern World in Rural Areas,' *International Education Year Series, No. 9,* p. 3.

23. Ibid.

24. G. Hunter, "Education for the Rural Community," in P. C. W. Gutkind (ed.), *Manpower and Unemployment Research in Africa 1, No. 2,* (1968): 7.

Part 2
Locating Educational Functions

Introduction to Part 2

To educate is to school. Such has been the implicit assumption of much past educational planning. The possibilities for locating educational functions outside the schools were rarely seriously considered. Yet much of what we know and most of the skills we possess were learned outside of formal schools. This is certainly true of underschooled societies. It seems also to be true of highly schooled societies.

Now the possibilities for locating important educational tasks outside the formal schools are being openly examined. Planners are beginning to include the question of location among other important educational decisions. "Can certain educational tasks be performed with greater learning efficiency and at less cost outside formal schools?" This is a question being asked with increasing frequency. This new option to decide the location of educational functions opens up a great range of possibilities for the development of education. The price of this greater freedom, however, is the need for better information about available possibilities and their relative merits.

Planners must now clarify the objectives of educational programs and identify their target populations in greater detail. Where the social demand for education and the manpower requirements of industry were routinely translated into school enrollment targets in the past, planners must now be more specific: Is the demand for education best met by schooling, or does schooling just create the demand for more schooling and increase social unrest? Can manpower requirements actually be translated into enrollments? Can the schools produce the needed skills, and will those they do produce be used where they are needed? Questions such as these open the way for a consideration of alternative locations for education.

A number of factors may influence the choice of location for educational functions. One may be the structural capabilities of formal and nonformal education to perform certain tasks. Brembeck, in chapter 5, develops ten propositions about the capacities of these two modes of education and draws certain implications about their appropriate uses in accomplishing certain educational tasks.

The degree of specificity of the initial educational objective will also influence the choice of location. Thus location of the learning of a particular vocational skill may be limited to a few institutions such as a vocational school or an apprenticeship program in a particular industry. But an adult literacy program with more general aims may be located in any number of institutions — in various types of voluntary organizations such as trade unions, cooperatives, neighborhood organizations, in government sponsored organizations, or in formal schools. But, as Grandstaff points out in chapter 4, the choice of location will itself further specify the objectives of an education program.

Paulston's study of National Youth Service Programs in Africa and the Caribbean in chapter 6 illustrates the need to consider the total environment and the needs of the target population. For the same type of program takes on different goals and forms of organization because of the different settings and the different needs of the target populations. Grandstaff's study also shows how tradition, social climate, class interests, and the distribution of power and wealth bear on the choice of location.

Cost looms as an important factor in deciding on the location of any educational program, and Paulston presents some illustrative data on relative costs of National Youth Service programs, but the economics of nonformal education will be considered more fully in a later chapter.

4

Are Formal Schools the Best Place to Educate?

MARVIN GRANDSTAFF

As the topic of nonformal education has developed, it has become clear that one of the central propositions is that formal schools are not adequate to all educational activities. Skepticism about schooling makes one of two claims. Either (1) formal schooling cannot accomplish a given objective, or (2) formal schooling is not the best means for accomplishing some given objective. These are quite different claims, and the difference has considerable importance for some questions. In the general case, however, both claims amount to an assertion that for some educational objectives or functions there is a more appropriate arena (or arenas) than that of formal schooling. Put another way, a claim that formal schooling is inadequate is a claim for the superiority of nonformal education. If that is accepted, then we have to admit to our deliberations the question of criteria by means of which the judgment can be made as to the most appropriate location of any given educational function. That is the problem to which these remarks are addressed. It is, incidentally, a question that usually does not arise in conventional discussions of education, since those discussions take as a given the assumption that formal schooling is the best, if not the only, vehicle of education.[1] But when we broaden our focus to include nonformal education, the problem of location of educational function immediately arises.

There is no question but that an adequate approach to the problem of criteria for the location of education function should have several dimensions. Here I will examine the problem from the perspective of the need structures of social groups. There are, in addition, at least two other dimensions that would seem indispensible to a comprehensive treatment of the problem. Let me mention those briefly. First, there is a financial dimension to the decision-making matrix. Which, among possible locations of function, promises the greatest return on investment? This dimension obviously anticipates some measure of educational effectiveness and experimentation with methodologies having different cost patterns, along with the development of accounting models for both formal and nonformal measures. Second, there is the general question of what may be called "learning style" and its mesh (or lack of it) with the measures contained in a specific educational program. For example, to what educational environment is the learning style of an adult in a peasant society best suited against, say, that of an urban adolescent in an industrial society?

Finally, I think we need to ask what is the relationship between objectives for educational development and the need structures of various potential educational contexts? That dimension is the subject of this paper. It is a complex problem and this analysis will probably answer fewer questions than it raises. Nonetheless, if we are to locate educational functions where they are most likely to be accomplished, we must have some way of deciding how our proposals for education fit with the character of the social groups for which the proposals are made. Let me explicate that question a little. What I would like to attempt is a rough schematization of dynamics that bear on educational activities in such a way that a consideration of them is an important component of making decisions about the location of educational function. Given that schematization, I will apply it in the analysis of a major case of relocation of educational function — the period in American history of roughly 1830-1860 — conventionally labelled "the Common School Revival." The basis of the schematization is the concept of "need."

The notion of "needs" is central to the question of functional location as I have stated it. What is posited is the sociological doctrine that the activities of human groups can be understood in terms of the status of those activities as attempts to meet the needs of the group. Although there are other perspectives on activity — activity as the drive to approximate an "ideal," and so on — most modern social inquiry proceeds from some construction of one of several theories of need.[2] *Needs* are conceived as dynamics within the social group that determine the shape of activity and, most important here, determine the specific shape of an activity that is nominally directed at the accomplishment of some generalized objective.

The need structure of the group may (almost certainly, will) give a distinctive shape to the objective as it is worked out in practice. To take a simple example, there are likely to be major differences between the shape of literacy education if it is lodged, in one instance, in a state-supported school and, in another instance, in a nonformal agency such as a worker's cooperative. The activity of pursuing the objective picks up a functional freight which, in turn, is rooted in other needs of the group. In piecing out the example, let me suggest two ways in which this shaping process might figure. We might expect the content of literacy education to differ in our two cases. Differences in content might arise from different political or economic needs of the two agencies. Perhaps the state needs, for purposes of national development, an extensive relocation of labor, in terms of occupations and geographic placement, while the worker's cooperative needs, for purposes of national development, an extensive relocation of labor, in terms of occupations and geographic placement, while the worker's cooperative needs, for purposes of internal cohesion and economic advancement, a commitment to the existing occupational structure and geographic stability. Given those differing needs, we might expect that the instructional materials of the state-supported program would incorporate information about urban life, industrial occupations, and so on, while the materials for the worker's cooperative would draw its informational content mainly from the existing occupational and valuational framework. Too, the administration of the instruction itself is a potent means of assigning prestige and rank within the group, especially in the perceptions of the learners. Those who give the instruction assume, just by virtue of their being instructors, an honorific place in group affairs — a place that may often be extended to enhance the instructor's power in deliberations unrelated to educational questions. It would not be surprising then, if a state literacy program selected personnel from among those having some connection with the state itself, or at least reserved to itself the prerogative of approval, licensing, and the like. Nor would we expect the worker's cooperative to do otherwise than to select from among its own membership for the prestigious spots in the program hierarchy.

There are, undoubtedly, other ways in which the need structures of the group act to shape the specific character of educational programs, but these suffice for illustration. It would appear, then, that the potential shaping dynamic of the comprehensive need structure of a group should be taken into account in deciding what context is most appropriate as the residence of some educational function.

Now let me employ this schematization looking at some of the events and changes of the period of the Common School Revival. I am interested in a process that takes the following rough form: Changes in the social, economic, or political character of the society occur, creating "imperatives" in the form of very generalized educational objectives. At the point that the objectives emerge, the society is confronted with an array of choices — to ignore the objective, leaving arrangements as they are, or to take up the objective and give it explicit attention. (This involves a choice between what we might call "informal" education — that is not given explicit attention, and "purposeful" education. This distinction may be an important one, but I will not explore it here.) If the decision is made for explicit attention, there are at least two possibilities — to locate the objective in some nonformal context or to locate it in an official, formal school setting. It is this second decision upon which this analysis will focus. In the period at issue the decision was, in almost every case, to locate the new objectives in schools. It would be interesting to analyze cases in which the decision was for nonformal agencies. At present, however, there are no major cases of that sort to examine, despite the efforts of Ivan Illich and others to win acceptance for the concept of "deschooling society."[3]

What I want to ask is why the objectives were located in the schools rather than someplace else, and I will try to answer in terms of the need structures of groups. It should be noticed that this is quite a different question from that of why the objectives themselves emerged. That question has been the almost exclusive focus of historians of the period, and fairly adequate explanations of the emergence of the objectives are available. The location question, on the other hand, has figured very little in the work of historians. The result is a partial and largely ideological picture: changing social conditions posed new educational imperatives and the schools were expanded to meet them (a partial picture because it was not just that the schools were expanded, but in addition, other agencies were ignored, replaced, or bypassed.) The ideological twist comes in the tacit message that whenever a new educational objective arises the appropriate strategy is to locate it in the schools. Educational historians have been major promulgators of the ideology that educational progress is equivalent to expansion of the formal school system.

The years of the Common School Revival provide an intriguing analogy to the situation in the developing nations of the present time. The era was marked by rapid industrialization, urbanization, the emergence of centralized commerce and its apparatus of mass markets, concentration of wealth, homogeneous communication and transportation networks, as well as by political popularization, social assimilation, and the struggle to find — within a society where wealth and human resources were in limited supply — an accommodation between the demands of a vital ideology and the pragmatic limitations of economic and social possibilities. The problems and imperatives of developing industrialism arose against a context of agrarian, in some cases almost feudal, society. Granted, the analogy is fairly crude. Still, this period of profound modernization in American experience makes it an attractive subject for consideration of the location of educational function.

Prior to about 1830, much — indeed, when the entirety of the population is considered, most — education was firmly within the context of the nonformal, to the extent that education received attention at all. The system of common schools — a fixture of Colonial America — had, during the Federalist years, become largely defunct.[4] Locally supported schools made a half-hearted effort at basic literacy training, but they reached a minority of their potential constituency and, except for the rural areas and small towns, the Colonial common school tradition was largely forgotten. In the industrializing Northeast (which is the primary referent of the Common School Revival), there was little or no formal provision for education, particularly for the children of the new industrial working classes. Indeed, a large percentage of working-class children entered the labor force at such an early age as to preclude most schooling. In the surviving crafts apprenticeship remained the norm, and other sorts of education — such as political enlightenment — were functions of family and community. Of course, until the early years of the century, limitations on suffrage had so limited participation in political affairs that there was little urgency for the political education of working-class children. Religious education and cultural induction, too, were still the province of the family and the immediate, often ethnic, community, even though Bible reading was still a staple of what schooling the children received. There was no systematic oversight of schooling; each city and town had the prerogative of setting its own requirements and standards. Nor was there any standard method of financing. Parents, in the case of middle and upper classes, paid for the education of their children; public support, almost always at the level of local taxing unit, was largely limited to "pauper schools."

By 1860 the situation was astonishingly altered. A list of reforms that were largely accomplished or well under way would include at least the following:

1. State participation in school affairs, through the founding of state departments of education, extended to state inspection of schools, establishment of minimum standards for offerings, leadership in curriculum and materials development, record-keeping and teacher-training and accreditation.

2. In all states of the industrial Northeast and the West, there was at least a start of free, publicly-supported elementary schools available to all children.

3. Programs of teacher training were beginning to be widely established.

4. The idea of compulsory attendance had been advanced and was beginning to win a measure of acceptance. In one state (Massachusetts) a compulsory attendance law was in effect.

5. Even though there was nothing resembling a universal pattern, the shape of an enlarged and reasonably consistent society-wide curriculum for general elementary school education was beginning to emerge. The new outline contained, in addition to the conventional "basics," such general education areas as science and history and "practical" subjects such as bookkeeping and applied arithmetic.

6. Although Bible reading, school prayers, and other sorts of religious observances were maintained, the schools began to take on a secularized tone, with religious exercises assuming a nondenominational Protestant character.

7. Educationists began to conceive the school as a multipurpose, social service institution, rather than as a limited agency concerned with a narrow list of immediate, pragmatic objectives. What events and dynamics had operated to produce such extensive and far-reaching changes in the short space of three decades?

The answer, of course, lies in the social imperatives of the rapid and massive transition of an agrarian, small crafts, independent entrepreneur economy and society to one of large-scale industry and manufacturing, centralized commerce based in corporate investment and bank financing, and mass merchandising. Industrialization is a very complex process, out of which a great many discrete social and economic influences may be analyzed. Let me mention a few that had particular significance for the schools. The new factories had quite different short-term and long-term impacts on the labor marketplace. The immediate impact, based in the rapid expansion of production and consumption, was a demand for large amounts of cheap labor. This demand brought thousands of women and children into the labor force (along with the many new immigrants.)

Over time, the increase of machine input into the system decreased the system's demand for human energy. That, coupled with the agitation of reformers against the brutalities of child-labor practices, began to remove children from the labor force. This, in turn, raised the necessity for a caretaker agency for the children of industrial workers. Political popularization and the extension of the suffrage was seen as posing an imperative for increased literacy. The rise of Jacksonian ideology and the tiny beginnings of worker welfare organization combined to articulate the idea of education as an instrument of class mobility. Industry and commerce, in converting to a centralized, mass base, required homogeneity of workers and consumers. The influx of immigrants from abroad and regional differences among domestic population groups presented a problem in homogenization which was attacked by expanding and unifying school attendance and programs, thus diminishing cultural diversity. The list could be continued, but let me move now to the question I framed earlier. We can see that social, political, and economic changes raised educational imperatives. Why were those imperatives located in the schools and what shaping effect did that location have upon the general educational objectives?

There are, to begin with, certain simple and obvious reasons for the selection of formal schooling. First, the reforms of 1830-1860 were greatly influenced by advocacy and many of the major advocates were schoolmen — James Carter, Henry Barnard, and especially Horace Mann.[5] It is not surprising that those advocates who recognized and articulated the imperatives of the emerging society should cast their reform proposals in the mold of schooling. Too, some of the new imperatives, especially literacy, had a strong schooling tradition. Finally, the society itself possessed a strong tradition of schooling, rooted in the Colonial experience and the Protestant world view. Still, important as these factors were, they do not as most educational historians seem to assume constitute an adequate single explanation for the location of the new objectives in the schools, nor for the generally held view that the expansion of schooling came about because it was uniformly and universally need-meeting. Let me demonstrate what I mean. To understand the large-scale expansion of the schools, we have to consider the need structures of the several components of society in order to see how the general objectives meshed with the needs of different social groupings. Although several kinds of educational reform — curricular, administrative, and so on — came about during the Common School Revival, I will center on the general objective of "enlightenment," as exemplified by literacy (broadly conceived to include arithmetic, speech, grammar, etc.) and general knowledge. The focus is general elementary education.

The conditions I have noted above brought the objective of universal, free, elementary education to the foreground. Now let us consider what happened to the objective once it was recognized. First, how did the objective link up with the needs of some important social groups? Let me stay with the urban context and delineate four groups:

1. The old elites and the newly wealthy industrial capitalists

2. Liberal, democratic reformers and intellectuals

3. Artisans, small-scale entrepreneurs and other groups who were members of or aspired to membership in the emerging middle class — that is, the bourgeois

4. The urban working class, particularly the industrial workers, immigrant workers from abroad and relocated rural people.[6]

Let me give a rough estimate of how the concept of universal elementary schooling linked with the needs of these groups.

The Elites. There was little direct linkage between public schooling and the needs of the elite groups. The elites provided for the education of their children out of pocket and, indeed, saw the concept of public schooling as a potential burden of taxation that they were not anxious to take up. There was a tenuous indirect linkage, rooted in the concern of industrialists to have effective work forces and the distaste and fear the elites felt toward the intemperance and criminality of the lower classes. Horace Mann exploited the indirect linkage in his advocacy of the common school, repeatedly extolling the virtues of a literate work force and affirming his belief in schooling as a vehicle for the promulgation of temperance and diligence, two qualities he much admired. In most instances, the elites possessed a greater need to preseve the privileged opportunities of their children and to avoid increased taxation than to gain the indirect benefits of public schooling, so they opposed it.

The Reformers. The reform sensibility of 1830-1860 was rooted in the concept of democratization. The extension of suffrage was a main strategic device, and the election of Jackson, followed by Van Buren, was the chief political accomplishment of the era. Jacksonianism was, in some respects, a mirror image of Federalism. As such it deplored local diversity and caprice in policy and administration, along with the investment in the political system of class distinctions based in wealth and position. Too, there was widespread abhorrence of the human evils in the industrial system — child labor, the destruction of family ties, long working hours, and so on. In this latter regard, few reformers exhibited respect for the potentials (or even the persons) of the working classes and took, instead, the stance that since the poor could not help themselves it was up to government to help them (a tradition still ubiquitous). Sympathy for the plight of the worker and his family there was, and a willingness to extoll the contributions of the workers to progress and prosperity, but there was no major assignment of economic or educational competence to the workers. Given this set of beliefs, the common school, more than any other thinkable set of educational arrangements, meshed with the needs of the reformers. The common school served the purposes of producing a homgeneous citizenry, possessed of the means for enlightenment — the Jeffersonian ideal — and at the same time could serve as a caretaker agency for the children of the poor — an instrument to lift them out of their degradation.[7] The common school seemed to present, too, an alternative to other forms of social change, such as the redistribution of wealth through socialist measures. It was among the reformers that the common school found its chief theoreticians, its most ardent propagandists and its most florid eulogists.[8]

The Middle Class. As homgeneity in language, dress, habits, and so on was brought to the fore by the needs of industrial capitalism, so those characteristics became a valuable currency in social mobility. For the middle classes and the upward-mobile, the common school was important as in instrumentality. It promised to give the children of the middle class a better footing in relation to the elites and — since the value systems of most of the reformers who were articulating the theory and practice of the common school were bourgeois, and since the values of the reformers were reflected in the schools — it promised to solidify the position of the middle classes. Too, the partially secularized school, with its tone of nondenominational Protestantism, seemed to the middle class a bulwark against the Catholicism of the lower classes, especially the European immigrants. As an indirect instrument for solidly held needs, the common school had a high positive valance for the middle class.

The Working Classes. Here, as is so often the case when the lower class is confronted with schooling, there was considerable ambivalence.[9] On the one hand, the common school seemed to provide the chance for mobility and for alleviation of some of the oppressive conditions of working-class life. It was wrapped up with a hope for the use of democratized politics to make the institution of government more responsive to the needs of the working class, and it was a staple of the reformers who constituted the main hopes of the workers for an effective alliance. There was, thus, both direct and indirect linkage between the common school and the needs of the working classes — direct in terms of mobility, child benefits, and the like, indirect as the common schools provided an indispensible point of unification with their liberal reformist allies. The literature of the early workingmen's movements are strong in their advocacy of the common school and those early "unions" provided considerable agitation in favor of free, public schooling. On the other hand, the common schools were touted, even by some of the most liberal reformers, as a barricade against speedy and fundamental social change. The ideology of the common school held not for the elimination of privilege, but for the extension of privilege to all — a program that many workers felt was at best slow and uncertain; at worst, an impossibility. The common schools, deeply committed to the reformist impulse for homogeneity, ran roughshod over the cultural backgrounds and, in the case of European immigrant minorities, the very language of the children. The non-English speaking child entered the school at a disadvantage and because he did, the school served him only partially as a tool for mobility. Finally, the question or religion in the schools was crucial, since a large portion of the working class was Catholic and the new common schools were nonsectarian. The specific issue was most often the use of the King James Bible in all school Bible readings, but the general issue was religious animosity compounded by class divisions. So severe was the religious issue that a number of riots occurred, the most serious of which was in Philadelphia in 1844, when perhaps a dozen people were killed and many injured. The Philadelphia riot also featured the burning of two Catholic churches, a seminary, and forty other buildings.[10] In several important ways, then, the common school failed to fit with the needs of the working classes and in some cases was antithetical to working-class needs. As the Common School Revival progressed — and as its meaning, in actual practice, became more clear to the working class — the strong advocacy of the common school in the rhetoric of workingmen's associations waned. Although it was usually preserved it received lower and lower priority. In addition, the workingmen's associations sponsored nonformal educational programs, such as mechanic's institutes, political forums, and library programs, indicating a recognition that the common school was decreasingly perceived as directly responsive to working-class needs.

At this point we can see the common school, one out of several think-able specific implementations of the general objective of "enlightenment," as the product of a limited set of needs: the need of reformers for a homo-genizing and caretaking institution, the need of the bourgeoisie for an instrument of social mobility, and the indirect need of the working class to accept the common school as a condition of their political alliance with the liberal reform movement. The triumph of the common school, then, is not a victory for the teleological power of the ideal of "enlightenment," but a testimony to the political power of the reformers and bourgeois acting influentially within a political movement that included much of the working class.

There were a number of conceivable ways in which the administra-tion and funding of the common school might have been structured. Grants-in-aid might have been made to several kinds of agencies — churches, work-men's associations, groups of artisans, agrarian communities, and so on — agencies that in our present concern we would label "nonformal" — with administration and policy-making vested in the funded groups and fostered a vigorous pluralism. Or, as some educationists — impressed by the schools of Prussia and loyal to the conservative tradition — advocated, a federal system of financing and control might have been implemented. That, in turn, would have strengthened the position of central government both politically and economically. Or education might have been attacked indirectly, through strengthening the economic and political positions of workingmen's associations and the like, or through measures to improve the general economic status of the working class. As the new labor movement became disenchanted with the common school, it increasingly advocated such indirect approaches to educa-tional reform — approaches that we might call supporting the contexts of nonformal education.

What did develop was a system of state oversight and local funding, within broad policies set by the separate states. This system served several indentifiable needs, while failing to serve others. It fitted well with the need of Jacksonian liberals for a politics of "anarchy with a constable." The individual became the primary unit of the polity, with a diminished role for the state — that of overseer, rather than initiator of policies. Perhaps no institution was as completely cast in the new liberal model as was the school. Legislation and finance were vested at the local level rather than in the state, with at the same time an expansion of the executive function of the state in the form of the new state education departments. Politically, the common school was a duplicate of laissez faire liberalism, with its emphasis on individual initiative. Too, by giving a legislative mandate to local politics — then, as now, importantly influenced by the elites — and a general credentialling mandate to the state, the structure of the common school mirrored the compromise with Federalist conservatism that liberalism struck in the wider setting of national politics. That compromise involved an acceptance of the broadening of political participation by the conservatives ("anarchy") and of mechanisms (local politics and state regulation) for the judicious control of popularized politics (the constable.) Finally, the political structure of the common school served the need of the existing power structure for acceptance of large regional differences. That acceptance helped, for a time, to avert the building conflict between North and South. The development of a federal system would surely have contributed to that schism, for the federal policy on education which has appeared in the past two decades has centered on regional differences. Indeed, contemporary concerns with such issues as school integration, national achievement norms, and education for "national goals" can be seen as long-delayed attention to needs that were unmet or legislated against by the political structure of the Common School Revival. The local funding/state oversight model did not serve the needs of ethnic groups for cultural integrity, nor those of Catholics for a unified school-church program, nor those of workingmen's associations for recognition and prestige. Neither did the common school model meet the more generalized needs — more easily seen in retrospect than at the time — of the underclasses (unskilled workers, immigrants, blacks) for political and economic protection. And most emphatically, the common school pattern did nothing in relationship to the slaves of the South. Instead, it allowed for the continuation of the practices and beliefs on which the slave system was built.

Here, as in the conception of labor, we find that the need-meeting character of the common schools was predicated on political and economic power and was by no means uniform in terms of meeting the needs of all constituent groups. Rather, the common schools were shaped in accord with the needs of those groups having political and economic control over them. By embodying a particular political model, the common school helped to build one of several possible politico-economic systems, serving the needs of some segments of the society, ignoring some needs and working against the fulfillment of some others.

What I have tried to do in this brief historical analysis is to illustrate the propositions advanced earlier — that the needs of social groups determine the career of education objectives in practice and that needs act to shape educational programs directed toward some generally stated educational objective. (I am also arguing, indirectly and in a speculative way, that had the educational objectives posed by industrialization been located in available nonformal agencies, the shape of education — and perhaps of society generally — would have been profoundly different.) This is, as yet, a fairly crude formulation and I am not even certain that the concept of needs will, over time, prove to be the best analytic tool. What I do hope is that I have opened up a central dimension of the problem of criteria for locating educational functions. If this dimension is to become a component in a calculus of decision-making for location of function, we need to develop a consistent and reasonably comprehensive way to determine and describe the need structures of social groups. I would like to see a number of more restricted and detailed studies than this on the relationship between group needs and educational objectives — especially the need systems of groups with a high potential for nonformal education. Such studies might be drawn from a three-way matrix with the following dimensions: (1) type of educational objective (political, occupational, valuative, cultural, etc.); (2) type of nonformal agency (family, worker's association, union, health professionals, church, youth groups, etc.); and (3) context of data collection (historical period, cultural group, geographical location, social group, etc.). Such studies might further test the workability of the concept of need as a descriptive tool and refine out capacity to characterize potential educational agencies in terms of the fit between educational functions and group needs. I remain convinced that the capacity to make informed judgments about that fit is an important element in what we hope will become a workable procedure for determining the most appropriate location for the educational objectives we hope to foster.

Notes

1. For an extended discussion of this point, see my paper, "The Family as an Educational Institution: The Lost Perspective," in *Social Foundations of Education,* ed. by Cole S. Brembeck and Marvin Grandstaff (New York: John Wiley and Sons, 1969), pp. 127-32.

2. This is widely true in the social sciences, less so in historical studies, where there remains widespread disposition to see activity as the manifestation of ideas at work in the world. This teleological view is particularly endemic in historical works on education. For a lucid discussion of this point, see George V. Plekhanov, *Fundamental Problems of Marxism* (New York: International Publishers, 1969), pp. 103-108. The work is a new translation of Plekhanov's essay of 1897, "The Materialist Conception of History."

3. Ivan Illich, *De-Schooling Society* (New York: Random House, 1971).

4. The Common School Revival is covered in nearly every standard work on American educational history. Especially useful for this study were: Rush Welter, *Popular Education and Democratic Thought in America* (New York: Columbia University Press, 1962), pp. 45-140; Merle Curti, *The Social Ideas of American Educators* (Paterson, N.J.: Littlefield, Adams, 1959), pp. 50-168; and Lawrence Cremin, *The American Common School: An Historic Conception* (New York: Teachers College, 1951). Other sources, especially useful for their presentation of the conventional coverage of the period, included Robert E. Potter, *The Stream of American Education* (New York: American Book Company, 1967), pp. 133-270; Elwood Cubberly, *Public Education in the United States* (Boston: Houghton Mifflin, 1934); John Brubacher, *A History of the Problems of Education,* (New York: McGraw-Hill, 1947); R. Freeman Butts and Lawrence Cremin, *A History of Education in American Culture* (New York: Henry Holt, 1953); William Drake, *The American School in Transition* (Englewood Cliffs: Prentice-Hall, 1955); and Newton Edwards and Herman Richey, *The School in the American Social Order* (Boston: Houghton Mifflin, 1963), pp. 291-356.

5. Curti, *American Educators,* provides an excellent discussion of the contributions of Mann and Barnard and Mann's *Annual Reports of the (Massachusetts) Board of Education,* 1843-1855, have long been recognized as classics in the analysis and advocacy of the common school.

6. Cubberly presents a more specific (and somewhat biased) listing of proponents and opponents of the common school, *Public Education,* pp. 164-65.

7. Curti, *American Educators,* pp. 114-119.

8. Consider, for example, the words of J. Orville Taylor: "The 'monuments of genuine glory' are the school houses raised by a free people. These humble but mighty institutions, scattered all over our soil, are the fairest ornaments of the land. . . . Our common schools are the sun of the people's mind, daily scattering light and warmth over the nation. They should be the idols of a free people, and around them all should gather to honor and elevate, for they are the sources and guardians of freedom." Quoted in Welter, *Popular Education,* p. 43.

9. Welter, *Popular Education,* pp. 45-46, provides a comprehensive discussion of the position of the working class on the common school, including, as few historians of the period have, the workingmen's reassessment of their early unqualified advocacy of the common school.

10. Potter, *American Education,* p. 229.

5 The Strategic Uses of Formal and Nonformal Education

COLE S. BREMBECK

This chapter inquires into the nature of formal and nonformal learning. The purpose is to examine the structural characteristics of each in order to find out their respective capabilities to perform educational tasks. The assumption is that if we knew more about what each is capable — or incapable — of doing, our uses of these two modes of education would be more economical, efficient, and effective.

The chapter is really a speculative essay designed more to stimulate argument than to prove a thesis. The perspective is sociological in that it concerns the characteristics of the social organization of two modes of learning and the impact of these characteristics upon people who participate in them.

I should perhaps apologize in advance for dealing with things commonplace and familiar. All of us have been in schools and our perceptions of them are based on firsthand experience. All of us have learned outside of school. Such learning is pervasive and certainly not novel. Still, I find ironical our familiarity with these modes of learning and our ignorance of them. Part of our problem may be that we tend to equate learning with instruction. The learning process so obviously involves instruction that we regard it to be the key shaper of what is learned. But the environment of instruction also teaches; it determines what is "caught" from the teaching, in contrast to what is "taught." And what is caught may have a more profound influence on human behavior than the cognitive learnings conveyed through formal instruction.

It is about the influence of the learning environment that we are most ignorant. To my knowledge there exists no satisfactory description or formulation of the environmental characteristics of school and nonschool learning that tells us very much about the respective capacities of each mode to perform certain educational tasks. I hope to probe this obscure region or at least walk around it and survey its boundaries.

Some Working Hypotheses

My explorations shall run in these ten directions, which I state in the form of working hypotheses:

1. The unique characteristics of formal and nonformal education may be

53

discovered in the structures of their respective learning environments.

2. That these unique structural characteristics equip each to perform certain tasks better than others.

3. That we have overloaded the formal system beyond its capacity with tasks it is not well suited to handle.

4. That we underutilize the nonformal system in terms of certain of its unique capacities.

5. That prescriptions of reform of the formal system which ignore its structural capacity are exercises in futility.

6. That one of the critical differences between the structural environments of education is their proximity to work, immediate action, and the opportunity to put to use what is learned. This difference is basic, for nonformal education is characteristically carried on within a context of action, work, and use. Formal education, on the other hand, takes place outside this context, just by dint of taking place in a school

7. That for this reason nonformal education is a better mode where the object is to change immediate action or to create new action, and formal education is superior where immediate action is subordinated to abstract learning or concept building, looking toward longer range change.

8. That future education policy must become total in the sense that it employs *all* the available means of education to meet increasingly diverse types of demands. The time when formal education could cope with all the learning demands of a complex society is past. We should realize it and adjust education policy accordingly.

9. That future education policy must reckon with life spans rather than school years. The education process must be viewed in the context of a developmental sequence that begins early in life and ends, if it ever does, with adults participating in the occupational sector of the economy and the responsibilities of citizenship.

10. That considering the changes that take place in an individual's educational needs over the life span and the variety of available modes of education, it becomes possible to sketch out a model for future educational policy and practice.

The Growing Interest in Nonformal Education

The current disillusionment with formal education may be due in part to our miscalculation about the capacity of formal education to perform certain tasks. We overload the system by adding more. Then we blame the system. Perhaps we should be blaming ourselves for not knowing more about the stress capabilities of the educational tools with which we work.

The same error in judgment could as easily be made now in the flush of enthusiasm for nonformal education. It too could be assumed to have magical properties which in fact do not exist, and its future could also be filled with sobering second thoughts. Presently, the assumption seems to be that formal education has fallen short: the task therefore is to develop nonformal education.

Perhaps the more fundamental assumption should be that *both* formal and nonformal education have built-in structural elements which condition their capabilities to contribute in defined ways to the attainment of certain educational objectives. Perhaps the fundamental task is to analyze more precisely the structural properties of each, to determine the potential of each for contributing to particular kinds of educational goals, and to build programs which utilize these strengths within a more unified and coherent policy of educational development. If this were done, investments in both school and nonschool education might yield better payoffs.

The question is, if formal education has performed badly, why? Could it perform better if used more wisely? If nonformal education is to perform well, how and under what circumstances? Some light on these questions may be gained by inquiring into the basic structures which determine their capacities to perform.

The Structure of Nonformal Learning

Something of the structure of nonformal education can be learned by reflecting upon the nature of learning in preliterate societies. Education itself is old, as old as man's capacity to learn, but schools, as we know them, are relatively new on the human scene. In primitive society, nonformal education was the mode. A child required no specialized training to learn the things he needed to know. He learned from his father and other adults the arts of hunting and food-gathering. In somewhat later societies he learned to cultivate, plant, and harvest. Tasks were unspecialized and easily transmitted from parent to child. The learning process was spontaneous, with both parent and child largely unaware that it was taking place.

But societies tend not to remain primitive in their outlook and simple in their organization. Endowed with the capacity to learn, man started to control his environment for his own purposes. He developed fire to keep him warm, clothing to shelter him from the wind and cold, baskets and kettles to carry more than his hands could, and, finally, the wheel, to which he transferred burdens from his back.

Some men were better at certain skills than others; they became artisans, making copper pots, weaving baskets, and making wheels. Young men came to watch and to learn. They became apprentices, helping and learning at the same time. Probably the first formal schools sprang up around such artisans and from such definable social and economic needs growing out of man's increasingly complex way of living.

My own appreciation of the structure of nonformal learning was deepened when I lived for awhile on the Northwest Frontier of Pakistan, near the Khyber Pass, where shepherd boys were a familiar sight along every country lane and road. When I began to observe one particular boy, my first reaction was: "How young to be tending a flock of sheep!" Yet it was obvious that this young shepherd knew well what he was about. He herded the animals with great skill along paths to and from the pasture lands. Where fences are unknown, he kept his flock within boundaries. He knew how to protect the sheep from menacing wild dogs and he could use his stick with great effectiveness. He recognized poisonous weeds and steered his flock away from them. At age ten he was a good shepherd.

This boy grew up in his vocation and was probably never aware that he was learning it. When he was very small, his father or older brothers took him along while they tended the flock. To protect him from the hot sun, they put him down in the shade of a bush. From there he watched and listened. As he grew older, he ran after the sheep, assisting his father in rounding up the strays. In the spring, at lambing time, he watched his father work with the ewes. He learned how to teach a new lamb to suckle. At shearing time he was there, assisting at first, then later, catching, throwing, and holding the sheep for the shearer. From his earliest years he knew the value of the flock to his family. He saw his mother and sisters use the wool to card yarn from which the family clothes were made. The flock provided meat for the table. The wool and sheep that were sold brought the family its meager cash income.

Here, then, is a learning situation in which the young learn what they need to know, first by observing their elders carry on significant tasks in which they are skilled. Then, by taking part first in simpler tasks and later in more complex ones, they are finally prepared to train others. The training cycle is complete.

What does the shepherd boy's education illustrate about the structure of nonformal education? First, it took place within the context of immediate and meaningful action, work. Second, there was no gap between learning and the use of it. Indeed, learning grew out of the need for it. Learning and doing were so mixed up that it would be hard to sort them out. Third, learning took place as a part of normal living; there was nothing of the apparatus of formal schools, no lessons or classes, no artificial rewards and punishments. Learning was so natural that the shepherd boy was hardly aware that it was taking place. Four, the learner saw a connection between one aspect of the task and the whole task. He could easily see what caring for a new lamb meant to his family's welfare, because he had observed the life cycle of a sheep and its relationship to what he wore and ate. The boy did not need to be told that caring for sheep was important; this was one of the accepted values by which his whole family survived. Five, the shepherd boy's "teacher" was associated with his "student" in carrying on meaningful action. In a sense the boy's father was a co-worker, superior only in knowledge and skill. The role of teacher and student blended harmoniously. Six, the shepherd boy's education incorporated within itself some important factors that stimulate learning. There was no arbitrary decision about what the boy should be capable of doing at a certain stage of his development. As he demonstrated his readiness he simply assumed new responsibilities. He needed no external rewards, such as grades and certificates. His satisfaction came from assuming an adult role early in life. His learning provided a kind of security which comes from takings one's accepted place in the family and among one's peers. It should have come as no surprise to me that by the age of ten this boy had already learned a vocation, perhaps his life's work.

Almost forty years ago John Dewey, the American philosopher of education, wrote about his conception of an ideal school. I find it of interest that Dewey incorporated many of these elements of nonformal education in his ideal school. Once he cast his ideas in the form of a fictional visit to Utopia. The purpose of the visit, he said, was to learn what he could about the educational system in Utopia.

Dewey's first observation was that in Utopia education was carried on without anything like schools, at least schools as we know them. He reported that children were gathered together in association with older and more mature people who directed their activity. They met in large grounds, with orchards, gardens, and greenhouses. No group was larger than 200, and most of them much smaller, the Utopians having found that people seem to work best in close, intimate, association. There were workshops which had all kinds of things for children to work with — wood, iron, and textiles, There were also museums, scientific laboratories, and books.

There were no arbitrary divisions of children into classes by age groups. Older children took part in directing the activities of those still younger. Some of those who liked especially to work with children later became Utopia's teachers.

How was learning carried on in John Dewey's educational Utopia? Here we see Dewey's sharpest departure from our present practice. Teaching was carried on much as the painters who were trained in, say Italy, when painting was at its height. The adult leaders combined their special knowledge of children with special gifts in certain directions. They associated themselves with the young in carrying on some line of action. As in older societies, where younger people were first apprentices who observed their elders and then took part with them in doing first some of the simpler things and then more complex tasks, so in these directed activities the adults first engaged in some work in which they themselves were competent, whether painting, music, scientific inquiry or observation of nature, or industrial production of some type. Then the younger children, watching them, listening to them, began to take their part in simpler forms of action, a minor part at first, until as they developed they accepted more and more responsibility for action.

John Dewey asked the Utopians about the objectives of their educational system. The Utopians at first did not understand what he meant. The whole concept of the school, of teachers, of students, of lessons had so completely disappeared that when Dewey asked about the special objectives of education the Utopians thought that he was asking why children live at all. The notion that there should be some special end which the young should try to attain was completely foreign to their thoughts. Dewey was led to the conclusion that what we regarded as objectives were so thoroughly engrained in the working activities of Utopian youth that they didn't have to think about them.

What are the main structural characteristics of nonformal education? They derive from its proximity to immediate action, work, and the opportunity to put learning to use. These elements of the environment close the gap between learning and doing, find intrinsic motivation in the learning situation, imbed objectives in work and activity, and associate learners and teachers in meaningful lines of action.

The Structure of Formal Education

We turn now to the structure of school learning. How does it differ from that of nonformal learning? What does its character tell us about its capacity?

First, formal schools are detached institutions, removed from indigenous practice. When the first schools sprang up around native artisans, they separated youth from their families for periods of time and made students of them. Schools became institutions for learning, teaching became a profession, and learning became a recognized pursuit of the young. Thus schools in a cultural sense were broken off from the main stream of work and action.

This separation of learning from action has a deep psychological impact upon the learner. He begins his formal education knowing that what he will learn is removed from the everyday reality of adult society. It is academic. This awareness is revealed in many ways. For example, the common urge of students to get "out" of school expresses a great deal about the meaning they attach to being "in." We speak of education as being "preparation" for the "real" world, thus denying it a reality of its own. Constant calls that schooling be "relevant" implies that by nature it is not. It must be made so.

All this is not to say that we do not value school learning. We obviously do. I am speaking about the *way* we value it, how that way illuminates the detached nature of schools, and how it subtly discounts the learning in the mind of the learner. Thus this structural characteristic of schooling modified and shapes its capacity to perform educational tasks.

Second, schools are in a sense ghettos of the young who create their own society and values. The detached nature of modern schools makes this inevitable, though we continue to express surprise, and frequently disgust, that it happens. Adults in schools are presumably caretakers of the young, but the young actually end up taking care of themselves within their own adolescent culture. The kind of meaningful working relationships between adults and children, which Dewey foresaw, do not thrive in an age-graded school society removed from action and where the only adults are professional teachers who can only talk about the world of work and action outside the school.

Third, not only do schools set children and youth apart from adult society: they further segregate them among themselves. Students progress grade-by-grade, year-by-year, in a constant pattern of severence with adult teachers and the reestablishment of relationships. The system works against the development of meaningful relationships among either older and younger children or among adults and children.

Four, the apparatus of the schools is admirably suited to *teaching;* whether the same may be said for *learning* is open to question. Anthropologists like to observe that in preliterate cultures children are in most cases far more eager to learn than the elders are to teach, whereas in machine cultures children are less eager to learn and adults are more eager to teach. To what extent this emphasis on learning in preliterate societies and on teaching in machine societies can be attributed either to the nature of preliterate and modern societies I do not know. I think the enigma does raise some interesting questions. Can it be, for example, that part of the answer may lie in the difference in modes of learning between preliterate and literate societies? In other words, in their different uses of formal and nonformal learning? Can it be that in substituting the discipline of classroom and the material rewards of grades for the pleasurable system of participating in adult-valued behavior we offend the basic social and biological nature of the young? Can it be that in spending the great resources we do on improving the arts of teaching we have actually failed to create stimulating environments for learning?

Fifth, formal education depends to a large extent on deferred rewards. The immediate present is devalued. Only the future is truly meaningful. Formal education, then, must find its target point in future time and teach students to deny the present for the sake of later rewards — for example, admission to the next level of education, a job, "success." By nature it does not carry within itself satisfactions sufficient for both the present and future.

Sixth, the structure of formal schools influences the methods of learning they employ. Consider first, that since schools operate largely outside the context of immediate action, they must depend more on telling than on showing; whereas the shepherd boy learned largely from observation and action, his counterpart in a formal school must learn largely by being told. The shepherd boy was active. The school student, passive. Second, as knowledge increases, more and more time must be given over to telling, either orally or in print, or in demonstrating outside the context of action. Third, the student must learn to follow the lesson through abstract written or oral language. This requires special skills that must be learned if a student is to achieve well in school. Finally, because it requires special skills, school learning becomes an art in itself.

These, then, are some of the conditions formal schools impose on learning, simply because they are detached institutions. The charge of irrelevance sometimes levelled at the schools can better be understood within this context;

their success as places of learning depends in part upon their ability to recreate within their walls a learning environment as naturally compelling as that existing on the outside. That environment must be created; it is not naturally built into the structure of school learning.

Achieving the Best Fit between Educational Means and Ends

I commented earlier that a new strategy in education policy should be to select from all the available means those with demonstrated capacity to achieve desired goals. The means also should be selected with due regard to such variables as: Who is to be educated? At what time in life? In what kind of programs? And for what purpose? The key is to find the best fit between means and ends. In this concluding section I would like to speculate about the fit of formal and nonformal education with respect to certain educational tasks.

The first task I would like to discuss is that of initiating and implementing developmental change. Considerable disappointment has been expressed about the ability of formal education to effect such change. This may be an instance of not using it well, for I suspect that initiating change and implementing change are two quite different ends and they call for the application of different means. Formal education may best fit the end of conceptualizing and planning change. Nonformal education may be better suited to implementing it.

The environment of formal education incorporates change agents, such as books written outside the indigenous setting, teachers trained in cosmopolitan centers, a systematic way of inquiring into subjects and organizing knowledge, and a tradition of research. The Western-type formal school is itself a foreign import in many areas of the world, introducing new values and practices into indigenous environments. Thus the structural characteristics of formal education equip it to work out on the cutting edge of change.

I doubt that these same characteristics equip it to carry through and implement change. This may be one reason why specialized formal institutions created to deal with certain social problems very frequently fail to live up to expectations. Missing in their structures are the linkages that would permit them to get at the infrastructures to be changed. Their detached natures are the flaw.

Nonformal education, on the other hand, is geared to action and the application of knowledge. Where both the initiation and implementation of developmental change are the goals, a wise course would seem to be to link the two in a sequence beginning in knowledge generation, conceptualization, and planning, and ending in application, work, and action.

The work in agricultural development carried on by American Land Grant Universities is an example. Most breakthroughs in the plant and animal sciences came out of classrooms, laboratories, and experimental stations. In themselves they would never have helped to revolutionize American agriculture. Beyond this formal system, and linked to it, was the nonformal which operated through extension programs. It was this system that penetrated the infrastructure of agricultural production. Here is a case where all the available means of education were well fitted to the tasks to be performed.

The second task I should like to discuss is that of preparation for the world of occupations. There seems to be little consensus on what should constitute a philosophy of occupational training. That there is a set of common competencies needed to undertake most jobs in modern society seems now to be accepted. The ability to read, write, and speak, to relate to one's society and culture, and to acquire some sense of citizenship are probably basic in occupational preparation.

When we come, however, to preparation for the performance of specific skills the issues sharpen considerably. What do the structural characteristics of formal and nonformal education equip each to do well? I would suggest that where the arena of action centers within formal education itself, the schools are equal to the task. Thus schools are a good place to train teachers to understand schools. They may be a poor place to train teachers to understand communities. In other words, when the arena of action is outside the formal school I begin to suspect that the school is a poor site for specific training. If, on the other hand, the school's detachment can be overcome by integrating it with the world of work, the results may be surprisingly good. The training of doctors in teaching hospitals where classroom, sickroom, surgical room, and laboratory are in close proximity is an example.

Now what are the implications of this for one of the very largest areas in which the schools engage in skill training: that of vocational and technical education? Here the general practice is quite different from that represented by the teaching hospital. Many vocational and technical education programs are isolated in formal schools and unrelated to the world of work. And too often these are ineffective. The reason may be that a formal system detached from the world of work where the knowledge is to be put to use is simply a poor choice of educational means to do the job. Could it be that these programs could better be set up within the shop, as a medical school in a teaching hospital, or that students could be better assigned to work for portions of each day on jobs for which they are training?

Not all school programs in vocational education are confined to formal schools. One such program that usually exhibits good teaching and learning is that of vocational agriculture. Here the program typically rotates between classroom and farm. In the classroom boys learn scientific knowledge of agriculture to which they are not exposed in the nonformal learning situation at home. On the farm they raise live stock, grow crops, and test in practice the validity of scientific concepts. Thought and action thus confront each other daily.

There are other aspects of this learning situation that are of interest. Teachers of vocational agriculture typically grow up on farms, a fact which gives them two qualities which Dewey found in Utopian teachers: skill in carrying on some line of action and credibility in the eyes of the students. Another element is that the nonformal system of learning on the farm is used to reinforce the formal system, giving it a kind of legitimacy it would not otherwise have in the mind of the student. Conversely, the formal system reinforces the nonformal learning, giving importance to the projects which boys conduct on the farm. The best of both systems thus combine to create a compelling environment for learning.

A third task of education is that of teaching young children. Recent evidence points to the critical importance of the preschool years in a child's learning. This period of nonformal learning seems to have great influence on how well the child learns during his years of formal schooling.

I would regard the elementary school as a reasonably effective means for teaching basic literacy and for introducing the child to the larger community in which he must live. The elementary school is an institution close to its surrounding cultural roots. It has a traditional linkage with the family; of all schools it probably finds it easiest to use nonformal appraoches to learning. Its teachers are probably the most creative and most sensitive in using the child's background to stimulate school learning.

The secondary school is a very different institution from that of the elementary school. Historically is comes out of a different tradition. While the elementary school sprang from a popular desire for education and its teachers were drawn from the people, the secondary school came out of an intellectually elitist tradition and its teachers were drawn from higher institutions and universities. Historically, it was a very formal school, detached and without linkage to action or the nonformal systems of learning. Even today when one works in elementary schools he can feel this difference.

Yet, it is this school to which modern society assigns the responsibility of educating, not just the elite, but the mass of our youth. It is this task of educating all the youth that I would like to turn to next.

The development of an appropriate strategy for the education of youth seems to me especially perplexing. We isolate them in formal schools at the very time when they are reaching for mature values and orientation. Instead of helping them develop really meaningful relationships with adult society and work we abondon them largely to their own devices, justifying our actions by saying that they are learning important things they will need in the future. We place youth in this holding pattern at the very time that biologically and psychologically they want to be "with it" rather than "out of it."

Large doses of detached school learning seem to me to be inappropriate for this age group and socially harmful. If the end of educating the young is to widen the generation gap, isolate them from the inherited culture, and sort out for election to the elite those who learn well through abstract symbols, then the formal secondary school is admirably suited to the purpose. If, however, the goal is something like that of John Dewey's Utopians, to associate youth and adults in a meaningful line of action toward the end of transmitting skills and culture, the secondary school is probably a poor educational tool.

In many ways I think it may be argued that formal education generally is more appropriate for adults than youth. Adult learning usually springs from genuine motivations growing from life experiences in nonformal learning. Detached learning for adults may have the value of giving new perspective on experience and of stimulating new ideas. It could be that in terms of the structural capabilities of formal and nonformal education to accommodate youth and adults our timing is just the reverse from what it should be. Perhaps it is the youth who most need nonformal education and adults formal education. I would therefore take some stock in the newer forms of secondary schools without walls which combine intellectual search and applied activity and reserve purely formal education as an option to be used when individuals feel the need for it.

Conclusion

Underlying my approach to this chapter is the conviction that learned behavior is determined by the environment in which it takes place. Behavior is shaped and maintained by its consequences. The learning environments of formal and nonformal education tend to be of a different character. They shape and maintain different kinds of behavior. The goal, then, of educational strategy should be to determine the kind of behavior sought and create those educational environments which most clearly support and encourage it.

Modern society requires a wide range of behaviors in order to perpetuate itself and do its work. Yet, our assumption to date has been that formal education is capable of producing nearly all of them. And when it doesn't we cry for its reform. It is quite possible that formal education, right along, has been doing what it is good at and that it ought to continue. The difficulty may be that we now want it to do some things it is not good at. Perhaps it is time to seek other means that are naturally good at doing them better.

6

Nonformal Educational Alternatives

ROLLAND G. PAULSTON

My purpose in this chapter is to examine why and how specific programs in the nonformal educational sector might more effectively be included in the educational planning process. I will first examine the growing awareness among planners that the process of designing educational futures must include more than formal schooling alone. Then I will examine a number of case studies of nonformal educational programs that have to a greater or lesser degree been planned and coordinated with formal schooling at a national level. These selected examples of national youth-service programs, unfortunately, offer no more than fragmentary data and a weak basis for generalization. They do, nevertheless, allow us to come to grips with a core problem of planning nonformal education, the widening of the data base to facilitate the conscious working out of realistic alternative educational programs before attempting to incorporate them in the existing educational complex.

Before moving into the body of the chapter, it may be helpful to define a number of key terms and to comment on the sources of data used. When possible, I have attempted to use Coombs' definitions so as to gain greater comparability with the results of his ongoing World Bank-UNICEF-International Council for Educational Development study of nonformal education in rural and agricultural development.[1] He defines education as any systematic, organized instructional process designed to achieve specific learning objectives by particular groups of learners. Formal education refers to the traditional, articulated school system that begins at the primary level and culminates in colleges, tertiary level institutions, and universities. Formal education is typically under the jurisdiction of national ministries of education which are responsible for the maintenance of established curricula, teacher corps, examinations and certificates, and the administration of major public financial support.

Nonformal education, in marked contrast, is a residual category. If loosely defined, it could conceivably include all socialization and skills learning processes taking place outside formal education — an overwhelming field of activity. For the purposes of scholarly study, and for educational planning as well, the parameters of nonformal education must be greatly reduced. For the purposes of this work, my operational definition of nonformal education includes any structured, systematic, nonschool educational and training activities of relatively short duration, where sponsoring agencies seek concrete behavioral changes in fairly distinct target populations. Programs examined here are further restricted by examining only those that operate at a national level, that are offered by governmental ministries or agencies, and that have occurred in developing countries. While recognizing that with modernization there is a growing functional blur between formal and nonformal education as here defined, an attempt is made in table 6-1 to chart some of the more salient identifying characteristics of these educational programs. These are, of course, only modal characteristics, and the range of each variable is apt to be rather wide.

It should be noted that a number of educational planners reject the term "nonformal". Marien, for one, finds it a misleading distinction. He proposes instead a model of the educational complex which "includes all organizations and parts of organizations involved with the provision of formal instructional services that proportedly enhance the learning process of students."[2] The four

Table 6-1. Some Modal-defining Characteristics of Nonformal and Formal Educational Programs

Nonformal, Nonschool Programs	Formal School Programs	Variable
On a continuum from high to low degree of structure, but usually the latter. Lateral transmission stressed. Little interrelatedness of components, i.e., a nonformal *sector,* not a system.	Relatively highly structured. Functionally interrelated sets of units hierarchically ordered, i.e., a graded (in time and content) sequential system.	Structure
Usually task- or skill-centered; dictated by functional needs of participants; low verbal. May reflect values conflicting with status quo and elites. Discreet content units.	Generally academic, abstract, and often "ethnocentric." Highly verbal, reflects status quo values of elites. Articulated content units.	Content
Short-term, present-time orientation; time and gain closely joined. Often part-time, nocturnal or diurnal study. Flexible timing of activities.	Future-time oriented; time and gain not joined. Full-time diurnal attendance stressed. Lock-step inflexible sequence of activities.	Time
Uncoordinated, fragmented, diffuse. Voluntary organizations predominate. Greater degree of local control. Decisions often made at program level.	Coordinated control, national, regional, or religious bureaucracies predominate. Centrical tendency. Elites influential in higher control positions.	Control
Low visibility, may be on the job, at home. Participants bear fairly low costs. High efficiency of locale utilization, i.e., functionally related to learning.	Highly visible, expensive, fixed in place. Often state-supported. Urban preference. Low efficiency of plant utilization. Learning physically isolated from application.	Locale

Great variation but stress is on resocialization, acculturation, and the learning of practical skills and knowledge to be used in work or community situation. Terminal, closed-ended. Seeks to bring distinct groups of people into conformity with principles and practices of another group — usually an agency or employer. Seeks to supplement or complement formal schooling.	Stress on socialization, enculturation, and perpetuation of educational bureaucracies. Legitimization of existing elites, their values and behaviors. Conferring status, selection for more schooling, and possible elite recruitment. Seeks to bring youth into conformity with controlling body — usually an elite, and adult institutions.	Functions
Payoffs tend to be tangible, immediate, or short-term gains related to work or daily life: i.e., increased material well-being, productivity, self-awareness and/or power to control environment.	Payoffs tend to be deferred promise of long-term gains in sociocultural and economic status.	Rewards
Teacher helps student interact with and master the material to be learned and applied. Content centered. Methods are relatively flexible and related to application and performance-standard needs.	Knowledge is standardized, transmitted from teacher to pupil in the classroom. Teacher-centered. Teaching methods dictated by policy and are relatively inflexible and noninnovative.	Method
Learners are from all age groups, i.e., not age- or place-defined. Job mobility concerns predominate. Great variety of teacher qualifications and motivations.	Students are age-defined, predictable. Usually urban in outlook and social mobility conscious. Teachers are formally certified with their status correlated with location in the school hierarchy.	Participants
Great variation in costs per program and per student vis-à-vis costs for comparable educational programs in the formal system. Economies of size not often possible. On a cost/benefit basis, little gained by nonformal education programs.	Costs are standardized by level and increase moving up the structural heirarchy. Economies of size possible.	Costs

major educational components, or subsystems, of the complex are: (1) a "core" of schools, colleges, and universities; (2) a "periphery" of structured educational programs entailing formal instruction such as adult education, management training, remedial training, and retraining youth activities; (3) "informal education" beyond classrooms involving mass media, cultural facilities, social institutions, political processes, and personal media; and (4) "international education" or knowledge inputs gained outside of national boundaries. The important difference here is that both core and peripheral educational activities are viewed as being "formal" if both teachers and students are involved in learning situations promising some reward (i.e., certificates, diplomas, job access, promotion, licenses, merit badges, etc.) beyond the inherent value in learning for its own sake.[3] Although this comprehensive model would facilitate analysis of systematic relations in the total educational complex, the means of distinguishing between core and peripheral activities is somewhat vague and difficult to operationalize.

Data used in this study were drawn from a review of the scant literature on planning nonformal education, from a recently completed critically annotated bibliography on nonformal education in development,[4] and from an examination of primary and secondary source materials on specific attempts to create national youth service programs in developing countries. In light of the scarcity of evaluative research findings on programs studied, the study should be viewed as exploratory, as an attempt to operationalize the concept of nonformal education, and, eventually, to facilitate the educational decision-making process. It is obvious that nonformal education activities and programs have existed with various success in most countries for a long time and, studied or not, they will continue. Thus our task is first to understand better their functions and operation. Only then should attempts be made to intervene in nonformal education as a means of seeking greater efficiency in the educational complex.

Enlarging the Scope and Utility of
Educational Planning

During the past decade, the field of educational planning has experienced considerable turbulence and rapid expansion. This growth, especially in developing countries, has often been a concommittant of the quantitative explosions in national educational systems. As school enrollments have grown in response to enormous pressures of social demand, educational planning has frequently been called upon to bring the explosion under some degree of greater control by introducing more rational goal-setting and allocation practices in human resource development.

Hindsight tells us that the effort was unrealistic in the extreme and, for the most part, a failure. The linear expansion of schools has, in fact, only been halted by the fearsome increase of educational expenses which in typical cases have been growing at least twice as rapidly as national economies and overall public budgets.[5] Planning, of course, can do little to influence the demand for schooling or the runaway expansion of enrollment in the past decade or so. Nor has it been notably effective in attempts to introduce substantial educational change — admittedly often of a utopian nature — in formal educational systems in underdeveloped or developed societies.

Given the relative ineffectiveness of planners in accomplishing their objectives in the past, what new strategies might be put forth to make educational planning more useful in coming to grips with the staggering problems facing educational decision-makers today? A number of proposed changes in the aims, methods, and scope of educational planning might be noted, but one of special interest in our present inquiry is the effort to enlarge the scope of planning to include nonformal education. For example, a key element of Coombs' nontechnical planning approach involves a change in the relationships and allocation of resources between the formal educational system and other educational activities. The scope of planning, he asserts, must be expanded to include all educational programs as a unified whole:

Each individual educational unit and program — formal and nonformal alike — must be designed with a careful eye to fitting the particular needs and social-economic circumstances of its local area. Such educational plans must be derivative of integrated rural development plans specific to each area because the productivity of education will depend heavily upon the presence or absence of complimentary development forces and resource inputs in the same area. The foregoing will require considerable better planning concepts and methods that are presently available; better information and more reliable assumptions as a basis for planning; greatly strengthened administrative systems for implementing plans; and, above all, creative new ideas about education itself and how it can be best provided.[6]

Coombs goes on to note that the rational planning and development of nonformal education has been a particularly neglected area to date. It has been largely ignored (except by the International Labor Organization and the private sector) by professional educators, researchers, and educational planners alike. Chesswas has also stressed the need for systematic data collection from all types of out-of-school training activities, such as literacy education, correspondence courses, and the like.[7] Such data could serve a number of useful purposes. It would widen the data base of planning and facilitate the inclusion of nonformal education — or at least its more structured and visible aspects — in national educational development plans, and thus facilitate coordination of the educational programs offered by all ministries and agencies. It would also help to strengthen manpower planning and allow additional cost-benefit comparison of formal and nonformal alternatives. At present even such basic data as enrollment by sex, level and type of instruction, completion rates, or agencies supporting nonformal education programs is not yet collected in any country.

Despite the near total lack of systematic study of the concept of a nonformal educational sector and of summative evaluations of such programs, there does exist a considerable body of material on experiences in the nonformal sector. It will be my purpose in the following sections to examine part of this experience in the hope of extracting useful observations as to how to strengthen the educational planning and decision-making process vis-á-vis rural areas of underdeveloped countries.

Some Case Studies of Nonformal Education

The following case studies of National Youth Service programs are examined to raise a number of questions about planning nonformal educational activities for youth: i.e., is it feasible, is it desirable, etc.? These programs have been selected because they comprise one of the few distinct areas of the nonformal education sector that has been more or less planned and coordinated at a national, or ministerial, level by governmental authorities concerned with a lack of jobs for school leavers, the need for more effective vocational training programs, more effective political socialization, and a host of other problems of out-of-school youth. This attempt, using a modified social systems approach, will hopefully move beyond the intuitive and exhortative studies that have been all too common to date.

I would also, by inference, like to probe some of the rather sweeping claims recently made for nonformal education as a "wonder drug," or cure-all for the inadequacies and so-called dysfunctionalities of formal educational systems. Two of these claims might be noted. One is made by Coombs who states that the critical educational gaps "can only be filled by well-conceived programs of nonformal education. . . ."[8] In a similar vein, AID concludes that "for many lesser-developed countries, the only opportunity for skill and knowledge development for the populace as a whole is through some kind of non-formal education. . . . It seems equally clear that this non-formal mode of learning could be very substantially increased in value and extended in scope by more imaginative planning, organization, and leadership."[9]

Given the obvious need for alternatives to formal schooling, the research agenda becomes one of examining the record of attempted innovations, of identifying significant factors in the success or failure of such programs, and of producing credible evidence and theoretical constructs which will enable us to explain, to predict, and to plan with greater precision.

A wide variety of National Youth Service Programs are found throughout the developed and developing nations.[10] For the purposes of this chapter, however, and its objective of helping to develop comprehensive action programs of nonformal education in the Southeast Asia Ministers of Education Organization (SEAMEO) member countries, it will be necessary to select cases that generally reflect program contexts that are comparable to Southeast Asia. Basic assumptions here are that out-of-school youth in developing countries are a critical, high priority problem, that voluntary National Youth Service programs offer a potential nonformal education mechanism for both youth and national development, and that their promise will be maximized if they are rationally planned and coordinated with the processes and outputs of the formal educational system as well as with the larger socioeconomic realities of specific national settings.

The criteria used to select case studies for analysis are:

1. Programs that have taken place in Third World countries

2. Programs that provide full-time residential training for varying periods from one to two years

3. Programs that have a marked nonformal educational component to teach new skills and behaviors

4. Programs that are aimed at the 15- to 20-year age group — they do not include essentially service efforts by elitist university student groups (as in Ethiopia)

5. Programs that are national in scope and administered by agencies of national governments

6. Programs that are largely "voluntary"

7. Programs that have been studied and/or reported and for which a minimal amount of descriptive or other data exists in the literature

Using these criteria, I narrowed the selection of possible illustrative case studies to three National Youth Service programs in Africa (i.e., Kenya, Tanzania, and Uganda) and two in the Americas (Jamaica and Cuba). Unfortunately, I was unable to find an example that met the foregoing criteria in Southeast Asia.

Although the experiences summarized here are limited, the problem of out-of-school and unemployed primary-school leavers is becoming increasingly critical in all developing countries. With over half of the total population in low-income countries under 20 years of age[11] and with rapidly expanding primary enrollments, the output of primary schools continues greatly to exceed the absorbitive capacity of secondary-schools training facilities and labor markets. Economic growth has not generally kept pace with the explosion of primary schooling and ever-greater numbers of youth are frustrated by being unable to enter secondary schools or find employment.

Given this crisis situation and the resistance of elite-oriented and academic formal schooling to basic change, what might educational planners contribute by way of "diagnosis" and proposals for innovation and alternative action as well? A comparative examination of attempts to create innovative nonformal educational programs that seek to train and involve out-of-school youth in the tasks of national development might be seen as one necessary first step in this direction.

African National Youth Service Organizations

Following the creation of the Ghana Young Pioneers in 1955, six other African countries (Kenya, Malawi, Swaziland, Tanzania, Uganda, and Zambia) have created national youth services. Generalizing from the Kenya experience, Griffin has noted a number of common stated and unstated objectives for the creation of these new national institutions.[12]

They have all more or less sought:

1. To help in the assimilation of militant youth who have been actively

engaged in preindependence struggles and who, once independence has been achieved, require reorientation to fit them for normal working lives. Although this is a transitory reason and has no place in long-range planning, it often gives a powerful initial impetus to the creation of National Youth Services.

2. To create a pool of trained manpower to support the army and police in matters of defense and internal security.

3. To help relieve unemployment. The practical value of this reason may be marginal, but its psychological value may be considerable.

4. To provide desirable new skills and behaviors through education and training. Remedial studies are often stressed.

5. To aid national development through project work (i.e., roadbuilding, erosion control, new agricultural settlements, etc.). National Youth Service men may cost as much or more than the minimum wages of unskilled workmen, but as a disciplined corps of volunteers they can be used in isolated areas where contracted labor would be difficult to employ.

6. To foster the creation of a national outlook and spirit among youth from various tribal or ethnic backgrounds.

African National Youth Service organizations, moreover, share a number of common features with respect to their rationale, administration, programs, costs, and achievements.[13] They all represent efforts by governments actively to make some provision for the educational and training needs of young people who are unable to enter the upper levels of the formal school system. They share the belief that out-of-school and unemployed youth must be provided (1) an opportunity for systematic vocational training *in situ*, (2) a chance to contribute with skills and volunteered service to national development, and (3) a follow-up program after service for job placement, apprenticeship training, or participation in some sort of agricultural resettlement scheme.

All six African Youth Services have been rather heavily influenced by the training formula developed by the Israeli technical-assistance mission which helped to create the Ghana Youth Pioneers. In what might be called the Israeli training model, young volunteers receive a period of basic training stressing discipline, drill, physical fitness, and willingness to do hard work. Nonformal education is offered, often of a remedial nature, in reading skills, civic education, as well as in particular skills training. Most frequently taught skills courses include carpentry, masonry, "improved" agriculture, and motor mechanics. The sole exception to this formula is found in the Uganda National Union of Youth Organization where training is carried out in local youth centers and not in a base-camp type of structure.

One of the recurrent battles fought by NYS programs dealing with primary-school leavers is the constant need to guard against suggestions of bookishness or academic content. If training courses offer academic content, aspirations for secondary schooling aroused in the course of primary schooling can easily be resurrected with a corresponding diminution in ultimately placing trainees in employment. When viewed in practical terms, programs will be required to offer skills training in at least a minimum of such basic subjects as communication skills, elementary bookkeeping, health and nutrition, and, where possible, family planning.

The problem of conflicting self-serving incentives and society-serving incentives in poor countries especially is, of course, not easily reconciled.[14] Some NYS organizations seek to create a service orientation by stressing group spirit and religious viewpoints. Where traditional religious behaviors and viewpoints are no longer acceptable, attempts have been made to motivate youth through "development studies" courses to heighten awareness of national development needs and the potential contribution of volunteers to nation-building.

All the African organizations are administered by government departments other than ministries of education and there appears to be little or no contact between the authorities responsible for planning and administering formal school programs and youth-service programs.[15] The youth services, in fact, have been able to establish a considerable degree of autonomy in their programs. They have their own budgets and provide most of their own supervisory personnel. They use a modified military uniform and a military-type chain of command. There is, however, a considerable variation in the degree to which military patterns are present.

The content and location of training programs varies with the development situation and priorities in each country. In Malawi, for example, agricultural development is viewed as the first priority and the Malawi Young Pioneers are used as an agency to introduce and promote improved agricultural practices into rural areas. Youth are provided instruction and experience in agricultural techniques comparable with inherited agricultural practices within the price range and technical competence of the average small farmers. No efforts have been made to introduce mechanized farming. In 1969 some 2,200 Young Pioneers were in service.

In Zambia and Tanzania, NYS programs have shifted from an emphasis on vocational trades training to the need to develop neglected rural areas. "Skills" camps near urban areas have been closed and relocated in rural settings. Training now seeks to prepare youth to establish cooperative farms through a system of support and loans from a number of government services and from agriculture. This development reflects a growing awareness among training organizations that youth-service training in itself is not a solution, that it must be followed by arrangements where the controlled application of new learning will be possible and, to some degree, profitable. Settler developments where ex-volunteers open up new agricultural areas have, in this regard, been an important innovation.

African Youth Service programs in general are small and becoming smaller. The Kenya NYS, for example, is the largest in Africa. In 1966-67, it enrolled over 5,000 members, but by 1969 this figure had declined to 3,500 young people, mostly boys. The Zambia Youth Service had 1,500 boys and girls in eight camps in 1964. Six years later 1,100 recruits were being trained in industrial skills, agricultural, or domestic science courses of one or two years' duration in nine camps.

Programs have diminished in size not necessarily for lack of volunteers or perceived value for developmental ends, but primarily because they are expensive. The real costs of training programs per trainee are very difficult to estimate. Programs receive funds and equipment from various national and external sources and working budgets, when available, give only a partial picture of total costs. It is possible, however, to establish something of a range which enables comparison of the costs of NYS programs with those of formal school programs. In Malawi without expensive training camps, for example, annual costs per trainee came to about £60, or a little over half of the total cost for a student in an average secondary boarding school. In Kenya, the £100 cost per service-man equalled that for a formal-school student, while in Zambia per-capita costs of trainees were approximately "three times that for secondary-school boarding students."[16] In general, however, it seems safe to say that the cost of keeping a youth in national service will be roughly comparable to putting him through some form of secondary schooling (i.e., between £100 and £200 p.a.)

The main factor inflating the cost of training has been the frequent insistence of consolidating training activities in urban institutions concerned exclusively with training. When training and resettlement activities are combined, however, bost costs and trainee-wastage rates are reduced. It can be demonstrated that training *in situ* encourages trainees to stick to the tasks for which they were trained. This slight trend away from institutional training must, however, be greatly intensified if the costs of African NYS schemes are to be lowered to the point where such programs will be able to make significant inroads into the vast training needs of out-of-school youth.

Equally imperative will be a greater reallocation of resources away from rapidly expanding formal-schoolsystems. Following a study of NYS in African Commonwealth countries, A.K. Wood concluded that in terms of the numbers of primary-school leavers who are unable to continue in the formal school system (an average of some 75 to 80 percent), "the national youth organizations have not been able to make any substantial contribution to their absorption and training. Such a contribution would appear to be unlikely whilst costs remain high and the primary concern of the educational efforts of governments is with the expansion of the upper levels of the formal educational structure."[17]

NYS Programs in the Caribbean

Before examining NYS programs in the Caribbean countries of Jamaica and Cuba — programs in Trinidad, Guyana, and Dominica exist on a lesser scale — it may be appropriate to contrast briefly some important differences between the regions of Africa and the Caribbean. In Africa, a large continental land mass with over 300 million people, the economic trend is from subsistence farming toward the production of supplementary cash crops for the commercial market. Life is rural and youth are relatively isolated. Formal education is restricted, ties to the industrial nations are weak, while family, clan, and tribal ties are strong. The Caribbean, on the other hand, with a population of some 4 million, is a region of small, scattered islands with plantation-type economies producing raw materials for export to the industrial nations of Europe and North America. The family is a comparatively weak unit, land is scarce, farming is generally deprecated by youth and parents alike, and the population is largely urban in orientation if not location. Mass media from North America saturates the area and along with the widespread formal schooling excites consumption and employment aspirations which are totally unrealistic given the existing economic systems and employment potentialities. With a rapid population growth, and with an unemployment rate among the 15-25 year group of over 30 percent, there is a considerable migration of youth seeking employment in the United States and Western Europe. The Caribbean youth, moreover, are profoundly alienated from agriculture and rural life. They share the general dissatisfactions of the youth cultures in more developed countries, attitudes that are reinforced by the awareness that with frighteningly high levels of unemployment, they have little chance of playing any kind of constructive of self-respecting role in their societies.[18]

Both African and Caribbean governments have responded to youth and development needs through the creation of a multitude of youth organizations which seek to provide disadvantaged youth with skills, social training, and better opportunities to prepare for employment in industry and improved agriculture. NYS programs in Africa are closely linked with political parties and ministries of agriculture and are especially characterized by attempts to prepare youth for agriculture and rural and community development. Youth training in the Caribbean, including revolutionary Cuba, is, however, more often viewed as part of the social welfare and educational apparatus. It seeks to resocialize youth with antisocial tendencies through encampments stressing remedial social work, character, and citizenship training. Youth attending camps are mainly from socially and economically disadvantaged backgrounds. They are provided skills or craft training, usually of an inferior quality because of unqualified instructors, and simulated working environments. Attempts at full skills training to recognized levels in youth organization programs, by and large, compare unfavorably in cost and learning with industrial training in formal education with on-the-job training.[19]

The oldest and best established NYS in the Caribbean, the Jamaica Youth Corps (JYC), offers an excellent example of difficulties in planning NYS organizations as innovative, nonformal educational institutions.[20] The JYC was created in 1956 as an educational and social welfare component of the 1957-67 National Plan for Jamaica and, although supposedly autonomous, retains links with the Ministries of Labor, Agriculture, Education, and Social Welfare. It is a two-year volunteer program for "those who fail to complete eight years of free primary and post-primary education."[21] These children, mostly rural black boys, have absorbed middle-class values and goals that they are largely unable to pursue. Their parents as well overwhelmingly desire that their children escape the grim and depressing conditions of rural life and obtain white-collar employment. Yet formal schooling is highly selective and "bookish." It offers no vocational or career guidance, but instead powerfully reinforces and extends the unrealistic occupational aspirations of lower-class youth and their parents.

With the rapid expansion of schooling in Jamaica following World War II, problems of unemployed youth, migration to urban centers, and "lawlessness and indiscipline" reached crisis proportions. The Central Planning Unit, attached to the Chief Minister's Office, was accordingly instructed by the Cabinet to draft a plan for a national youth service. In this plan, economic and social objectives greatly superceded educational objectives. To wit, the JYC was designed to take 7,000 youth out of the labor market and to use their labor for the creation of capital assets. Costs were not to exceed £40,000 for capital equipment and an annual recurring expense of £100 per volunteer. The scheme would be administered initially by the Ministries of Education and Social Welfare and, once established, would be transferred to an autonomous Statutory Board appointed by the Governor and located in the Executive Council.

How the plan should be implemented and how the JYC's goals are to be accomplished has, however, been a source of conflict and disagreement. The Ministry of Education has continually sought to introduce a full-scale program of rather specialized vocational training to help alleviate shortages of skilled workers. The Youth Corps administration rejected this approach because of chronic and critical shortages of funds, equipment, and qualified staff. Instead, they have developed a one- to two-year program stressing training in rudimentary agricultural skills in rural camps, literacy and remedial studies, civic education, and on-the-job training "sustained by sheer resourcefullness."

This chronic lack of funds has necessitated great emphasis on local self-help and volunteered services, and on gifts of land and other resources from large international corporations. Because qualified staff will not work for the low salaries offered, in-service training programs are constantly underway. But, as soon as a staff member achieves some competence, he leaves for a better-paying job. Attempts to make agriculture more attractive through use of mechanized equipment such as tractors and sprayers, etc., have also been defeated by lack of funds.[22]

Another serious problem is the reluctance of the Ministry of Education to pass on the powers of financial control, and the ministry's continuous interference in staff and program content matters. Throughout the JYS's early years, the Ministry of Education insisted on "keeping a restraining hand" despite the statutory powers of the Board of Management. Efforts by the board to gain national acceptance of the corps as an integral part of the national educational system following independence have been consistently blocked by the ministry.

Incentives used in the JYS include: (1) recognition of "good" work and behavior in organizational and national publications, (2) "gold-edged certificates" and Youth Corps badges for "first-class campers," (3) prizes (never monetary) and trophies, (4) group "treats and holidays," and (5) the promise of recommendations to prospective employers on termination of service.[23]

Primarily because of financial restrictions, the JYC has never accomplished its basic goal of placing 7,000 of the some 40,000 school leavers joining the labor force annually in camps. The corps has nevertheless helped to make productive use of the otherwise unwanted and unused manpower of some 1,000 youth every year. Several camps and a variety of rural developments have been built with volunteer labor, and over 50 percent of the ex-campers "return to rural areas to utilize their training in agriculture and trades."[24]

As the number of applicants applying to the Corps is over four times as great as the number of available places, it seems reasonable to assume that the program would expand rapidly if increased resources could be provided. At best, however, it would seem that the JYS could absorb no more than about ten percent of the total population of unemployed, out-of-school youth. Moreover, follow-up studies of early graduates show that less than 30 percent are able to secure employment (20 percent in agriculture, 18 percent in trades and mechanics, 16 percent in construction trades, 15 percent in industry, 9 percent in business, and the rest in tourism, tailoring, the police, etc.). As less than two percent reenter the formal-school system, the JYC may be viewed as a relatively effective "cooling-out" institution.

Revolutionary Cuba offers another Caribbean case of attempts to plan and implement voluntary youth service programs falling entirely in the nonformal sector. With the revolution in 1959, Cuban authorities have given a high priority to the mobilization of both in-school and out-of-school youth. All secondary-level students are required to spend a minimum of six weeks a year in agricultural work camps as an integral part of their schooling. A wide variety of other work-study and voluntary development projects in rural areas involve nearly all post-primary youth.[25]

Despite impressive gains in making schooling available to all classes and in all parts of the country, the number of secondary school-age children who repeat classes or drop out is still considerable.[26] These youth are mostly 13- to 16-year-olds from rural and urban working-class families. They are for the most part unskilled, unmotivated, and lacking in "consciencia," or the willingness to sacrifice personal for collective gain.

Rather than allow a "generación perdida," i.e., a lost generation of lower-class youth (antisocial and sometimes delinquent behavior will supposedly not be present in the generation growing up entirely in the new revolutionary society), Cuban authorities have sought to resocialize this group through their incorporation in the "parallel" or nonformal educational system.

In close collaboration, the Ministry of Education and the Young Communist

League evolved a plan (in 1968-69) for a national youth service which would identify and mobilize both in- and out-of-school youth for technical training and productive work in the sugarcane harvests. Called the Centennial Youth Column in honor of Cuba's century of struggle for for national independence, the organization seeks three basic objectives: (1) to provide remedial learning in basic education, (2) to prepare agricultural workers who are qualified and motivated to support the introduction of mechanized agriculture, and (3) to inculcate socialist consciousness in work, study, and play.[27]

Although participation in the column is voluntary, one sees large signs all over Cuba exhorting youth to enlist. There is at the same time a good deal of pressure brought to bear on eligible youth (i.e., unemployed, failing in school, and nonrevolutionary in behavior) by educational authorities, the Young Communist League, and other mass organizations. Recruitment of youth for the column, however, is difficult, or as stated by Prime Minister Fidel Castro, "A hard job that calls for the cooperation of everybody in this country." He has not, perhaps, made this job any easier by insisting that volunteers must willingly learn to do as free men that which was formerly done by slaves (i.e., to cut sugarcane without pay).

More than half of the 24,000 volunteers currently completing three years of service (i.e., 14,717) come from the province of Oriente in eastern Cuba, where the majority of Cuba's canecutters, for the greatest part black, have traditionally lived. The work contribution of the column takes place in the Province of Camagüey, a relatively underdeveloped agricultural area. The service is organized along military lines and located in camps near centers of agricultural production. Youth of 13 and 14 years of age spend the majority of their time in remedial studies, while the 15- and 16-year-olds do field work, build roads, and participate in on-the-job training. According to Castro, of the 24,000 young men being demobilized in 1971, over 6,000 have become agricultural machine operators, 800 have qualified as sugar industry workers, and 1,200 have become teachers in the Worker-Farmer Education Plan.[28] Gains in basic education, in agricultural production, and in political and revolutionary "self-improvement" are also noted.

Costs of the column, which are covered by the Ministry of Education budget, are not available. It might be reasonably assumed, nevertheless, that the cost-benefit ratio would be a favorable one. Camp staff is provided by the Young Communist League, and volunteers provide the greatest part of their food requirements through their own efforts, so these expenses are low. An indication of high productivity might be seen in the fact that the 16,000 members of the column who worked in the 1971 harvest cut more cane than did the 60,000 to 80,000 mostly adult volunteers who worked the Camagüey sugarcane harvests in Pre-Column years. The need to place demobilized volunteers in positions where they will be able to utilize their new skills, abilities, and knowledge is viewed by Castro as a major problem. He is concerned that only some 500 of the 24,000 ex-volunteers plan to stay and settle in Camaguey. Approximately 2.5 percent plan to re-enter the formal school system, while the vast majority will return to their provinces and help to meet the pressing need for skilled agricultural workers. Although the cost efficiency of the program is not known, the program's effectiveness in relation to the basic objectives of the revolution, i.e., the building of socialism, would seem to have been fairly impressive.

As an experimental program, the column is in no way seen as a solution to problems of failure and desertion in the formal educational system. It would appear, nevertheless, that the program offers possibilities of wider application. In its attempts at resocialization and ideological formation through productive labor, the column has been at least moderately successful. Large numbers of youth who failed in formal schools have through nonformal educational experiences learned new skills and knowledge important for both national economic development and for individual growth into productive and responsible citizens.

Conclusions

In this chapter I have attempted two related tasks. One has been to examine the growing awareness of educational planners concerning the need to enlarge the scope of planning to include selected activities in the nonformal sector in designing alternatives for human-resource development. A second has sought to assess some of the more viable efforts to plan and implement a particular type of nonformal education activity, i.e., national youth service organizations in developing countries.

What tentative conclusions might be made after examining the case materials presented here from an admittedly narrow area of the nonformal sector? How might this data help to offer a more unified explanation of a wide range of empirical phenomena which until now have been given *ad hoc* interpretations and has defied attempts at conceptualization as a discreet development sector? The following might, I believe, be proposed.

National youth service organizations where they exist in the developing countries among the most elective part of a country's network of adult-making agencies that are concerned with the socialization of the child into an adult.[29] They offer adolescents valuable opportunities to learn adult roles without having to compete with adults or meet adult standards. Where formal schooling offers few opportunities for voluntaristic involvement and social change, nonformal educational programs in youth organizations provide a wide range of programs and modes for adolescent participation.

National youth service as nonformal education, however, has frequently been used to "cool down" aspiration for formal schooling, to remove youth from the labor market, and to co-opt peer groups and enable adult-making agencies to influence the youth culture. Nonformal education must not be seen as a means of avoiding qualitative change in schools and in other basic social institutions. If this tendency continues, there will be little likelihood of linking up the formal and nonformal educational sectors so that the former largely serves to prepare youth for continuing nonformal educational involvement as adults.

The contribution of educational planning, it might be noted, revolves around three basic tasks: (1) the definition of alternative objectives that education might serve given national development aims, (2) designing of educational programs in terms of components, costs, methods, etc., and (3) analysis of program costs, benefits, and feasibility in any given socioeconomic setting. If the nonformal sectors viewed as an integral part of the national educational complex, is to be included in part in the designing of alternative educational objectives and programs, a number of steps must first be taken. Obviously we will first need a working definition of nonformal education, a rigorous assessment of the current state of the art, and research on, and evaluation of, promising new programs.

I should like to propose that for many developing countries NYS organizations may well serve as effective supplements to secondary schooling in seeking alternative objectives. It should be possible for educational planners to design such programs so that they are both feasible and beneficial for goals of youth development. The basic problem, however, lies not in the technical work of planners, but in the ability of national decision-makers to set new priorities and goals for both society and schools, and to allocate resources accordingly. Nonformal education is no *deus ex machina,* no happy new solution to complex problems of inefficiency and inequality in human-resource development. Rather, as with formal education, nonformal education will continue to reflect and be constrained by the realities of power, wealth, and status of the reward structure and organization of the society in which it functions.

Notes

1. P.H. Coombs, "Outline of Research Project on Non-Formal Education for Rural and Agricultural Development," Essex, Conn.: International Council for Educational Development, 1971.

2. M. Marien, "Notes on the Educational Complex as an Emerging Macro-System," in E.O. Ottinger (ed.), *Global Systems Dynamics* (New York: Karger, 1970).

3. Ibid.

4. R.G. Paulston, *Non-Formal Education: An Annotated International Bibliography of the Non-School Sector* (New York: Praeger, forthcoming, 1972).

5. P.H. Coombs, "The Need for a New Strategy of Educational Development," *Comparative Education Review* 14, no. 1 (February 1970): 81-82.

6. Ibid.

7. J.D. Chesswas, "The Basic Data Needed for Educational Planning," G.Z.F. Bereday, J.A. Lauwerys (eds.) *The Yearbook of Education, 1967: Educational Planning* (New York: Harcourt, Brace and World, 1967).

8. Coombs, "Outline of Research Project on Non-Formal Education for Rural and Agricultural Development," op. cit., p. 3.

9. Agency for International Development, Bureau for Technical Assistance, Office of Education and Human Resources, "Non-Formal Education: Action Program and Work Plan," Washington, D.C., USAID, 1970, p. 3.

10. See A. Gillete, *One Million Volunteers: The Story of the Volunteer Youth Service,* Harmondsworth, England: Penguin Books, 1968.

11. See International Labor Organization, "Vocational Preparation and Out-of-School Youth in Developing Countries," *Carnets d'Enfance,* June 1968.

12. In Commonwealth Secretariat, *Youth and Development in Africa: Report of the Commonwealth Africa Regional Youth Seminar, Nairobi, November 1969* (London: The Secretariat, 1970).

13. Ibid.

14. See J. E. Eaton, "Education and Public Service," *School and Society* 95, no. 2294 (October 1967).

15. See G. Skorov, *Integration of Educational and Economic Planning in Tanzania* (Paris: UNESCO/International Institute for Educational Planning, African Research Monographs, no. 6, 1966).

16. C. Angi and T. Coombs "Primary School Leavers and Youth Programs in Zambia," *Education in East Africa,* 1, no. 2 (1970): 37.

17. Commonwealth Secretariat, *Youth and Development in Africa,* pp. 158-59.

18. See Commonwealth Secretariat, *Youth and Development in the Caribbean: Regional Youth Seminar, Port of Spain, Trinidad,* August 1970, London: The Secretariat, 1970.

19. Ibid., p. 27.

20. V.H. Lawrence, "The History and Role of the Jamaica Youth Corps in the Social and Economic Development of Jamaica," Master's Thesis, Graduate School of Public and International Affairs, University of Pittsburgh, 1962.

21. Ibid., p. 29.

22. Ibid., p. 74.

23. Ibid., p. 102.

24. Ibid., p. 126.

25. C. Mesa-Lago, "Economic Significance of Unpaid Labor in Socialist Cuba," *Industrial and Labor Relations Review,* 22, no. 3 (April 1969): 340.

26. L. Nelson, "The School Dropout Problem in Cuba," *School and Society* 99, April 1971.

27. F. Santié "La Precolumna Juvenil Del Centario: Expresión del sistema

paralelo dentro del Marco de la Educación Permanente en Nuestro Páis." Paper presented at the Interdisciplinary Seminar on Continuing Education, Havana, Cuba, December 1970.

28. F. Castro, "Speech Delivered in Honor of the Centennial Youth Column Who Have Just Completed a Three-Year Work Stint." *Gramma Weekly Review,* July 25, 1971.

29. J.E. Eaton and M. Chen, *Influencing the Youth Culture: A Study of Youth Organizations in Israel,* (Beverly Hills: Sage Publication, 1970).

Part 3
Non Formal Education and Individual Change

Introduction to Part 3

The fit between educational programs and the demands of national development, especially the manpower demands of economic development, has been of prime concern to educational planners. Their planning has usually relied on formal education for manpower development.

The search for nonformal alternatives to schools derives from a greater concern for the fit between educational programs and individual needs than has characterized educational planning in the past. Even where this concern has not been the initial motivating force in the search for alternatives, it has been a goal in most nonformal efforts. In fact one of the hallmarks of most nonformal education is voluntary participation. A program which does not meet at least some of the individual's needs cannot hope to attract participants.

This growing concern for individual needs is yet another example of the overall effort to push back the frontiers of educational planning in order to plan and design more effective learning programs. Concern for individual needs does not necessarily imply a neglect of national manpower requirements; it may, in fact, facilitate meeting these requirements. Manpower planning, as usually practiced, has been based on an assumed link between educational programs and the productive use of knowledge and skills developed in them. But the growing unemployment among educated youths in many developing countries is an indication that the link between manpower development and manpower utilization cannot be taken for granted. The focus on the fit between educational programs and individual needs may indeed encourage more effective manpower utilization.

The problem is twofold: (1) to identify the educational needs of individuals, especially those needs which are perceived as such and which are closely linked to development goals, and (2) to design educational programs which effectively meet these needs. It is to these problems that the following three chapters are addressed.

The educational needs of modern man — the learnings, skills, and personal qualities he must acquire to actively participate in the developmental process — go beyond those needs provided for by the explicit curricula of formal schools. The task of identifying the needs of modern man has occupied Inkeles and his associates for the past decade. Some of the results of their massive study are briefly recounted in chapter 7. According to their findings, the formal school has been one of the major agencies of individual modernization. There have been other agencies as well, but many critics rejected Inkeles' hypothesis that the factory was one of them. He presents the objections to his hypothesis, examines their bases, and answers them. He goes on to offer empirical evidence to substantiate the role of the factory as a potentially positive influence in individual modernization.

It must be recognized, however, that the potential of the factory, like that of the school, may not be fully realized. The failure of a program to bring about individual modernization may be due either to the individual's receptivity or to the program itself. Waisanen, in chapter 8, reports evidence from his studies in Costa Rica to show that individuals participating in the same program are not equally responsive. So, in some instances, the failure of a program to realize its potential may be due to the receptivity of its subjects. Usually, however, there is also room for improvement in the design of the educational program itself.

Inkeles has shown the potential of the factory as a place for learning, and Waisanen has provided an example of nonformal learning in a rural setting. The factory and rural program can reach people with little or no formal education, and what they learn can be of immediate use to them and to their society. To realize more fully the potential of such settings for education, greater attention should be given to making them effective places for learning. That is the concern of Ward, McKinney and Dettoni in chapter 9.

The task of designing an effective program for nonformal learning is a complex one. And the systems approach outlined in chapter 9 does not simplify the jobs to be done, but it does provide a framework for ordering the problems and viewing their interrelationships. The chapter analyzes a sequence of problems that arise in designing, implementing, and evaulating nonformal education programs, and it offers some guidelines for solving them. One of its contributions is to show the interdependence of design, implementation, and management evaluation.

7

The Role of Occupational Experience

ALEX INKELES

Since 1962 a group of my colleagues and I have been working to understand the impact on the individual of his participation in the process of modernization. In the pursuit of this goal we devised a complex and comprehensive questionnaire, touching on a wide variety of life situations and intended to measure a substantial segment of the range of attitudes, values, and behaviors we conceive as particularly relevant to understanding the individual's participation in the roles typical for a modern industrial society.[1] This questionnaire we then administered to some 6,000 young men in six developing countries: Argentina, Chile, India, Israel, Nigeria, and East Pakistan. All three of the continents containing the overwhelming majority of developing nations are represented. The sampled countries cover the range from the newest nations that have only recently won their independence to those with a long history of self-governance; from those only now emerging from tribal life to those with ancient high cultures; and from those furthest removed from, to those most intimately linked to, the European cultural and industrial social order. The men interviewed were selected to represent points on a presumed continuum of exposure to modernizing influences, the main groups being the cultivator of the land still rooted in his traditional rural community; the migrant from the countryside just arrived in the city but not yet integrated into urban industrial life; the urban but nonindustrial worker still pursuing a more or less traditional occupation — such as barber or carpenter — but now doing so in the urban environment even though outside the context of a modern large-scale organization; and the experienced industrial worker engaged in production using inanimate power and machinery within the context of a more or less modern productive enterprise. To these we have added sets of secondary school and university students who enjoy the presumed benefits of advanced education. Within and across these sample groups we exercised numerous controls in the selection of subjects and in the analysis of our data, both to understand the influence and to prevent the uncontrolled effects of sociocultural and biosocial factors such as age, sex, edcuation, social origins, ethnic membership, past life experience, and the like.

Our interview included almost 300 entries. Some 160 of these elicited attitudes values, opinions, and reports on the behavior of others and oneself, touching on almost every major aspect of daily life. The questionnaire included various tests of verbal ability, literacy, political information, intelligence, and psychic adjustment. In some cases it took four hours of interviewing to complete — a demanding experience for both interviewer and interviewee.

We believe our evidence shows unmistakably that there is a set of personal qualities which reliably cohere as a syndrome and which identify a type of man who may validly be described as fitting a reasonable theoretical conception of the modern man. Central to this syndrome are: (1) openness to new experience, both with people and with new ways of doing things, such as attempting to control births; (2) the assertion of increasing independence from the authority of traditional figures like parents and priests and a shift of allegiance to leaders of government, public affairs, trade unions, cooperatives, and the like; (3) belief in the efficacy of science and medicine, and a general abandonment of passivity and fatalism in the face of life's difficulties; and (4) ambition for oneself and one's children to achieve high occupational and educational goals. Men who manifest these characteristics (5) like people to be on time and show an interest in carefully planning their affairs in advance. It is also part of this syndrome to (6) show strong interest and take an active part in civic and community affairs and local politics; and (7) to strive energetically to keep up with the news, and within this effort to prefer news of national and international import over items dealing with sports, religion, or purely local affairs.

What are the influences which make a man modern? Education has often been identified as perhaps the most important of the influences moving men away from traditionalism toward modernity in developing countries. Our evidence does not challenge this well-established conclusion. Both in zero-order correlations[2] and in the more complex multivariate regression analysis, the amount of formal schooling a man has had emerges as the single most powerful variable in determining his score on our measures. On the average, for every additional year a man spent in school, he gains somewhere between two and three additional points on a scale of modernity score from zero to 100.

Our modernity test is not mainly a test of what is usually learned in school, such as geography or arithmetic, but is rather a test of attitudes and values touching on basic aspects of a man's orientation to nature, to time, to fate, to politics, to women, and to God. If attending school brings about such substantial changes in these fundamental personal orientations, the school must be teaching a good deal more than is apparent in its syllabus on reading, writing, arithmetic, and even geography. The school is evidently also an important training ground for inculcating values. It teaches ways of orienting oneself toward others, and of conducting oneself, which could have important bearing on the performance of one's adult roles in the structure of modern society. These effects of the school, I believe, reside not mainly in its formal, explicit, self-conscious pedagogic activity, but rather are inherent in the school as an *organization*. The modernizing effects follow not from the school's curriculum, but rather from its informal, implicit, and often unconscious program for dealing with its young charges.[3] The properties of the rational organization as a hidden pursuader — or, as I prefer to put it, as a silent and unobserved teacher — become most apparent when we consider the role of occupational experience in shaping the modern man.

The Factory as a School in Modernity

That the school might modernize was quite readily accepted by almost everyone. But our idea that work in factories should be a modernizing experience was met by skepticism or outright rejection from a surprisingly large number of persons to whom we initially described our project. Their reasons were by no means substantial.

First and foremost, they challenged the assumption that basic changes in personality could occur with any regularity in individuals who had already reached maturity. The OM scale (overall measure of modernization) measures some patterns of response which lie at the core of the personality; these include the sense of personal efficacy, cognitive openness, trust, orientation to time, and modes of relating to social "inferiors." Modern psychology considers these attributes as "basic" in the sense that they are assumed to be laid down in childhood and adolescence, and thereafter to be stable or relatively unchanging, certainly much more so than are mere opinions. Consequently, our critics were led to express the same view as Professor Bloom when, in his famous review of research, *Stability and Change in Human Characteristics,* he concluded: "We are pessimistic about producing major changes in a (personal) characteristic after it has reached a high level of stability."[4] Bloom had in mind mainly such attributes as intelligence or congitive capacity, but a large segment of the community of personality psychologists takes essentially the same pessimistic view of the prospects for bringing about significant change in basic characteristics of personality after the age of sixteen or eighteen.

The second reason our critics advanced was doubt that the factory provided a sufficiently powerful environment to bring about changes in basic value orientations and need dispositions. Some psychologists hold that there are almost no circumstances under which really basic traits of personality laid down in early childhood can be substantially altered in adulthood. Most would, however, agree with Bloom that under extreme environmental conditions — such as are prevalent in concentration camps, prisons, or "brainwashing" sessions — "one may encounter considerable deterioration in characteristics which are ordinarily quite stable."[5] This concession to the idea of adult change, however, is limited largely to instances of deterioration or retrogression: it does not apply to long-term positive transformations, that is, to growth and new development in adulthood. Those who assumed such extreme conditions to be necessary for bringing about transformations of fundamental personality characteristics in adulthood were, therefore, convinced the factory could not produce the sort of changes we anticipated.

The third line of attack was based on a challenge to our interpretation of the factory as a social organization. Our critics saw the factory in a quite different light. They argued that even if the factory could bring about significant personality change in adulthood, the kind of change it produced would probably make men less rather than more like the project's model of a modern man.

They pointed out, for example, that factories are hierarchically organized, and argued that therefore one should not expect them to stimulate the sort of participant citizenship required by our model of the modern man. Since technical considerations must always be uppermost in making decisions in industry, they noted, there was little likelihood that the factory would train men to pay respectful attention to the opinions of subordinates and others less powerful or prestigious than they were. Our critics went on to point out that most factory workers are in a dependent and passive position. They perform routine repetitive functions, often dull and deadening, and do so mainly on the initiative of others. According to this view, workers are coerced and harried by the clock and the inexorable pace of the machine. Changes in the machinery or in the arrangement of their work, are likely to require that they work harder, or faster, and may even threaten some of them with a layoff. Therefore, our critics claimed, factory work would encourage passivity and dependence, foster fear of and resistance to change, and stimulate a reaction against the domination of strict schedules and a preference for more spontaneously arranged work.

We challenged our critics' interpretation on all three grounds. Of course, we did not rest our case on the mere assertion that our critics were wrong. There were sound reasons for doubting the validity of their assumptions. And the issues they raised are sufficiently fundamental to warrant turning aside briefly from the presentation of results to clarify our theoretical position.

Theoretical Foundations

Our first task was to look more closely at the assumption that the main features of individual personality are laid down in early childhood and adolescence and persist basically unchanged into adulthood. We were at once struck by how little sytematic empirical evidence there was to support that assumption. Since the idea seems to accord so well with most people's practical experience, there has been little incentive to challenge or even test this theory, which has nevertheless become almost a dogma of the psychoanalytic age.

Benjamin Bloom performed a great service by pulling together the research available on the stability of responses to a variety of psychological tests. These included the Kuder Personal Preference Record, which tests interests such as the mechanical and artistic; the Strong Vocational Interest Test; the Allport and Vernon Test of Values; the Thurstone Personality Scale, and others. One striking fact which emerged from Bloom's review was that virtually all of the available longitudinal studies on which so many of our conclusions about the stability of personal traits rested had been done with high school and college students. These researches, therefore, typically covered only two years or so of elapsed time, and in very few cases really extended very far into adulthood. Most, therefore, simply have no bearing on the question of how far basic attitudes, values, and dispositions are stable throughout adulthood. Even these few studies which covered a period of three or four years, however, indicated that a good deal of change may have taken place in that short interval, because the correlation of test scores over that span of time was generally only about 0.60 on tests such as the Allport-Vernon value scale, Plant's tests of ethnocentrism, and Thurstone's personality scale.

How much stability or change there will be depends, of course, on the area of personality one is testing. Apparently there have been very few, if any, truly longitudinal studies of features of personality which are strictly, or even remotely, comparable to those dealt with by the OM scale. Furthermore, how much personality change one observes in a given group will, in our opinion, depend greatly on how far the group's environment has been changing. It is noteworthy, therefore, that after reviewing the evidence with regard to the stability of adult characteristics Bloom concluded:

Much of the stability we have reported in this work is really a reflection of environmental stability. That is, the stability of a characteristic for a group of individuals may, in fact, be explained by the constancy of their environments over time. (p. 223)

The essential feature of our modernization study, however, is its emphasis on the *change* in the social and physical environment which men experience as they shift from the more traditional settings of village, farm, and tribe to city residence, industrial employment, and national citizenship. We believed that in such circumstances the stability of personal characteristics commonly observed under conditions of social and cultural continuity must give way to a more rapid and profound rate of personal adaptation. We proceeded, then, on the assumption that the personality can continue to develop and grow well into adulthood, and that basic change, even in fundamental characteristics such as the sense of efficacy, was more than merely possible. Rather, we assumed it to be highly likely, at least when men lived under social conditions conducive to personal transformation, such as those prevailing in the sectors of developing countries experiencing the process of modernization.

Our second challenge to our critics rested on the belief that basic personal change can be stimulated by experience in settings less extreme or stark than prisons and concentration camps. While taking this position, we were not unaware that on completion of his intensive review of stability and change in personal characteristics Professor Bloom had stated that "a central thesis of this work is that change in many human characteristics becomes more and more difficult as the characteristics become more fully developed," with the consequence that "to produce a given amount of change . . . requires more and more powerful environments and increased amounts of effort and attention as the characteristic becomes stabilized."[6] In our view, the factory qualified as such a "powerful environment," one which should be able to infringe upon individuals with sufficiently concentrated force to bring about changes in core features of personality.

We noted, first, that contact between the individual and the factory system was not fleeting or irregular. To work in a factory means to expose oneself to its regimen for at least eight hours a day, five to six days a week, and continuously, week in and week out, over a period of years.

Second, we believe this involvement with the factory is serious and engaging for the participants. Work is one of the most important elements in most men's lives. Moreover, in developing countries, jobs with the pay and steadiness of industrial employment are rare. That alone makes factory work particularly desirable. In addition, such employment often confers prestige. Most men in industry in these countries are, therefore, not merely sojourners casually passing time in the plant.

Third, and most important in conferring on the factory the quality of a "powerful environment," are certain features of its activity and organization. Technical constraints, the objective standard of productivity, and strict requirements of profitablity all act to give the factory a firm and relatively invariant character. It does not so much adapt to men as it requires that they adapt to it.

The essential logic of machinery and mechanical processes must be rigorously observed, else the machine, or its attendant, or both, must break. It requires only a few instances in which hair, or a flowing gown, or fingers get caught in the machine, to impress the point indelibly on all who come in contact with it. This same sharpness of outline tends to be manifested in the organization of the factory. Departments, shops, even individual machines are distinctly set off and clearly demarcated. Division of labor is generally precisely and rigorously maintained. Hierarchies of authority and technical skill give a definite structure to interpersonal relations. Standards of performance tend to be objective and precise. And the system of rewards and punishments is highly relevant to all the participants, unambiguous, powerful, and by and large objectively calculated.

These characteristics of the factory that make it a "powerful environment" point to the basis for the third challenge we addressed to our critics, namely, that the factory's effect would make men more rather than less modern.

In our view, the organization of the factory and its mode of functioning embodied a series of fundamental principles to which men from a traditional background would respond favorably. We anticipated that rather than respond with confusion or react defensively, traditional men would be open to the lessons the factory had to teach, incorporating and adopting as their own standard the norms embedded in modern factory organization. This learning, we believed, would come about through the same processes of socialization identified by us above as the basis for learning modern attitudes and values in the school—modeling, generalization, exemplification, and reward and punishment. These processes can be observed at work across the whole range of the main themes which defined our analytic model of the modern man, but it should suffice to illustrate the point with reference to a select few.

Efficacy.

By the very nature of the forces at work in it, the factory exemplifies efficacy, since in it is concentrated the power to convert obdurate materials into new shapes and forms far transcending the capacity of the unaided individual to do so. In the factory the worker sees large pieces of metal or mounds of ore given new shape: coal and coke become steel, bauxite powder becomes aluminum, thick bars of steel are twisted and bent, small globs of plastic molded to complex, intricate, and even beautiful contours—sometimes with little more visible human effort than pushing buttons or moving levers. The total working of the factory affirms man's capacity, through organization and the harnessing of mechanical power, to transform nature to suit man's needs. One worker we spoke to in Nigeria expressed the basic idea for us perfectly when, in reply to our questions about how his work left him feeling, he said: "Sometimes like nine feet tall with arms a yard wide. Here in the factory I alone with my machine can twist any way I want a piece of steel all the men in my home village together could not begin to bend at all."

The factory provides models of efficacy in the person of the engineer, the technician, and the more highly skilled workers such as tool and die makers. These men have the professional responsibility to solve problems, to develop new combinations of elements, to convert ideas blueprints into concrete mechanical reality. In bringing their technical training and experience to bear on the production problems of the factory, they should provide regular, sometimes daily, personal models of efficacious behavior.

The system of reward and punishment in the factory should also serve to reinforce the lesson in efficacy it offers. The inducement to greater personal efficacy is probably most immediate in a piecework system, although the learning it induces may quickly be extinguished if management response be continuously raising quotas. Nevertheless, efficacious behavior in the plant may be, and often is, stimulated by direct reward, such as bonuses, reclassification to higher skill categories and promotion to more responsible work.

Readiness for innovation and openness to systematic change, the struggle to keep costs down to competitive levels, and the constant pressure to keep up with the demands of the market, oblige factories to be outstanding among large-scale institutions in the introduction of new machinery, techniques, and administrative arrangements. We recognize that the main responsibility for effecting such changes usually lies with management, and with its associated engineering and technical personnel. We assumed, therefore, that in stimulating men toward openness to new experience and readiness to accept change, the factory would work mainly through the process of modeling.

In so far as the factory as an institution is generally receptive to innovation, readily adopting new techniques for processing material, new machinery and new personnel policies, it should also encourage openness to new experience by exemplification. Managerially sponsored innovation may, of course, mean harder, faster, or more dangerous work for the employee. In most reasonably modern factories, however, technical innovations are more likely to lead to safer, less strenuous, and more evenly paced work. Technical innovation may also result in higher individual productivity and elevated skill ratings. Although there is, again, no guarantee that these gains will be fed back to the workers in the form of increased earnings, in many instances the technological innovations of management do redound to the interest of the workers. Insofar as their experience was thus positive, we expected workers to generalize the lessons of the factory to other situations in which openness to new experience and readiness for change are called for.

By bringing together a much wider variety of men than one commonly finds in the village, the factory offers the worker an encounter not only with new ways of doing mechanical things, but with new people whose thinking and customs may be quite different from his own. Since the factory is a culturally neutral ground, since it presents a firm structure which it applies more or less equally to all its members as a guide to their interaction, and since it holds up certain common standards of evaluation such as objective skill and productivity, much of the uncertainty that usually surrounds contact with strangely different people may be eliminated or at least be made more bearable in the context of the factory. A more secure basis is thereby provided for exploring new customs and for discovering common interests and propensities, which are otherwise typically maksed by the more salient dissimilarities with which people from different cultures initially confront each other. In the context of the factory, the cost of exploring new ways is low, and the rewards may be quite gratifying. Such success in opening up relations with people who are culturally rather different from oneself may, furthermore, be generalized into a lessened fear of strangers and a heightened confidence in one's ability to understand foreign people and ways.

Planning and Time

To attain its goal of maximizing productivity the factory must emphasize planning. The principle of planning is exemplified in the very layout of the factory, designed to permit the most rational movement of goods from their point of entry as raw material to their exit as finished product; in the flow of the work, as the product is subjected to one process after another in the technically prescribed succession; and in the coordination which insures that despite extensive division of labor, the required tools and material will be available at the appropriate place and at the right time.

The management of time is intimately related to planning. Industrial production requires precise scheduling in bringing together the diverse elements entering into the production process. This requirement is most evident with the assembly line, since it rigorously imposes the necessity that everyone start and stop at the same time, that each process be allocated a precise amount of time, and that each step be completed as scheduled. According to the socialization principle of exemplification, men working in factories should come to internalize a concern for orderly advanced planning and precise scheduling. This learning should be facilitated by the system of factory reward and punishment since persistent lateness brings reprimands and may lead to discharge, and bonuses are often paid for completing important jobs on or ahead of schedule.

Respect for Subordinates

The predominance of rules and formal procedures in the factory should teach respect for the rights of subordinates and of other individuals of inferior standing in the hierarchy of status. Of course there are still factories run by cruel and vicious bosses, and even in the best run plant a particular foreman or other supervisor may be able to hound and even persecute a man. By and large, however, the norm of treatment in the factory emphasizes relatively just, humane, respectful treatment of subordinates, at least compared to what goes on in many other settings in underdeveloped countries.

Factories are generally owned by public corporations. This may make them places in which authority is cold and distant, but their public character generally also insures that the extremity of personal, vengeful treatment by harsh bosses is much less manifested in them than in other types of work situations. Generally the factory is dominated by men of relatively higher education, in whom a more civilized standard of personal conduct is likely to have been inculcated than will be commonly found among absentee landowners or their overseers. Industrial managers and engineers are likely to look for their "ego tonic" outside, in the larger community, rather than seeking it vicariously through abusing the dignity of their subordinates in the plant. In addition, the trade union, generally totally absent in the countryside but quite common in urban industry serves as an additional important source of restraint to insure that the men in the plant are treated with respect in accord with objective rules for decent supervision.

The interdependence of men in the complex production process of the factory requires that there be a substantial flow of information up as well as down the status hierarchy. Inexperienced engineers and foremen quickly learn, often to their dismay, that their own success is heavily dependent on the cooperation and goodwill of their subordinates. The men in most immediate contact with machines and materials see and know things which are vital to the fulfillment of the factory's production goals. To be effective, therefore, supervisors cannot merely tell the men what to do; they must also pay attention to what the men tell them about how things are going.

In general, then, by modeling and exemplification, men working in factories should have an opportunity to learn lessons in showing consideration for subordinates and in respecting the feelings of those weaker or of lesser status than themselves. To the extent that their views are listened to and given some weight in the decision-making process, they should also be learning to see the value of diversity of opinion as opposed to unanimity.

All of the other themes built into our analytic model of the modern man should also, in some degree, be reflected in a man's work experience in an industrial establishment. Belief in the calculability of the world and the people in it should be encouraged by the regularity of work and pay in the factory, by the fulfillment of its imperatives for close coordination in the division of labor, and by the model of responsible norm-oriented behavior usually presented by the engineering and technical personnel. A preference for universalism over particularism might well be fostered by the factory organization's embodiment of bureaucratic principles of governance through impartial rules, and its conformity to technical and normative standards. A rejection of fatalism and its replacement by optimism and active striving should be fostered by several attributes of the factory, including the steadiness and relative security of industrial work, its mastery over materials, and its evident ability to exercise some substantial control over natural forces.

Of course we are completely aware that none of the effects we anticipated is a necessary concomitant of industrial employment. Our description of the factory was cast in what Weber call "ideal-typical" form, in order to highlight the theoretical basis for our expectations. In doing so, we meant neither to assert that the factory was unique, nor to deny that in many, perhaps most, concrete instances it might fail to live up to its potential.

Summary and Conclusions

We selected work in factories as the special focus of our attention in seeking to assess the effects of occupational experience in reshaping individuals according to the model of the modern man. Just as we view the school as communicating lessons beyond reading and arithmetic, so we thought of the factory as training men in more than the minimal lessons of technology and the skills necessary to industrial production. We conceived of the factory as an organization serving as general school in attitudes, values, and ways of behaving which are more adaptive for life in a modern society. We reasoned that work in a factory should increase a man's sense of efficacy, make him less fearful of innovation, and impress on him the value of education as a general qualification for competence and advancement. Furthermore, we assume that in subtle ways work in a factory might even deepen a man's mastery of arithmetic and broaden his knowledge of geography without the benefit of the formal lessons usually presented in the classroom. Indeed, the slogan for our project became, "The factory can be a school—a school for modernization."

Although our most sanguine hopes for the educational effects of the factory were not wholly fulfilled, the nature of a man's occupational experience does emerge as one of the strongest of the many types of variables we tested and is a quite respectable competitor to education in explaining a person's modernity. The correlation between time spent in factories and individual modernization scores is generally about 0.20[7] With the effects of education controlled, the factory workers generally score eight to ten points higher on the modernization scale than do the cultivators.[8] There is little reason to interpret this difference as due to selection effects since separate controls show that new workers are not self- or pre-selected from the village on grounds of already being "modern" in personality or attitude. Nevertheless, we can apply a really stringent test by making our comparisons exclusively within the industrial labor force, pitting men with few years of industrial experience against those with many—for example, five or more. When this is done, factory experience continues to show a substantial impact on individual modernization, the gain generally being about one point per year on the overall measure of modernization (OM).

It is notable that even when we restrict ourselves to tests of verbal fluency and to tests of geographical and political information, the more experienced workers show comparable advantages over the less experienced workers. To choose but one of many available examples, in Chile among men of rural origin and low education (one to five years)—and therefore suffering a double disadvantage in background—the proportion who could correctly locate Moscow as being the Soviet Russian capital rose from a mere 8 percent among the newly recruited industrial workers to 39 percent among those with middle experience and to 52 percent among the men who had eight years or more in the factory. Even among those with the double advantage of higher education (six to seven years) and urban origins, the proportion correctly identifying Moscow decidedly rose along with increasing industrial experience, the percentages being 68, 81, and 92 for the three levels of industrial experience, respectively.

It should be clear from these data that the factory is serving as a school even in those subjects generally considered the exclusive preserve of the classroom.[9]

To cite these modernizing effects of the factory is not to minimize the greater absolute impact of schooling. Using a gross occupational categorization that pits cultivators against industrial workers, we find the classroom still leads the workshop as a school of modernization in the ratio of 3:2. Using the stricter test which utilizes factory workers only, grouped by length of industrial experience, it turns out that every additional year in school produces three times as much increment in one's modernization score as does a year in the factory, that is, the ratio goes to 3:1. The school seems clearly to be the more efficient training ground for individual modernization. Nevertheless, we should keep in mind that the school has the pupil full time, and it produces no incidental by-products other than its pupils. By contrast, the main business of the factory is to manufacture goods, and the changes it brings about in men—not insubstantial, as we have seen — are produced at virtually zero marginal cost. These personality changes in men are therefore a kind of windfall profit to a society undergoing the modernization process. Indeed, on this basis we may quite legitimately reverse the thrust of the argument, no longer asking why the school does so much better than the factory, but rather demanding to know why the school, with its full time control over the pupil's formal learning, does not perform a lot better than it does relative to the factory.

Notes

1. Some sixty-eight of the questions are listed, in abbreviated form, in table 1 of Smith and Inkeles 1966. A complete copy of the questionnaire may be obtained by ordering Document 9133 from the Chief, Auxiliary Publication Project, Photoduplication Service, Library of Congress, Washington, D.C. remitting $13.50 for microfilm or $117.50 for photocopies.

2. The correlation (Pearsonian) between education and overall measure of modernization ranges from 0.34 in Pakistan to 0.65 in India. The size of these coefficients is substantially affected by the educational "spread" in each sample. That spread is largest in India, with the cases rather evenly distributed from zero to thirteen years of education.

3. In most of the current discussions of the effectiveness and ineffectiveness of our schools, this aspect of the school's impact has been generally neglected. For an importatn exception see Dreeben 1968.

4. Bloom, Benjamin S., *Stability and Change in Human Characteristics* (New York: John Wiley and Sons, 1964), p. 218.

5. Ibid., p. 223

6. Ibid., p. 229-30

7. However, in India it was only 0.08. We believe this to be not a condition peculiar to India, but to our industrial sample there. Everywhere else we sampled from 50 to more than 100 factories, including all types and sizes of industry, but in India our sample was limited to eleven factories, mostly large, and two of these were not truly industrial; they processed minerals.

8. Keep in mind that the test has a theoretical range from zero to 100, and an observed range in our samples almost as great. With samples of our size, differences so large are significant at well above the 0.01 level. This test of significance and many of the other statistics presented in this report require that one meet certain conditions, such as random sampling, which our data do not meet. Nevertheless, we present such statistics in order to provide a rough guide or standard of judgment, in the belief that to do so is preferable to leaving the reader without any criterion by which to evaluate one figure as against another. The reader must be cautioned, however, not to interpret any single statistic to literally. Conclusions should be drawn not from single figures but from the whole array of evidence across the six countries.

9. It will be noted that the pattern manifested in the other five countries is

not shown in Israel. There the new workers are as well informed as the experienced. We attribute this not so much to the qualities of Israeli industry as to the nature of Israeli society. In that small, mobile, and urbanized environment, information tends to be rapidly and more or less evenly diffused throughout the nation and all classes.

8 Individual Modernity and Nonformal Education

FREDERICK WAISANEN

To the degree that there is a measure of success in a program designed to stimulate development, it is evident that the impact of such programs is not uniform on all individuals to whom the change program is addressed. Whatever or wherever the target population, individuals in it will be dispersed along a continuum from innovativeness to laggardness, from change readiness to change resistance, and, some would assert, from traditionalism to modernity.

The introduction of the concept of "modernity" takes this issue of differential response to change programs out of a context of truism and puts the matter into the center of controversy. It is self-evident that actors who seek new ideas, i.e., actors who are change-oriented, will be more responsive to programs that involve the introduction of new ideas. It is quite another matter, although tempting, to conclude that this differential responise can be interpreted in the context of individual modernity, i.e., a "set of attitudes, values and ways of feeling and acting, presumably of the sort either generated by or required for effective participation in a modern society."[1]

The tenability of the concept of individual modernity is dependent upon the specification of the attitudes and behaviors that differentiate modernity from traditionalism. In this validation process, there is particular need to distinguish between relatively specific indicators — which may be culture-bound — and variables that are theoretically relevant and that have cross-cultural applicability.

Questions asked about the modernity concept are for the most part predicated upon this issue. When the criticism is advanced that modernity, in the predominant mode of presentation in the literature, carries a Western, entrepreneurial, and ideological bias, these criticisms are generally based more upon the specific indicators used in the measurement process, like the saving and the loaning of money, the deferral of gratifications, and a commitment to programs of upward social mobility. My own work on the subject is an open to these charges as anyone else's.[2] It may well be that the data used in this discussion — because they are from a study designed and executed several years ago[3] — are conspicuously contaminated by similar biases.

Elsewhere,[4] I argued that individual modernity might be viewed in terms of four behavioral dimensions — with analogous attitudinal correlates: (1) information-seeking, (2) planning and investment, (3) multisystem participation, and (4) innovativeness. These four dimensions were held to be accumulative and developmental; i.e., information-seeking is a prerequisite to planning, planning a prerequisite to multisystem participation, etc. I noted, additionally, that these four dimensions have a parallel with several and distinct functions of education (formal or nonformal), namely: (1) the awareness function; (2) the skill acquisition function; (3) the participation function, which involves skill application; and (4) the research function, which is predicated upon the quest for new ideas and characterized by the state of innovativeness.

While I believe such a conceptualization is not without promise, there is still need to attempt placement of the concern for individual modernity into a more parsimonious and theoretically connected framework. In this regard, I believe there is particular promise in the concepts of self-perceived autonomy and the perception of ability and opportunity to influence one's life trajectory. Figure 8-1 provides a two-axis representation of this view.

Figure 8-1. A Two-Dimension Conceptualization of Individual Modernity

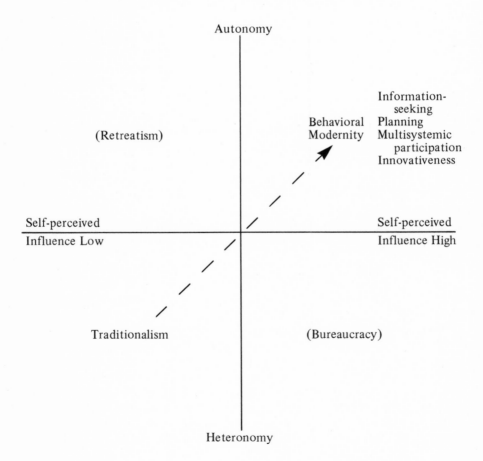

The vertical axis order individuals by the degree to which they feel dependent upon, or constrained by prevailing norms. The heteronomy pole represents an orientation to the system, an absolutistic view of the rules of the game, and a resistance to change. The autonomy pole is characterized by a recognition of options in lifestyles and by the perception that such options are subject to individual and independent choice.[5]

The horizontal axis orders individuals by the degree to which existing social structure is perceived to lend itself to individual impact. The low influence pole can be characterized by, among other qualities, fatalism and resignation; the high influence pole by a recognition that change can occur as a consequence of individual inputs into the system.[6]

From a social psychological perspective, the modernization process becomes defined in terms of increasing autonomy and efficacy, with the dotted arrow indicating the direction of predominant long-term change.

The labeling of the quadrants of the model is, of course, open to argument. The labels suggested in figure 8-1 are at best tentative and exploratory. At worst, they may be oversimplifications and distortions.

While this concern for individual modernity may not be at the center of our concern, its relationship to nonformal education is undeniable. Returning to the assumption expressed earlier, response to nonformal educational programs is a variable; and the central thesis of this chapter is that those persons who are in the "modernity quadrant" of figure 8-1 will be the most responsive.

The data that I will bring to bear upon this issue are not as direct and full as they might be; there is a *post factum* and *ad hoc* quality about them that gives cause for concern. To ignore their relevance, however, might be the greater error.

A Field Experiment in Nonformal Education

During the period 1963-66, I directed the Costa Rican phase of a UNES-CO-supported, comparative study of communication and rural development.[7] The experiment involved an assessment of the impact of two nonformal educational strategies — the radio forum and functional literacy stimulation.

In brief summary, the design of the study involved: (1) The selection of fourteen rural communities in Costa rica. (2) The selection of twenty-three recommended practices in agriculture, health, and education. (3) The interviewing of all heads of households in the fourteen villages in order to obtain knowledge, evaluation, and adoption measures for each of the twenty-three practices, as well as an extensive set of measures on socioeconomic, demographic, and attitudinal characteristics of the heads of households. (4) Villages were assigned, on matching basis, to radio treatment, literacy treatment, or control village status. (5) Fifty-two weeks of once-weekly, one-half hour radio forum broadcasts were directed to four of the villages. Fifty-two pamphlets were produced and distributed, one per week, to another four villages. The content of both treatments dealt with the recommended practices, presenting arguments supporting their adoption, including payoff potential and specific practice instructions. The control villages received no direct treatments. (6) Following termination, heads of households were reinterviewed, again for the purpose of obtaining measures of knowledge, evaluation, and adoption of the twenty-three recommended practices. (7) Before-after comparisons were along several relevant dimensions. The before-after measurements were available for 286 heads of households.

The data from this study enable at least preliminary answers to three questions of central concern:

1. Can measurable individual change be effected by a nonformal educational strategy?
2. What degree of change can be effected?
3. What type of individual is most likely to be affected?

The data suggest that the answer to the first question is that there can indeed be measurable change consequences, although they may not be uniformly dramatic and emphatic. Table 8-1 provides change data for forum participants, nonparticipants, and control villagers in the Costa Rican field experiment. For the nine practices at issue, the differences between forum participants and nonparticipants are substantial.[8]

Table 8-1. Impact of a Nonformal Educational Program upon Adoption of Some Recommended Practices in Agriculture, Health, and Social Education

Recommended Practice	Changes in Adoption Rates (as a Percentage of Change Possible) Attributable to Experimental Treatments		
	Forum Participants	Nonparticipants	Control Villagers
Seed Selection	32	0	−2
Fertilizers	51	10	40
Insecticides	29	0	26
Fungicides	27	3	5
Weed Control	45	0	37
Boiling Water	29	7	18
Using Mobil Health Unit . . .	31	8	10
Loans	39	−2	22
Cooperatives	11	−13	3

Source: Adapted from P. Roy, F. B. Waisanen, & E. M. Rogers, THE IMPACT OF COMMUNICATION ON RURAL DEVELOPMENT: AN INVESTIGATION IN COSTA RICA AND INDIA (Paris: UNESCO, 1969), p. 53.

The comparison of forum participants with control villagers is clouded. The substantial changes favoring forum participants in adoption of selected seed, fungicides, and the mobile health unit are balanced by minor differences in increased use of fertilizers, insecticides, and weed control. At least some of the action that occurred in the control villages may be attributable to (1) the increased attention that the six control villages may have received from other change agencies during the period of our study, (2) a special searching for new ideas by the control villagers — perhaps consequent to perceived exclusion from the experimental treatments and the desire to demonstrate their responsiveness to extension education, and (3) special measurement error.

In any case, comparing forum participants with nonparticipants enables one to suggest that the answer to the second question ("What degree of change can be effected?") is determinable, and may be significant. For example, agricultural specialists can, with some confidence, translate selected seed use to increases in production, other things equal. If one adds to the increased production effect of use of selected seed the effect of increased use of fertilizer, insecticides, fungicides, and weed control, the payoff of the nonformal educational program could far exceed the $8600 actual costs of production, including personnel.

The third question ("What type of individuals are most responsive to a nonformal educational strategy?") touches both social policy and social theory, for it is here that the issue of individual modernity is salient and relevant.

Consider table 8-2, which again summarizes data adapted from the Costa Rica field experiment and dealing with the correlates of two dependent variables, knowledge and adoption of the twenty-three practices at issue in the nonformal educational program. Firstly, the twenty-one independent variables represent, in my judgment, more than a fortuitous fit with the characteristics of individual modernity discussed earlier. Their conceptual fit with information-seeking, planning, multisystem participation, and innovativeness is evident. Secondly, the variables that provide a measure of conceptual fit with self-perceived autonomy and efficacy (particularly variables 15 through 20) and which bear upon the earlier discussion of modernity (and summarized in figure 8-1 provide at least partial and indirect supportive evidence.

Table 8-3 presents data from another analytic mode. Using partial and multiple correlation techniques, we can order the independent variables by their interpretative value; i.e., we can rank the variables in terms of which "say most" about knowledge and adoption of the twenty-three recommended practices. The pattern of individual modernity implicit in the ordering of variables ie evident enough — and again it is possible to classify the variables along dimensions of information-seeking, planning, participation, and innovativeness. Taken together, and expressed as a multiple correlation value, the variable sets "explain" 42 percent of the variance of adoption and 48 percent of the variance in knowledge.[9]

Table 8-2. Correlates of Knowledge and Adoption in Costa Rica

Independent Variables	Dependent Variables	
	Knowledge	Adoption
1. Education	.36	.31
2. Educational aspirations for son	.33	.33
3. Literacy	.33	.21
4. Income	.27	.35
5. Organization membership	.20	.20
6. Mobility	.32	.41
7. Contact: agricultural (index)	.45	.55
8. Contact: social, educational (index)	.37	.45
9. Contact: neighbors	.42	.37
10. Mass media use	.46	.46
11. Newspaper reading	.41	.33
12. Radio use	.22	.14
13. Channel evaluation change agents	.28	.29
14. Channel evaluation mass media	.32	.29
15. Modernity	.35	.30
16. Self-autonomy	.18	.21
17. Ease of Self-change	.17	.22
18. Self-concept innovative	.26	.33
19. Perception of innovative climate	.18	**
20. Risk orientation	.18	.27
21. Forum participation	.26	.35
Opinion leadership	.30	.38

Source: Adapted from P. Roy, F.B. Waisanen, & E.M. Rogers, THE IMPACT OF COMMUNICATION ON RURAL DEVELOPMENT: AN INVESTIGATION IN COSTA RICA AND INDIA (Paris: UNESCO, 1969), p. 56.

Discussion

All this leads to the dilemma that change agents have confronted through all the years of development effort: the populations most in need of reaching are most difficult to reach; they who are most responsive to nonformal programs are those in lesser relative need for such programs.

The dilemma is probably not a true one, for the alternatives are not equally and inflexibly unattractive; there are steps that can be taken to increase the receptivity to new ideas of those who are in greatest need. Taking these steps is largely in the hands of formal organizations in developing societies, and hope is in the process of institution building.

If there is validity and relevance to the conceptualization of modernity summarized in figure 8-1, then the quadrant labeled "Bureaucracy" may deserve our special concern. Clearly, a formal organization that has become bureaucratized in the worst sense of the word — putting it into the far lower right

Table 8-3. Prediction of Total Knowledge and Adoption in Costa Rica by Stepwise Multiple Regression Analysis

Independent Variables	Partial Correlation	Percentage of Variance Explained in the Dependent Variable
TOTAL KNOWLEDGE		
1. Forum Participation	.117	2
2. Education	.270	8
3. Radio Use	.147	2
4. Modernity Index	.221	6
5. Agricultural Contact	.209	8
6. Educational Contact	.121	4
7. Newspaper Reading	.164	6
8. Contact with Neighbors	.137	4
Percentage of Total Variance		42
TOTAL ADOPTION		
1. Mobility	.183	6
2. Forum Participation	.200	5
3. Education	.239	6
4. Agricultural Contact	.343	17
5. Educational Contact	.196	7
6. Self-Concept in Innovativeness	.170	4
7. Risk-Orientation	.128	3
Percentage of Total Variance		48

Source: Adapted from P. Roy, F. B. Waisanen, & E. M. Rogers, THE IMPACT OF COMMUNICATION ON RURAL DEVELOPMENT: AN INVESTIGATION IN COSTA RICA AND INDIA (Paris: UNESCO, 1969), p. 58.

corner of the quadrant — will be immobilized by its own red tape, insensitive to changing times, unmindful of human needs, and concerned only with the maintenance of itself in a larger bureaucratic struggle.

By contrast, a bureaucracy in the better sense of the word would direct its resources to the task of continued and controlled change. It would provide a balance between caution that is born of experience and settled in positions of power and the adventuresomeness and innovativeness of the young. As it does this, it moves upward along the autonomy dimension and frees itself from the calcifying consequences of singular concern for self-perpetuation.

Formal organizations that fail to keep step with (or some steps ahead of) changing times will invite the populations they should be serving to either attack or retreat. The former response brings chaos, the latter despair and deterioration. Retreatism, as viewed in figure 8-1, is both antipodal to, and a consequence of, excessive bureaucratization. The quadrant might include, as examples, the cult follower, the tenured but inactive professor, and a Janis Joplin. They share a degree of resignation and apathy toward the larger society.

The central and guiding policy of institutions being built and formal organizations that are being transformed should be directed toward the stimulation of *mobility experiences* for a maximum number of people. The mobility rubric obviously covers many (and only superficially different) behaviors: travel to the city; reading the newspaper, book, magazine, or letter; listening to the radio; talking to the school teacher or extension specialist; talking with the child who is a student; or (and most powerful of all) being oneself in the educational experience, in classroom or field.

Lerner argued that, "Mobility is the agent of social change. Only insofar as individual persons can change their place in the world, their position in society, their own self-image, does change occur."[10] I agree.

The essence of the role that mobility plays in the modernization process is in the dissociative experiences that mobility generates. Mobility brings awareness of alternative behavioral modes, enabling assessment of their relevance to one's own life; and, given perception of relevance and payoff potential, the final consequence is change.

Notes

1. David Horton Smith and Alex Inkeles, "The OM Scale: A Comparative Socio-Psychological Measure of Individual Modernity," *Sociometry* 29, no. 4 (December 1966): 353-77.

2. For example, F.B. Waisanen and H. Kumata, "Education, Functional Literacy, and Participation in Development," forthcoming, 1971 in *The International Journal of Comparative Sociology;* and F.B. Waisanen, "Actors, Social Systems, and the Modernization Process," Carnegie Seminar Publication, Department of Government, Indiana University, 1969.

3. The study is reported in Prodipto Roy, F.B. Waisanen, and Everett M. Rogers, *The Impact of Communication on Rural Development, UNESCO-NICD,* 1969.

4. Waisanen and Kumata, *Education.*

5. From a social structural perspective, the vertical dimension would relate to the degree to which the structure is conducive to making alternatives available and encouraging independent choice among options.

6. The horizontal dimension, again in a structural context, represents something like a "reality line," and would reflect the degree to which a system is responsive to change.

7. The transnational comparison was with India. See Roy et al., *Impact of Communication.*

8. The decision to measure change as a "percentage of change possible" was based upon the central need to assess the differential impact of the experimental treatments. Were one interested primarily in total impact on, say, agricultural productivity, other change measures may have been more appropriate. For a discussion of this issue, see Roy et al., ibid., p. 41; and Carl I. Hovland et al., "A

Baseline for Measurement of Percentage Changes," in P. Lazarfeld and M. Rosenberg (eds.), *The Language of Social Research* (New York: Free Press of Glencoe, 1955), pp. 78-82.

9. These data are not a fair sample of the full pattern of findings that emerged from the study. Indeed, the overall effects were discouraging. For example, we were not able to show effects in intervillage comparisons. The crucial anticipation that there might be a "spin-off" effect, i.e., that forum participants would be influential agents in the continuing idea diffusion process in the experimental villages was not realized, so a more appropriate answer to the question, "Can measurable change be effected by non-formal strategies?" might be, "Yes; but it isn't easy."

10. Daniel Lerner, "Toward a Communication Theory of Modernization," in L. Pye (ed.), *Communication and Political Development* (Princeton: Princeton University Press. 1963).

Designing Effective Learning in Nonformal Modes

TED WARD, JOHN DETTONI,
LOIS MCKINNEY

Although educators, and especially educational administrators, concern themselves with managerial and political matters, any educational effort must be concerned primarily with *learning.* In nonformal education, more than in formal education, the emphasis is usually on *functional* learning, learning that bears an immediate and direct relationship to the life style of a learner. Learning is effective to the extent that it relates to important needs and characteristics of the learner or to a "target group" of learners.

The functional value of learning derives from the culture in which the learner is patterned and shaped. He becomes *what* and *whom* his cultural circumstances permit. His needs are molded by his social setting and economic condition; to a large extent, social and cultural factors make him what he is. Characteristics of the learner, especially his perceived needs, are the part of the learning system that is "given." Designing an instructional system for effective learning begins, not only with an acceptance of the learner as he really is, but also with a recognition of the social and cultural factors that give functional value and potential effectiveness to what he learns. In the experimental sense, learning variables within the learner or set of learners are *dependent* variables, not subject to direct intervention or treatment. For the practical-minded planner of nonformal education, the *independent* variables (those things which he can control, change or influence directly) are the instructional factors. The instructional factors of a learning system can be altered, and the consequence can be the increasing of learning effectiveness.

The searchers for nonformal alternatives in education include many angry people. Some are frustrated over the tendency of formal education to enrich and perpetuate an elitism within their societies. They charge that such educational systems do little or nothing to solve the problems of massive ignorance, poverty, and isolation from the determination of governing authority. Others have more specific criticisms of weaknesses of the "establishment" that they would attempt to relieve through alternative ways and means in education. Thus many reformers in American education find themselves in company with the educational revolutionaries of South America, Africa, and Asia, whose major concerns may be substantially different. The contemporary worldwide kinship of reformers and revolutionaries derives primarily from the fact that they are all seeking alternatives — for somewhat different reasons, toward somewhat different objectives, and using a wide variety of essentially different means. But, in a more basic sense, they share an identity with a long line of educational reformers, from Rousseau to Dewey, innovators and curriculum reformers, whose common quest is for effective learning.

The need for effective nonformal education is usually expressed as an imperative to find alternatives in response to one or more of the following goals:

1) to bring education to people who are not being reached by the formal educational establishment;

2) to provide education at lower cost; and/or

3) to direct educational objectives toward goals that are more practical or more closely related to the learners' needs within their society.

Designing an instructional framework for effective learning hinges on three factors:

1) relationship of the planned educational goals to the social values of the learners (what they see as important for satisfactions in life);

2) accommodation of the pedagogical expectations of the learners (how they expect to be taught); and

3) accommodation of the cognitive style of the learners (through what mental processes, strategies and meditations do they learn?)

Education is concerned with ways to bring together people and educational resources. Whether the people learn and the relative value of what they learn are issues sometimes overlooked. It is not enough to build schools or to provide teachers. To assure effective learning demands that ends and means (goals and procedures) be aligned with significant values of the society. Thus those who are concerned about effective learning must evaluate the degree of fit between the planned educational experiences and the expectations of the learners, in the light of the social values and needs in the society.

Increased Effectiveness Through Systems Development

Certain improvements and refinements in instructional design are beginning to make an impact on educational planning. Until recently, much planning remained nonarticulated and generally vague, or, erring in the opposite direction, overly preoccupied with specifics to the exclusion of broader areas of educational concern. A present trend reshaping educational planning practices seeks to relate the planning sphere to the total systems environment within which education functions.[1]

Recent improvements in educational design have come from increased understandings of learners and environments for learning. The mysteries of mental processes remain stubborn, yet within the past decade there has been important changes in instructional technology. These changes have evolved through application of scientific observations of learning processes, social interactions, and patterns of human responses to environmental stimuli. "Learning effectiveness," as typically used in nonformal education, develops its meaning from this recent pragmatic and rationalizing orientation—especially in relationship to the substantive planning issues indicated earlier (need to reach other populations, need for lower costs, and need to achieve different goals).

Some of technologies of formal education may be appropriate for nonformal education—to the extent that they can be used to reach the objectives of the nonformal sector and reach them at allowable costs. For example, a particular teaching procedure from formal education commonly employed in nonformal education is the illustrated lecture; but, when it appears on broadcast television and is received by community-based action groups, its objectives and costs (per unit) distinguish its present nonformal use from its original academic use. Creative and original procedures for instructional design in nonformal education are coming from new data, theoretical constructions, and models. Especially valuable is research in small group dynamics, organizational processes, social systems linkages, and psychological theory. The proliferation of useful information demands an orderly process for selection and design. Further, since the improvement of an educational operation depends heavily on evaluation, a concept of the operation as a system (or, in fact, a subsystem) is useful. Thus, cogent planning for effective learning is facilitated through a social systems perspective and methodology. Especially for the planner and developer of nonformal education, the use of instructional design procedures based on a rudimentary systems development concept of education can result in a more accountable and relevant educational program.

A simple systems model applied to educational planning suggests the following concerns:[2]

Problem I: Specify the Learning to be Achieved

Nonformal education is typically concerned with learning that has a high degree of "practical" usefulness. Thus the specification of learning, as indicated in a systems development procedure, is especially concerned with learning in exactly the form it is most likely to be applied. For example, assume that the practical problem for which the nonformal education is being designed is to meet the need for operators of tractors for community farms. The training program should specify learnings as skills of tractor operation and tractor maintenance. The learning would be specified in terms of its practical use, not in terms of abstract or theoretical understandings. In another illustration, the learning objectives for a family planning program would not be specified as understandings or as "knowing about birth control techniques," but as the composite of understandings and behavior changes that represent the actual adoption and practice of family planning procedures.

The emphasis on practical and behavioral learning achievements is a concern not only of nonformal education. Formal education, in some countries, has undergone a similar shift in emphasis toward behavioral objectives in the past few years. Nevertheless, it is in nonformal education that investments in education or training are expected to achieve very specific developmental goals based on very pragmatic values.

Problem II: Describe the Target Population

The target population for programs of nonformal education are usually rather specific and delimited. It is within *formal* education that the education-for-everyone approach has been most often applied. Indeed, one of the continuing dilemmas of schooling is the need to provide educational experiences for a diverse population. If populations are not carefully defined, the educational experiences may prove to be appropriate for only a limited segment of the target population.

One of the most important requirements for effective learning is a matching or interlocking of the planned experiences and the learners. Each proposed target population must be carefully studied and understood in terms of three major factors that vitally relate to effective learning: 1) the motivations, value systems and reward systems within which learners live and work; 2) their cognitive style and learning capabilities in terms of previously acquired skills; and 3) their expectations about learning and about the pedagogical environment. Precise description of the target population is absolutely essential for successful application of a system development procedure for instructional planning.

Problem III: Specify the Instructional Tasks

Jerome Bruner[3] was among the first of the psychologists of learning to warn that teaching and learning objectives is only one step; after the learning to be achieved is specified, it remains as a separate task to propose the sort of instructional alternatives (experiences) that would achieve the learning.

Specifying instructional experiences consists of 1) identifying and/or creating (at least describing) the possible instructional procedures that promise to achieve the learning objectives; and 2) making choices among the alternatives in order to move ahead in the development of the instructional system. (It is important to recycle an instructional system, revising the instructional procedures—sometimes even making other selections from among the alternatives—in order to improve the system on the basis of the data from evaluations of the system.)

Problem IV: Specify the Support and Management Tasks

As soon as the first decisions about instructional tasks are made, the support tasks can be defined. For example, if it is determined that the instructional tasks are to be performed through the medium of television, the support tasks can be defined (even before the instructional materials—"software"—are developed.) The support tasks for an instructional system ordinarily involve the system "hardware" and its maintenance. Nonformal education typically goes one of two directions: 1) uses existing resources ("hardware") and puts the new instruction through these channels with minor modifications; or 2) develops new resources to use as instructional channels. Generally the first option is elected when the system is to be very widely disseminated; the second option is used if the system is to be more precisely focussed on smaller (but perhaps widely scattered) target populations. For the first alternative, the specification of support tasks involves negotiations and joint planning with other agencies whose resources the instructional system will share, such as radio and television. For the second alternative, the efforts are apt to be more heavily invested in preparing the support system personnel, often necessarily recruited and organized as an altogether new team. In any case, the development of an effective management procedure must begin at this point.

Problem V: Specify the Level of Performance to be Learned

The effectiveness of systems development rests less on its "scientific" nature than on its careful organization of the sequences of decisions which must be made. In designing an instructional system for effective learning, it is usually advisable to make a separate step for the specifying of the level of performance to be learned. There is a difference between the learning task itself and the level of performance. The level of performance is concerned with accuracy, rate, or quality level of skill. For example, in the tractor-operation example used earlier, after it is determined what the learning task is and how it will be taught, the question remains, what level of competency will the system attempt to achieve? Since a systems development approach to instruction is usually based on a "mastery learning" model, the important issue to be determined in this step is what will constitute the lowest acceptable level of performance for any learner. For example, the system might specify a 100% frequency for learning to "check the oil level before starting the engine," but be satisfied with 70% frequency of performance of the lesson "shut off the fuel line before leaving the tractor at the end of the day." In matters of quality, the straightness of a furrow might be judged to be very important or not very important. Since the next step (preparing instructional materials) must take account of these judgments about importance, frequency and quality, the specification of the levels of performance to be learned should be made before the actual design of the instructional materials. Especially in education built on the "mastery" model, it must not be assumed that all learners are to learn every skill to a perfect level of performance and exhibit them 100% of the time. The "mastery" model instead very deliberately establishes a set of standards that represents the acceptable level of mastery of the skills or understandings and then designs a set of procedures whereby all appropriate learners will attain those levels.

Problem VI: Prepare Instructional Materials

The preparation of instructional materials is a set of tasks guided by the decisions made earlier in the specification of instructional objectives and in the specification of level of performance to be learned.

Regardless of the apparent "scientific" or technological approach to instructional systems design suggested by block diagrams and flowcharts, instructional design is a creative matter. With data about the target population and the learning objectives, a creative designer or team of designers is ready to sit down to think through the many different ways that learning experiences can be provided. The success of this step depends heavily on the degree to which the instructional designers observe the data on the target populations and the specified objectives. There are also two other highly important factors: 1) awareness of the full range of possible instructional materials and resources; and 2) insights into the relevance of the alternative instructional resources to the past and present cultural practices of the target populations.

Revising or adapting instructional materials that were designed for one purpose in order to make them useful for another purpose is difficult at best, hazardous at worst. Fortunately, it is common in programs of nonformal education to develop special new instructional materials rather than use in appropriate instructional materials designed for formal education. The difficulties of surmounting incompatible linguistic demands, conceptual levels, degrees of abstraction, and basic differences in learning needs and objectives may be more satisfactorily overcome by developing new materials than by attempting to excerpt from and revise existing instructional materials.

Now that nonformal education has become a matter of worldwide interest, there is an additional hazard: inappropriate use of instructional materials that have originated in another culture.[4] From research on programmed instruction has come evidence that instructional materials must be attuned to the culture. Especially when using the more specialized print media (particularly various forms of programmed instruction) and the visualized media (motion pictures and television), there should be an attunement between the instructional materials and two sets of factors within the culture: the cognitive style and pedagogical expectations of the learners. Instructional procedures in general—especially instructional *materials*—should be designed to relate to the cognitive style of learners; even within one culture, differences in cognitive style should be accommodated to increase the effectiveness of the learning. Across cultures, where difference of cognitive style may be large, it is especially important that appropriate transformation be made. Until recently it has been common for educators to make generalizations and to treat cognitive style too simplistically, but recent studies show that even within limited geographic areas and among people of similar ethnological backgrounds the differences in cognitive style can be pronounced. For example, Hovey points out evidences of a wide range of cognitive styles within twelve societies of Sub-Saharan Africa.[5] These differences in cognitive style suggest that very different procedures would be advisable in order to enhance the effectiveness of learning. But research indicating the degree of importance of accommodations to cognitive style is still lacking.

Problem VII: Train Human Resources

The people who will operate (manage or deliver) the major instructional experiences, as well as the people who will operate the support systems, must be trained. Although they need not be trained together, it is necessary for the training programs to be articulated or even overlapped to assure that the various human roles will be compatible and supportive. In a thorough systems design, the training programs for delivery system personnel and for the support system personnel are planned as thoroughly and precisely as the main delivery system itself. Personnel to be trained are analyzed as target populations, their needed skills are specified, and the instructional tasks and materials for training the personnel are specially designed.

Problem VIII: Design Evaluative Procedures

The success or failure of an instructional system usually depends on its ability to gather evaluative data and to recycle its design and operation (make changes for improvement) on the basis of indications from the evaluation data. Plans for evaluation should be completed before operating the system. The design for evaluation of the effectiveness of the system must be thorough. In a systems approach to "mastery" learning, the evaluation procedures are based on assessing the strengths and weaknesses of the system in terms of reaching its specified objectives. With reference to formal education, evaluation is more often concerned with the accomplishments of the *students,* whether a student "passes" or "fails". In terms of the "mastery learning" approach, it is the instructional system (including the input screening processes) that is under test. Thus the evaluative procedures must include data collection (testing) at the beginning and at several points during the learner's progress through the stages of instruction; it is important to be able to identify the exact breakdown points or weaknesses of the system for learners of given characteristics.·

Problem IX: Operate the System

This problem is self-explanatory, except that in a systems approach to instruction, the operation of a system, especially at the first, is a sort of trial or experiment. In the early months of the operation of a given delivery system of nonformal education, the major objectives of the operation is to gather evaluative data. Many well designed instructional systems begin their operational phase on a small scale, even operating under the constraints of field trials in given test sites where the characteristics of the environment and the learners are well known. It is important that these test sites be carefully selected for their equivalence to the broader populations for whom the system has been designed.

Problem X: Evaluate the Learning

The primary purpose of evaluating is to get information that can be used to *recycle the system.* "Recycling" refers to making changes (adjustments, alterations, corrections) in the instructional system in order to increase the effectiveness of the learning resulting from the system. In a "mastery" approach, evaluation also is used to *recycle the learner* until his learned performance is able to meet the level of performance specified as mastery of the learning. Especially in well planned nonformal education, testing is highly behavioral and task-oriented, in keeping with the learning specified by the system. For example, in the tractor-operation illustration, the testing program is likely not to use written examinations, but would rely heavily on evaluative observations of performance. The best evaluations are unobtrusive measures to gather data in such a way as that to reduce learner's awareness of being evaluated.

Basic Questions for Planning

In the process of planning, the creation of valid alternatives calls for examination and definition of the relevant and important variables of the field under consideration. For educational planners, the same process holds true but is complicated by the very fluid nature of the educational process. In simplest terms, learning can occur when educative experiences are brought to bear on a learner. But learning always occurs in complex environments. No simple model of learning is adequate for purposes of instructional design. The planned educational experiences are but one part of a more complex universe of experiences in which the learner himself is a contributing part. Further, the learning outcomes result from interaction of the deliberate educative experiences, the totality of general environmental influences, and the learner as a unique personality.

Identifying all of the significant variables within this model of learning is obviously impossible. Thus it is necessary to decide which factors are the most important and to plan well for their development. Following is a list of sociopsychological and ethnopedagogical issues most basic to the problems of designing nonformal systems for effective learning. Of major concern are the motivations, expectations, and abilities of learners and the rewards and reward systems in which the learners and the learning experiences operate.

		Sociological	Psychological
What brings a person to the learning experience?	Motivations	Conformity Societal norms Enforcement Requirement	Curiosity Anxiety Ambition Anticipation of rewards
What will he get from the experience?	Rewards	Prestige Recognition Status Income	Self-fulfillment Gratification
What does he hope or believe the experience will be?	Expectations (pedagogical, topical, value)	Roles: teacher Roles:learner Content Utility	Abstract/concrete
What is he able to do and what is he capable of learning to do? (what constraints on learning?)	Abilities Learning style	Role acceptance	Mental ability Cognitive sytle Affective invovlement

The questions following are suggested as inquiry tools to identify the factors that should be considered in the design of nonformal education if it is to be 1) alternative to existing systems; 2) less costly; and 3) able to deliver more effective learning.

Concerning the *motivation* of learners:

What motivations will exist?

Which of the extant motivations are appropriate to (consistent, in harmony with) the educational goals?

How can these be enhanced, emphasized, dramatized?

What are other motivations consistent with the educational goals?

Which of these are worth inducing (creating, establishing)?

How can they be induced?

Which of the extant motivations are inconsistent with the educational goals?

Which of these would it be worthwhile to minimize or suppress?

How can they be reduced?

Concerning *rewards:*

What rewards (reward systems) exist in the personal-social-occupational environment of the learners?

Which of the extant rewards are appropriate to (consistent, in harmony with) the educational goals?

How can these be enhanced (emphasized, dramatized)?

What are other rewards that would be consistent with the educational goals?

Which of these are worth inducing (creating, establishing)?

How can they be induced?

Which of the extant rewards are inconsistent with the educational goals?

Which of these would it be worthwhile to minimize or suppress?

How can these be reduced?

Concerning *abilities* and *learning styles:*

What is the level of ability to comprehend abstractions (of both the verbal and symbolic sort)?

What is the reading skill (comprehension)?

What are the mechanical and manipulative skills previously developed in the learners?

What are the factors of health, attention span, alertness, concentration and application of effort that will affect the learners?

What are the learning styles (in terms of cognitive styles and habits of response to pedagogy) that must be accommodated by the instructional design?

The questions specified above are primarily concerned with understanding and describing the target population. Appropriate accommodation of these factors can result in increases of learning effectiveness in nonformal modes of education.

Suggested Guidelines for Planning Effective Nonformal Learning

Planning for effective learning is a complex problem. There is no way to simplify the tasks; it is only possible to define them more clearly and to arrange them in convenient and manageable sequences. Basic to these sequences and to the designs which they will enable are several understandings. Designing effective learning in nonformal modes depends on these understandings.

Understanding the Historical and Cultural Sources

Within every society there are sources in the traditions and the value systems that have given rise to what education has become. That which a culture has produced cannot be overlooked in the planning of something new. Before attempting to augment or significantly alter the educational resources of a community, region or nation, these historical and cultural sources must be examined and, to the extent possible, understood. Such understanding is necessary if new nonformal resources are to have an ultimate accommodation (interlock) with the existing formal and informal systems of teaching and learning. With reference to these factors a guideline is offered: *For Effective Learning Nonformal Education Should Be Designed to Interlock into the Cultural and Historical Traditions of a Society.*

Understanding the Target Populations

Of all the many variables in an instructional system, the description of target population is likely to be the most complex. The three sets of factors that must be understood are 1) the motivations that drive and learners and the sorts of psycho-socio-economic rewards that will sustain them as learners; 2) the habits and expectations that their previous learning experiences have induced; and 3) the styles of mental processes and learning characteristics that have been induced by previous formal and informal learning experiences. Education without an outlet for the learning is apt to be seen as useless. With reference to the first set of factors, motivations and rewards, a guideline is offered: *For Effective Learning, Nonformal Education Should Provide Experiences For Which There Is A Practical Use.*

Incentives for learning should be perceptible to the learners and should be specifically rewarded within a relatively short period of time. Further, the learning situation and experiences themselves must be acceptable within the learner's frame of reference. He must see a worth and validity in the experience. Thus another guideline is suggested by the *expectation* factors: *For Effective Learning, Nonformal Education Should Utilize Instructional Procedures That Are Recognizable To The Learners As Being Valid Learning Experiences.*

This guideline might be incorrectly interpreted as suggesting that only "old" methods should be used; however, there are many occasions wherein learners can be carefully and gently reeducated to recognize the learning potentialities in new procedures and forms. Thus it is possible to introduce new media and methodologies if the plan provides for the necessary reeducation needed to accept the new procedures.

The third set of factors, *learning characteristics,* suggests another guideline: *For Effective Learning, Nonformal Education Should Employ Instructional Materials Designed Specifically For The Dominant Characteristics Of The Learning Styles And Mental Processes Of The Learners.*

To the extent that the dominant characteristics of learners' styles are in common within a society, this guideline can be employed. Not enough is known about cultural factors that affect learning style. We can never be sure, however, that we are taking everything important into account, but to plan instruction that will be effective, whatever is known about learning styles common within the society should be utilized.

Understanding the Administrative and Managerial Demands of an Instructional System

The instructional system consists of far more than a plan for the delivery of educational resources. As important as the delivery system itself is the management and evaluation components and functions of the system. Nonformal educational operations and agencies have two characteristics that place special demands on the managerial role:

1) the specificity of focus and purpose requires a discriminatory decision-making style in order to keep the operation on its main course;

2) the relative independence and autonomy of nonformal educational agencies and operations result in a constant necessity for defining and redefining the borders and boundaries, jurisdictions and overlaps with other nonformal and formal organizations and agencies. Thus a special demand on management is skill in communicative correlation with all other related human and physical resources. With reference to this matter, another guideline is offered: *For Effective Learning, Nonformal Education Should Be Designed To Operate Within A Management System Capable Of Correlating Human And Physical Resources As Well As Articulating All Potentially Contributory Agencies.*

Further, and an adequate and accurate supply of continuous data on the consequences of the educational operation is crucial in managerial decision-making. Without feedback and evaluatory structures and routines, reduction in discrepancies between intentions and outputs cannot be achieved. With reference to this concern, a final guideline is suggested: *For Effective Learning, Nonformal Education Should Operate Within An Evaluative Structure That Provides Data For Continuous Improvement Of The Instructional System.*

An instructional systems approach to nonformal education accepts the view that objectives are important as determinants of procedures. Many formal education programs are a result of valuing the perpetuation of procedures more than the achievement of goals. It is recommended that nonformal education be planned so as to respect the relationship of objectives and procedures as follows:

a. Make a general statement of the problems and/or needs to which the nonformal education is to relate.

b. Make a statement of goals and objectives for meeting the needs.

c. Determine and operate a set of procedures that will likely achieve the goals (construct the system).

d. Carry on a continuous evaluation and modification of procedures to assure that they achieve the goals.

e. Periodically assess the problems and needs in order to modify the goals and objectives of the system.

In such a relationship, the procedures of the system must be consistent with the goals; and the value of the goals is dependent on their relationship to the reduction of problems and the meeting of needs. As needs and problems change, the goals and objectives must change. When evidence indicates that goals must be more effectively achieved, procedures must be changed.

Summary

Designing nonformal educational programs for effective learning must deal with three vital concerns: establishing the aims or goals of the system; identifying and engaging the interests and motivations of the learners toward whom the system is directed, and developing the delivery system and whatever organizational structure it requires. Nonformal educational alternatives must be attuned to areas of identified human needs, should demonstrate relevance to developmental goals, and yet must maintain involvement of the individual learner. Additionally, these programs must be flexible enough to adapt to changing human needs and social environments through carefully built feedback linkages (systematic processes of evaluation, redesign and change). The tendency of human beings and formalized systems to routinize activity and to ossify (either personally or bureaucratically) must be offset — an especially urgent concern for educational planners; the developing nations of the world can scarcely afford wastage of human or material resources in pursuit of illusory promises. Critical questions of values, purposes, and direction (What educational experiences are appropriate? Decided by whom? What are people to become? Why?) must be carefully and defensibly explored; planning must take account of these findings.

Developing new strategies for educational development has become one of the demanding social obligations of our time. Conscientious educators and planners are aware of the moral dimensions of development and of the human outcomes of nonformal education which form a significant part of the development process. Systematic procedures of instructional design can result in increased learning effectiveness for nonformal educational programs and thus better contribute to societal development.

Notes

1. For a delightful and engaging book in this area (systems approach) — amenable to lay and specialized audiences — see: C. West Churchman, *The Systems Approach*, Dell Publishing Co., Inc., New York, 1968.

2. Popham, W. James and Baker, Eva L., *Systematic Instructions*, Prentice-Hall, Inc., Englewood Cliffs, New Jersey, 1970, p. 13.

3. Jerome Bruner, *Toward a Theory of Instruction*, Cambridge, Massachusetts: Harvard University Press, 1967.

4. Patricia Howieson, Elaine Hagland and Ted Ward, "Cross-Cultural Adaptation of Programmed Instruction," East Lansing, Michigan: Human Learning Research Institute, Michigan State University, 1970. (mimeographed)

5. Richard Hovey, "Cognitive Styles in African Cultures: The Global Articulated Dimension," unpublished dissertation, Michigan State University, 1971.

Part 4
Issues in Planning Nonformal Education

Introduction to Part 4

Previous chapters considered the need for finding alternative locations for educational functions, indicated the multiplicity of options available, and revealed the complexity of designing programs for effective nonformal learning. We now attempt to chart a path from theory to practice, by considering some central social and economic issues in the planning of nonformal education.

The search for new futures in education reveals many possibilities. It presents an array of options and calls for decisions which may have far reaching social implications. How will the future shape of education be determined? How can a path to that future be mapped? What does it take to make a plan for reality? These are some of the questions to which the chapters of this section address themselves.

One way to measure the impact of an education system is to examine the way in which its benefits are distributed over the population. In many cases access to education, hence access to its benefits, is differentiated by factors of age, sex, ethnic origin, and social class. What values guide the distribution of educational benefits? In chapter 10 Guyot suggests that equality and efficiency are two values that operate strongly in many developing countries. Deformalizing education, as he describes the process, can be an attempt to achieve greater equality and efficiency in the distribution of educational benefits. But the two values, equality and efficiency, are not always compatible. Moreover, the political consequences of such efforts can be far reaching. An examination of these consequences is a most realistic starting point for planning nonformal education, for in any educational program politics can play an important part in determining success or failure.

Even politically feasible programs may fail, however, if they are poorly implemented. One key to successful implementation is an adequate plan of action. In chapter 11 Hilliard outlines the elements of such a plan. An underlying principle of his plan is an awareness of, and respect for, the ethos of nonformal education — "usefulness to life, participatory learning, entertainment, using the vehicles of art as well as the concepts of science and technology." Such a plan will build upon existing resources to meet national needs in order to "enrich the lives of more people at a cost their country can bear."

Coombs' contribution in chapter 12 offers some insights on how educational planning must operate if it is to develop action programs capable of providing nonformal education for developing nations. The challenge he puts to planners is to move beyond a concern for schooling, which in the past was considered in an isolated and mostly quantitative way at the national level, to a broader concern for all of the activities which make up nonformal education. This move cannot be made in one step; it may require many small ones at the outset.

The final section of Coombs' chapter reiterates a concern expressed by many previous writers, a concern for evaluating the productivity and efficiency of nonformal education. For limited resources and growing demands for education make efficient allocation of these resources most important for the poor countries. In chapter 13 Hardin takes up the problem of economic evaluation in greater detail. After reviewing some efforts to evaluate nonformal education in the United States, he offers some observations on the requirements and procedures for program evaluation in developing countries. Evaluation requires careful planning and special skills if its results are to be of use in decision-making. Since evaluation also makes demands on the already limited resources of poor nations, it would be a mistake not to profit from other's experiences or to squander these resources by evaluating in a way that can have no effect on policy. The relevance of Hardin's chapter is not limited to economic evaluation; it can be applied as well to an evaluation of equality of access to education.

In considering the evaluation of equality of access we come back full circle to Guyot's question of who gets what. And we are reminded that educational planning and the search for new futures in education cannot be carried out in a linear fashion. Educational planning does not have a clear-cut beginning and end; it cannot be accomplished in a set period of time, for education is an ongoing process in constant need of revision and evaluation. This is particularly true in nonformal education. Programs can be designed to meet a specific need, but they must be dropped when the need has been met so that resources can be shifted to meet other demands.

10

Who Gets What When Education Is Deformalized?

JAMES F. GUYOT

A nation's system of education plays politics on both the input side and the output side of government. A major input to politics in the Third World has been the mobilization of new groups via the expanding institutions of formal education. And as schools mobilize they also socialize their charges, engendering both support and criticism for the reigning political formula. On the output side education functions as a gatekeeper, providing differential access to positions of power, wealth, and status for groups and individuals. Such is especially the case in postcolonial societies, where a highly structured system of formal education had been fashioned to shape and sort out the human resources needed to man the machinery of empire. It is this aspect of the output function — the answer to the question, "Who gets what?" — that will engage our attention as we contemplate the consequences of certain deformalizing changes in the educational systems of postcolonial countries.

Before proceeding with the argument it might be good to set out several leading characteristics of formal education, the alteration of which constitutes deformalization. This will be no attempt to draw up a firm definition by default for the concept nonformal education. It is intended only to provide some rough handles for holding on to ideas that appear in other forms in other chapters of this book. For these purposes formal education may be characterized as:

Academic. Formal education is general and abstract rather than specific and applied. As in the distinction between education and training, it is "about" a large number of things rather than "for" specific purposes. It is at least one level of abstraction removed from the actual world.

Economizing. Formal education operates in an economy of scarcity. Access to successive levels of education is progressively restricted, usually by a sequence of examinations or other qualifying hurdles calculated to hold back those less able to profit from the administration of heavier doses of education.

Incubatory. Formal education is something that takes place prior to other significant events in an individual's life. It is an incubatory phase that preceeds the operational phase. In a way, the object of education may be viewed as a child's wind-up toy which must be wound before it runs, and after running stops.

Documented. Formal education certifies the quality of its products in terms of public standards or credentials assigned by some relatively objective method.

These are often thought to represent "achievement" rather than "ascriptive" criteria when used for recruitment purposes.

Who Gets What Out of the System?

Individual ascent up the educational ladder has group consequences for social mobility since ethnic, regional, class, and other groups vary systematically in the degree of success with which their members play the education game. This variation follows from group differences in access, in interest, or in aptitude. Higher educational institutions are concentrated in cities and attendance is often costly. Consequently, rural folk and the poor generally have reduced access to higher education. Cultural differences in the value attached to modern education also play a role in determining which ethnic groups will push their children farther up the educational ladder. And finally, there are some real differences in aptitude patterns among ethnic groups. We need make no assumptions about the inheritability of IQ or racial differences in aggregate levels of intelligence in order to understand that for whatever cultural or other reasons members of one ethnic group will show, for instance, a greater aptitude for routine bureaucratic competence, and another for poetic imagination.[1]

In recent years the colonial formula for translating academic achievement into occupational opportunity has come under several challenges. One line of attack questions the appropriateness of academic credentials as indicators of ability to perform the new kinds of tasks that confront new nations. For instance, some suggest that the liberal arts education of the administrative generalist might have been appropriate in the days of limited government but that it ill fits him for the technical, economic, and managerial chores of national development.[2] Another line of attack is the political demand of ethnic groups, social classes, and regions of the country for fair shares in the apportionment of power, income, and status. These two challenges — one made in the name of efficiency, the other in the name of equity — are at some points complementary and at others contradictory in the changes they required of the formal education system.[3]

Five Deformalizing Changes and Their Political Consequences

Broadened Admissions

Perhaps the most direct way of democratizing the output of the educational system is to democratize the input. If the criteria for passing through each stage in the educational stream are broadened so as to permit a larger and more diverse population to collect their credentials at successive points in the passage, then the benefits for which these credentials act as counters will in the end be more evenly distributed across the several classes, communities, and localities that make up the nation.

How might this be accomplished? Let us try some variations on the academic and economic elements of the formal education system. For one, the academic hurdles could be eliminated by a policy of automatic promotion or open admissions throughout the length of the educational production line. To be really effective such a program would have to eliminate the economic hurdles as well by providing compensatory financing for those less able to pay school fees or forego earnings during the incubatory period and for the transportation or boarding costs of students from rural areas. In all, the total financial costs of this policy would be so great as to require either across the board, impoverishment of the educational program, or a severe limit on the total amount of education available to all. Furthermore, unless jobs are brought into greater equality of responsibility, income, and status, such a system will produce a Niagara of educated underemployed and necessitate some criteria other than educational qualifications to allot different levels of work among candidates.

Equality in distribution could be accomplished at less cost by employing a sequence of random filters to reduce the stream of students reaching the higher and more expensive levels of education. Random selection will provide a more representative distribution of educational benefits than a system of quotas for disadvantaged groups since some bias is bound to operate within the quota categories: those selected to fill the ethnic quota will be the more wealthy of each ethnic group; those filling an income based quota will be the more urban of the poor; and so on through the various combinations of quota categories. If random screening provides a more representative sample at each level, then this new mix of motivations and aptitudes will require compensatory inputs of educational resources if we are to achieve the same quality of output as would have been produced with student populations selected by academic criteria.

A more modest proposal for change which may improve both the equity and the efficiency of the educational system would be to search for more powerful predictors of educability than the current formal academic criteria. The subject matter matriculation examinations used for university admission are often less reliable predictors of performance at the university itself, than simple verbal aptitude tests.[4] The substitution of abstract aptitude tests in place of previous academic performance for selection to successive levels of education should help correct the bias against students from rural or poor backgrounds, especially where these backgrounds are associated with inferior educational resources. Thus this change would serve the goal of equity as well as efficiency. Whether it would redress racial imbalance will depend upon which aptitudes are tested.

Another selection device, partially introduced in the Soviet Union in the late 1950s and carried out in China following the Cultural Revolution, is a party directed evaluation by one's peers in a work situation. This method of admission certainly sharpens the student's motivation to perform well in the educational setting, and shapes his continuing devotion to the purposes for which he is being educated. Peer-political selection will usually have a broadening effect since that is one of the purposes for which it was adopted.

The political consequences of broadening admission to the higher levels of the educational system reach beyond the simple redistribution of values to alter the dynamics of the political system itself. The admission of new groups, or of new proportions of old groups, into urban elite life sets up a reverberating cycle in which the new men of power demand a yet broader redistribution of power and other social benefits.

From Art to Science and Theory to Practice

The curricular shifts commonly said to be required by the manpower needs of economic development programs are a general movement from arts to science and technology, from general education to specialized training, and from the purely academic to the practical and vocational. In the majority of new nations the natural trend is in the opposite direction, in response to forces operating on both the supply and the demand side. On the supply side lies the relative ease with which arts enrollments can be expanded compared to the financial and technical costs of developing new institutes with a more vocational, practical, or scientific bent. On the demand side is the reality in the postcolonial world that a liberal arts B.A. is truly the most vocationally rewarding certificate.[5] In other countries, where education is less open to free-market forces, some such shift in enrollments toward science and technology has taken place.

The implications that a shift in priorities from arts to science bear for the distribution of educational benefits are mixed. By and large vocationalization of primary and secondary education carries particular benefits for those groups economically less well off. On the other hand, science and technological training at the middle and higher levels are less available to the rural population as the higher costs for equipment and specialized teachers require concentration of facilities in urban areas. On the ethnic dimensions, expanding educational opportunities outside the arts field would also tend to be "regressive," with urban minorities such as the Chinese and Indians in the Southeast Asian setting multiplying their general educational advantage by their special interest and aptitude in science and technical studies. Countervailing governmental policies may take the form of special commercial and technical institutes reserved for the less advanced majority ethnic group, such as the Institute Teknoloji MARA in Malaysia, or strict ethnic channeling within the university itself as in Burma, where the Revolutionary Government diverts the non-Burman students into the arts courses.

If there is an expansion of specialized and technical education, and the development of appropriate job openings follows suit, then such deformalization should have an influence on the distribution of employment benefits. However, we should distinguish this employment effect from any effect we can anticipate in the structure of status and political power. Status and power may well remain frozen in the colonial mold if the dominant position in the civil service is maintained by a generalist elite cadre along the lines of the Indian Civil Service and its cousin services in Pakistan, Burma and Malaysia.

Intermittent Education

In postcolonial countries one typically finds the wind-up model of education conjoined with what Ralph Braibanti has characterized as an "achievement-ascriptive" career system, or one in which level of entry is set by achievement criteria (educational qualifications and a tough examination) while subsequent progress follows purely ascriptive lines (entry level and time in grade).[6] This conjunction of education and occupation means that many individuals find their life course fairly well fixed within the first score of years.

In place of the wind-up model in which an individual's full stock of education is imparted at the beginning of his life cycle, a more flexible program would provide a little education now and then, as appropriate to recharge his conceptual batteries over the course of his career. This pattern of intermittent educational intervention offers advantages in terms of efficiency and equity as well. First of all, it forges a closer connection between education and work life, presumably increasing the contribution one makes to the other. Secondly, it loosens up individual career patterns by offering a second or third chance to those who didn't score so impressively on the first time around in the occupational sweepstakes.

Reallocating Investment from Elite to Mass

The strategy of producing more literates and fewer Ph.D.s in the developing countries has much to recommend it. It certainly opens up a large number of nonformal options: adult education, the training of military recruits, and part-time village schools. Improvements in both efficiency and equity might be expected. Depending on the composition of the existing stock of educated manpower and the structure of the economy, the marginal return in the form of increased GNP may well be greater for investment in primary than in university education. Since about forty or fifty villagers can be pushed through the threshold of primary education for the dollar cost in teachers salaries and capital investment it takes to carry an undergraduate through to the B.A., a dollar spent on primary education spreads the benefits of education much more broadly. And finally, raising the average educational level of the masses is thought to reduce the "elite-mass gap."

This would be true if the effect of reallocation were to reduce the height and broaden the base of the pyramid of social values obtainable by means of education. Here a switch from Egyptian to Southeast Asian imagery, from the pyramid to the pagoda, may give us a clearer picture of what is likely to happen. A shift in emphasis from university level to primary education will probably not wipe out university and postgraduate education altogether. Hence the height of the structure remains the same. What changes is its shape. It comes to resemble the stupa of a Therevada Buddhist pagoda with its broad high base which rapidly narrows down to a thin ascending spire. There remains, then, an elite enjoying disproportionate income, status, and enlightenment. The difference in this form is that there are proportionately fewer of them and consequently their power is more concentrated.

Demonetizing Existing Credentials

A fundamental deformalization of education would come about if the connection between particular educational credentials and the qualifications for particular jobs were broken or at least loosened up. The linkage between credentials and qualifications is loosened to the extent that other criteria are taken into account in sorting candidates out among jobs. Such criteria are:

1. Experience in similar work at a lower level of skill or responsibility.
2. Performance tests or tests for knowledge quite closely connected with the requirements of the job. A very valid but quite expensive form of a performance test is a trial period of employment in the actual job.
3. Ascriptive qualifications such as race, age, sex, region, etc. In some cases these may actually be quite relevant to the requirements of the job. For example, Malay District Officers have a legitimacy in the eyes of Maylay peasants which a Chinese or Indian officer would be hard put to match.
4. Political merit as earned by party work or especial loyalty.
5. Random rewards. This criterion is usually applied only after other standards have been met, as in determining which of two civil servants entering duty on the same day shall be counted as senior.

The question of who benefits from such loosening of connections depends largely on the shape of the new connections, for instance, how much of which criteria enter into the employment decision and in what sequence.

As the aftermath of China's Great Proletarian Cultural Revolution has once more demonstrated, any program of deformalizing or destructuring implies an eventual restructuring. If we are to assess the political consequences of nonformal alternatives in education, we must consider carefully the implications of the new forms that such alternatives will take.

Notes

1. James F. Guyot, *Aptitudes and Academic Performance in a Sample of Malay and Chinese Students at the University of Malaya,* Southern Asian Institute, Columbia University (mimeo.) 1970.

2. John D. Montgomery and Milton J. Esman, *Development Administration in Malaysia,* Report to the Government of Malaysia, Kuala Lumpur, 1966. Ralph Braibanti, "The Civil Service of Pakistan: A theoretical Analysis," *South Atlantic Quarterly 58* (Spring 1959).

3. Several good examples of conflict in the joint pursuit of equity and efficiency appear in C. Arnold Anderson, "Central-Local Tensions and the Involvement of Education within Developing Countries," a paper prepared for the ACLS-SSRC Conference on Subnational Politics in Africa, May 1971.

4. James F. Guyot, *Aptitudes,* pp. 31-43.

5. Philip J. Foster, "The Vocational School Fallacy in Development Planning," C. Arnold Anderson and Mary Jean Bowman (eds.), *Education and Economic Development* (Chicago: Aldine, 1965), pp. 142-66.

6. The "achievement-ascriptive" pattern is perhaps most evident in Japan where it operates in both the civil service and in large business organizations. It is also prevalent in colonial civil service systems and often lingers on or even intensifies after independence, as evident in the Malayan Civil Service, where 90 percent of the variance in rank standing of Superscale MCS officers could be explained by their standing five years earlier.

11 Elements of an Action Program

JOHN F. HILLIARD

Throughout history the vast majority of people have acquired social, economic, and political skills through nonformal learning experience. Traditionally this process of inculcating knowledge and skills was based in the family, the tribe, or was an integral part of the whole culture. Although it was central to the system of "governance," it was only in the most marginal way a responsibility of the "government."

The Colonial period introduced two fundamentally new educational concepts: (1) that education, for purposes of Colonial administration, was a necessary responsibility of the governing power, and (2) that such education was the accepted mode of vertical social and economic mobility. Even those countries which never experienced colonial status were strongly affected by these concepts. As a result, the high value traditionally placed on nonformal education and learning deteriorated. Formal education along essentially European lines acquired a pervasive value system, often far out of proportion to its relevance and usefulness to society.

During the past fifteen years the developing countries and external assistance agencies have tended to concentrate their educational efforts on the development of formal school systems. Given the historical background, such concentration was perhaps inevitable. By products of this drive, however, have been continuing neglect of traditional modes of nonformal education and failure, until recently, to perceive the vast gap which could not be filled by the formal educational system.

Growth in populations and changes in the economics and aspirations of the developing countries render impossible a return to ancient forms of traditional education. On the other hand, formal education is becoming prohibitively expensive for many countries, given their increasing numbers of students and lack of financial resources. In most countries educational costs are increasing at a rate faster than national income and gross national product.

A considerable proportion of the present and future populations of most developing countries will receive little or no formal education at all. For many, the only opportunity for skill and knowledge development will be through some kind of nonformal education.

The only possible escape from this educational dilemma appears to be a far more perceptive and purposeful effort to make education and learning an

137

integral part of life where people live and work. It now appears clear that the skills, knowledge, and capacities of the labor force (and indeed the whole population) are developed as much through experience, on-the-job training, recreational, and cultural activities as they are through formal schooling. It seems equally clear that this nonformal mode of learning could be very substantially increased in value and extended in scope by more imaginative planning, organization, and leadership.

Within the more developed countries, nonformal education makes an extremely important contribution to all manner of human resources development, of both a general and a highly specialized nature. One of the important characteristics of such activities is that they often begin in order to meet real needs and end when the need no longer exists. In this sense, nonformal education efforts frequently are more responsive to real needs and new concepts than are formal and traditional educational endeavors.

Emphasizing nonformal education does not necessarily mean deemphasizing formal education. It does mean developing a new dimension of education which can provide useful learning experiences for a much larger proportion of the population in the places and environments in which they live.

The Concept

Considering the crucial role which nonformal education has played in the more developed countries, and its growing importance in the less developed ones, it has proved extremely difficult to evolve a definition of the term which is understood by and acceptable to educators. This is caused largely by (1) our present inadequate knowledge of educational activities carried on outside the formal school system, (2) the tendency of educators to think of education only in terms of formal, graded systems and (3) the wide-ranging and amorphous nature of nonformal educational activities, frequently private in origin and management and often achieved as a by-product of a venture primarily directed at objectives other than education (e.g., rural cooperatives, trade unions, health and nutrition clinics, political participation).

Equally difficult has been establishment of the concept of nonformal education *systems,* which would be potentially capable of providing nonschool populations with educational services systematically and in ways which would significantly serve individuals, societies, and the purposes of national development.

For purposes of this chapter, the definition of nonformal education is that suggested by Professor Frederick Harbison: "Nonformal education may be defined as skill and knowledge generation which takes place outside the system of formal, graded schooling." The concept of nonformal education as a system implies a conscious relationship between the various kinds of nonformal education and a reasonable degree of compatibility with the formal system of education.

During the past two years, considerable progress has been made toward establishment of acceptable definitions and concepts of nonformal (or out-of-school) education. However, these terms need further refinement to make them fully understood and acceptable in the international development community. Toward that end, it may perhaps be useful to make several points about what nonformal education is, what it is not, and what it can become.

1. Nonformal education can be valid, high quality education for imparting "life", skills and knowledge. It is not third-rate formal education.

2. It is education designed to reach large numbers of people where they live and work. Its objective is to impart useful knowledge, skills, and recreation without removing people from their normal environments and responsibilities.

3. Nonformal education can be highly diverse in organization, funding and management. It can emphasize local initiative, self-help, and innovation on the part of large numbers of people and their local institutions. Every successful learner can become in some degree a teacher.

4. It is education designed to pay its own way through increased employment, productivity, and social participation.

5. Its objective is to make learning a national, lifelong learning experience, compatible with the interests of individuals and communities, for all economic levels of a society.

Nonformal education cannot achieve all these things immediately. If properly developed, it can do all of them increasingly well.

Taking Stock

On the basis of incomplete studies made thus far, it seems certain that far more nonformal education and learning are taking place in every country than are known to development planners and educators. These activities range from small privately sponsored projects to large, well-organized programs established through legislation. They include everything from infant nutrition to computer technology, from better farming practice to industrial management.

In no country has there been an adequate, systematic inventory and analysis made of nonformal education. The educational benefits of employment have remained largely unrecognized. Few countries have made the vital distinction between schooling and learning. Even fewer have expressed this distinction in national policies, budgets, and actions. The basic operating assumption is that *schooling* is planned, purposeful learning, but that *learning* outside of school is essentially accidental and unplannable.

These concepts are changing. But they are not changing rapidly enough to meet the needs of people for useful education, or the needs of countries for better educated people.

Perhaps the first important element in an action program for nonformal education is, therefore, a careful inventory of efforts now taking place. Such an inventory should be designed to (1) identify all significant nonformal educational activities, both public and private, their objectives, organization, methodology, and funding (2) their clienteles: rural, urban, mothers, industrial workers, armed forces, craftmen, union members, school dropouts, illiterates, (3) coverage of client groups, gaps, and overlaps, and (4) an informed impression of the degree to which they are achieving their objectives.

Such an inventory could form the basis for looking analytically at the overall national problem of education to meet the requirements of development. This is, of course, a difficult and long-range task. However, to undertake it almost immediately brings into a different focus the whole concept of educational planning. It begins to identify private and public institutional resources that are or can be made available to enhance nonformal educational activities under way; it can relate these activities to each other and to national needs in a more rational way. It can clarify and emphasize the roles of industry, agriculture, and other economic and social groups. It can, frequently for the first time, identify educational goals as involving both formal and nonformal education as major components of a *national learning system*.

It should be emphasized that "taking stock" does not mean "taking over." Indeed, one of the great virtues of nonformal education is that responsibility for it can be so widely shared.

Another important dimension of the inventory is international in character. Nearly all developing countries are at different points of experience with nonformal education. A few are well advanced. Others have hardly made a start. All can profit from serious, systematic efforts to learn from other countries.

It could be very instructive for those concerned with nonformal education to visit other countries which have a record of extensive or comparable experience. To facilitate this, a number of international assistance agencies are now preparing case studies in countries that have had exceptional success with nonformal education.

Educational Requirements and Resources

Countries already hard pressed to find resources for their formal education systems are understandably concerned by the possible costs of a system of nonformal education. However, at this point few countries, if any, have any accurate idea of what an adequate program of nonformal education would cost, the sources of funding for such education, or what resources it now has which could be utilized more efficiently at little or no additional costs.

A wide variety of development services — rural cooperatives, health clinics, labor education programs, and the formal education system itself — are potential "delivery systems" for better nonformal education. Public sector and private industries are particularly suited to provide educational services. Large numbers of workers are brought together by employment, and productivity increases can often more than offset the costs of additional educational services.

In the formal school systems, around 95 percent of the total costs are for salaries of teachers and staff. In nonformal education, offered as an important but ancillary service, these costs can be minimal.

Modern communications media, particularly radio, television, and audiovisual materials, are already being employed for a variety of purposes. A better organized, higher quality educational content can be produced for out-of-school populations at relatively modest additional costs.

This is not to argue that good nonformal education can be had for nothing. The point is that the next important action step is to design an overall education program and relate present or potential resources to it in a rational way.

Motivation and Incentives

For every human being, nonformal learning is a basic aspect of life, particularly during the first twenty years. For many, it is a lifelong process. But in the great majority of countries this learning is haphazard, and circumstantial, frequently based on outmoded concepts and traditions.

With modern educational concepts, organization and technologies, there is no basic reason why this "accidental" learning cannot be made more purposeful, prolonged and include a much larger proportion of both young people and adults.

The impulse to learn is a basic aspect of human nature. Its inhibition arises primarily from lack of significant opportunity. This inhibition can be greatly ameliorated by making learning opportunities available (and making people aware of them) which can (1) improve the economic position of the individual, family, or community (2) enhance social, cultural, and political participation, and (3) stimulate interest and provide entertainment.

The last point deserves particular attention. All traditional nonformal education had a strong entertainment feature. Its vehicles were almost always the languages of the arts: drama, music, the dance, epic narratives. It spoke forthrightly to the primeval emotions; love, hate, conflict, loyalty, physical prowess, victory and defeat.

On the other hand, formal education has tended to be a solemn, monastic business, suffering from an obsession with facts, discipline, and order. It emphasizes information, rather than understanding; objectivity but not subjectivity, knowledge rather than behavior. Its ethos was (and still is in most places) hard and solitary labor. In our return to faith in and larger reliance on nonformal education, it is essential that the ancient ethos of nonformal education be painstakingly retained: usefulness to life, participatory learning, entertainment, using the vehicles of art as well as the concepts of science and technology.

If nonformal education observes these precepts, its clientele can become virtually every human being. This is particularly true with the rapid development of the new communications media.

Organization and Management

Most nonformal education originates because the formal system cannot or will not serve the purpose. The result has been a remarkable variety of activities, organized and managed in many different ways. Generally speaking, governments, and particularly ministries of education, have viewed such efforts with indifference or antipathy. In those instances where government programs were directed at development objectives, for example in agriculture, health, and industry, the educational component was usually considered as a necessary means to a noneducational end. There was seldom recognition that this kind of education is potentially very important to the whole behavior and function of the individual in society. One of the distinctive features of nonformal education is that it aims far more explicitly at changes in behavior than does formal education. Although there are important exceptions the main point of nonformal education is to induce changes in attitude and behavior: fewer and healthier babies, improved agriculture, better repair of automobile engines, greater productivity in steel production, more effective participation in solving villages problems.

Yet the principal custodians of development in these sectors are different people, with different professional skills and usually in different organizational units. The results has been an almost complete absence of organized planning for nonformal education in terms of national goals.

Moreover, those concerned with nonformal education tend to view the ministries of education, and educators generally, as tradition-bound and lacking sympathy with all education outside the traditional mold. Many have expressed the fear that if nonformal education becomes an organized function of the ministry of education, it will either die or be so rigidified as to lost its special value. There is, of course, an element of legitimate concern: ministries of education *are* inclined to see education outside the formal system as something less than true education, ungraded, unstandardized, and without the authentication of certificates, diplomas, and degrees.

There has even been considerable dispute regarding the matter of more planned and organized nonformal education. Some seem to argue that its essential genius is its very lack of planning and organization.

Dispite the merits of these contentions, accident or anarchy obviously are unacceptable as approaches to building an important segment of a national learning system. Equally unacceptable is to have it designed and operated as a bastardized form of formal education.

It is difficult to see how a national system of nonformal education can be developed without a reasonable measure of national planning, organization, and leadership. Many programs are possible only through legislation and direct or indirect funding. The use of modern communications technology can hardly escape some form of national operation.

The next action step would therefore be to create mechanisms within the government which would have the primary responsibility for leadership in (1) enunciating the philosophy and principles of nonformal education, (2) analyzing national needs for nonformal education, (3) proposing broad programs to meet these needs, and (4) encouraging and assisting both public and private agencies to conduct their activities in consonance with these programs.

The management of nonformal education should be as widely distributed as possible. To the maximum extent possible, the locus of decision and action should be at the point where the individual and the community confront their problems. Government intervention should be avoided when private agencies are effectively meeting an educational need.

These, then, would appear to be the essential elements of an action program in nonformal education: (1) creation of a philosophy and concept of nonformal education as a part of the national learning system, (2) making an analytical inventory of national activities and selected international experience, (3) design of a national program based on systematic study of national needs, (4) examination of national resources for carrying out the program, and (5) creation of mechanisms within the government to provide leadership and coordination.

These elements should lead to a sensible form of organization and management in each country. Perhaps the basic objective to be sought is improved planning and organization of nonformal education, and deformalizing much of the subject matter and methodology of formal education. After all, the proper goal of all education is not to produce or preserve a "system," but to enrich the lives of more people at a cost their country can bear.

12 How Shall We Plan Nonformal Education?

PHILIP H. COOMBS

There is growing recognition that developing nations will need to give much greater emphasis in the 1970s to out-of-school education, especially in rural areas, in order to supplement and enhance the yield of their earlier investments in formal education and to help narrow the huge educational gap that will continue to elude the capabilities of their financially-strained formal education systems.

This requirement confronts planners and decision-makers with a new set of perplexing questions to which there are no adequate answers as yet. For example: How should out-of-school education be planned, and who should be responsible? What should be the division of labor and relationships between out-of-school and formal education? How can out-of-school education best be integrated with broader national development goals and plans, and more particularly with local plans and schemes for economic and social advancement? What are the costs of out-of-school education and how can they be financed without fatally handicapping formal education? How can the relation of costs to benefits be assessed? Can out-of-school education make a major contribution to equalizing educational opportunities for seriously disadvantaged groups such as rural youngsters, girls, and young women?

This chapter, it should be said at the outset, offers no solid answers to these questions. Its more modest purpose is to provoke discussion among experienced practitioners and students of educational planning that may shed fresh light on this dark and relatively unexplored area. Therefore the statements made should be considered tentative hypotheses, not proven and immutable truths.

In particular we will direct attention to:

1. Some critical shortcomings of educational planning as presently practiced
2. Some important features of out-of-school education that differentiate it from formal education and condition its planning
3. Some logical steps reguired in planning out-of-school education
4. A few hypotheses about the potential productivity of out-of-school education

The Present State of Educational Planning

It will be useful to start by looking briefly at the present state of the art of educational planning, since this must be the point of departure for seeking ways to plan out-of-school education.

Only ten years ago educational planning was still in a primitive state in relation to the greatly increased and more sophisticated demands that history had suddenly thrust upon educational leaders. Then planning concepts and rhetoric soon emerged and gained currency — such as the idea of 'comprehensive' educational planning 'integrated' with social and economic development planning, and such methodologies as the 'social demand approach,' the 'manpower approach', and the 'cost-benefit approach' to educational planning. It became clear to all by the early 1960s that new and stronger forms of planning were urgently needed to make sense of the pell mell expansion that educational systems had entered into. But as attractive as these new ideas and labels seemed, they were still largely theoretical and had not yet been widely tested in practice. Nor were many nations equipped with the necessary human talents and institutional mechanisms needed to apply them.

Fortunately it can now be said that during the 1960s rapid and impressive progress was made in both the theory and practice of educational planning, thanks in no small measure to the efforts of international organizations, particularly UNESCO. Even so, it must also be said in candor that a large gap still remains between the theoretical concepts and methodologies of educational planning and their practical application and implementation. Four limitations of present educational planning are especially worth noting for the bearing they have on out-of-school education.[1]

First, virtually everywhere educational planning has thus far been limited to formal education, and in many cases only to primary and secondary education (particularly where colleges and universities are beyond the jurisdiction of the education ministry). Thus, while its scope has been broadened compared to earlier days, educational planning is still far from comprehensive in the sense of covering the whole of a nation's organized educational efforts.

The most serious omission practically everywhere has been out-of-school education — all those organized, systematic educational programs lying institutionally outside the 'formal' educational system such as farmer training and agricultural extension, accelerated skill training of various sorts, community development efforts in the fields of health, nutrition, childrearing and homemaking, functional literacy projects and special programs for out-of-school youth.

For purposes of official educational planning, education by implication has been narrowly defined to mean 'schooling' and only publicly financed schooling at that. If instead, one defined education in terms of its main objective, namely *learning,* then clearly the scope of national educational planning would have to be considerably broadened. This is more than a theoretical point, it is a very practical point for any nation that is anxious to make the best use of its available resources to promote overall social and economic progress. If educational planning is to address itself to the full realities of the matter, it must be liberated from the limitations of parochial institutional jurisdictions.

A second serious limitation of educational planning thus far has been its overwhelming preoccupation with the quantitative expansion of the existing formal educational system, with little serious attention to effecting necessary qualitative changes in the system's structure, methods, content, and management needed to make it function more efficiently, effectively, and equitably.

This tendency to concentrate on the quantitative aspects at the expense of the qualitative ones is, of course, quite understandable. For one thing, it is a great deal easier to make an educational system larger in its old image than it is to transform it in major respects — particularly when the precise *kinds* of changes and innovations that should be made and the practical ways of achieving them are not at all clear. Equally important, however, the intensifying popular pressures of the past two decades to expand the supply of education has kept educational authorities everywhere preoccupied with trying to keep pace with the rising demand. Though most were well aware that the old structure, curriculum, and methods were becoming increasingly obsolete in the new situation, there was little time or resources for attacking this especially difficult aspect of the problem.

For these reasons virtually every nation pursued an additional strategy of linear expansion aimed primarily at making the old system bigger as rapidly as possible to accommodate a larger number and percentage of young people at every level. Educational planning became an instrument of the expansionist strategy.

This strategy of linear expansion accomplished — much measured by its own criteria of success — the upward movement of statistics of enrollments and particpation rates. Indeed, it was so successful that, together with other forces at work, it propelled nation after nation into a worldwide educational crisis by the start of the 1970s.

On its face it was a crisis of rising student numbers, rising unit costs, and growing financial constraints. Down deeper, however, it was basically a crisis of maladjustment between educational systems that had grown remarkably in size but in the process had changed their ways far too little to keep apace with the rapidly changing world around them. It was and is as much a qualitative crisis as a quantitative one and can be overcome only by a new strategic emphasis on educational change and innovation. Further expansion is clearly needed, but to continue concentrating on quantitative enlargement to the exclusion of qualitative changes can lead only to educational disaster in the 1970s and beyond.

But how should educational planners plan for change? How can educational planning become a major force for change and avoid being a force that entrenches old educational habits still deeper? This, along with learning how to plan out-of-school education and tie it to the planning of formal education, represents the most challenging and urgent frontier of educational planning today.

It is probably fortunate that these two challenges have come together. The need for a new emphasis on out-of-school education may prove a blessing in disguise for formal educational institutions that are having the devil's own time trying to change their old ways. While it is true that we still know little about how to plan out-of-school education, at least we do know that it is an educational realm where inherent resistance to experimentation and innovation is far less stubborn than in the traditional formal system. Hence out-of-school education can, among other things, become a major laboratory for new ideas and approaches from which the formal system can benefit.

A third major shortcoming of recent educational planning has been its rather exclusive concentration on national aggregates and its failure to translate these into detailed subplans. There is no doubt that overall national educational plans are highly important for setting general targets and guidelines and for allocating national resources among major sectors of the economy and of the educational system itself. But 'macro' plans of this sort formulated in the national capital often with little or no reference to specific local circumstances, should not be mistaken for *action* plans. To implement an outline, national plan requires reducing its broad aggregates to specific action plans for each subsector of education, each geographic subarea, and ultimately each institution and program. To translate a macro-plan into a series of micro-action plans requires not only competent central planning but a planning process that runs from the bottom up as well as from the top down. This in turn requires competent planners and planning machinery throughout the system, right down to each individual school and classroom. Thus the training requirements of the 1970s are enormous — not only for professional full-time educational planners but, even more importantly, for educational administrators and teachers at all levels who can participate effectively in the whole planning process.

Our fourth and last point about educational planning concerns the integration of education with social and economic development. Here again considerable progress has been made, but much remains to be done. Large gaps still exist between talk and theory and practical action, and between generalizations and their translation into specifics.

There is no longer much dissent from the view that formal education should be seen not simply as an end in itself but as an essential means for preparing young people for a productive and effective life in the kinds of circumstances in which they are likely to find themselves, and as a means for promoting the social and economic advancement of society at large. This seemingly innocuous proposition, however, carries far more drastic implications for the reform of traditional educational structures, content, methods and practices than have yet been reckoned with. The implications are by no means adequately satisfied by a limited 'manpower approach' to educational planning (as useful as this may be) which in fact applies to only a small proportion of students in the higher and more specialized echelons of the system and mainly to urban employment. The implications for change, however, are no less drastic for primary schools whose traditional overriding aim has been to prepare pupils for secondary school, or secondary schools mainly oriented toward university entry, when in fact the great bulk of their students have no prospect of going on and will terminate their formal schooling at that level to enter the world of work. Only in a small minority of cases, unfortunately, has educational planning yet come firmly to grips with this essential heart of the problem.

To sum up, we have mentioned four critical shortcomings of educational planning as it now exists: its lack of comprehensiveness (particularly in excluding out-of-school education); its too exclusive concern with quantitative expansion to the detriment of educational change and innovation; its confinement largely to global plans that offer little guidance for practical implementation throughout the system; and its failure to come sufficiently to grips with the realistic needs of young people and of social and economic development. These shortcomings are not cited in criticism and should not obscure the considerable progress recently made in educational planning by many nations. But to ignore these weaknesses or treat them lightly would blind us to important clues to future improvement, not least of all in the planning of out-of-school education.

Special Problems of Planning Out-of-School Education

Against this background, we move now to examine several features of out-of-school education that distinguish it from formal education and are bound to affect the methods and feasibility of planning it.

To avoid misunderstanding, confusion, or fruitless debate, let us agree first that this dichotomy between formal and out-of-school education is in many respects an unhappy one, including the terminology itself. We all know, for example, that good teachers often get good results by making 'formal' education quite informal, and conversely that some programs classified here as 'out-of-school' are as formal in approach as ordinary schools. Participants in some evening adult education programs, for example, have complained that they were being treated like 'school children'.

Granted all this, there are still some important practical differences between, say, an agricultural secondary school and a farmer training center, a primary school and a functional literacy program, a vocational high school and an apprenticeship or on-the-job training scheme that have practical consequences for planning and administration. The differences, to be sure, are mainly *institutional* and man-made. The actual learning objectives of comparable formal and out-of-school education programs may be quite similar, but the organization framework and the educational 'delivery system' employed to pursue them are strikingly different — in structure, instructional methods, sponsorship, terms of admission and completion, finance duration and frequency.

Their most significant difference perhaps is in their conceived relationship to surrounding educational activities. Each component of the formal education system is considered to be (at least in theory and by regulation) an integral and interdependent part of a coherent total system, generally organized according to age and chronological progression, each annual step or multiannual cycle being prerequisite to the next. Out-of-school education programs by contrast are neither conceived of or treated as interrelated parts of a coherent system. Rather they are seen as (and are in fact) a motley assortment of separate educational activities, each with a life of its own, covering an astonishing variety of educational purposes and clienteles, and sponsored by an equally astonishing variety of sponsors, public and private.

Formal education is accepted as the business and prerogative of the Ministry of Education; out-of-school education, on the other hand, is practically everybody's business and therefore tends to be nobody's (especially when it comes to overall advocacy, planning, and fund-raising).

By and large, formal education enjoys far greater prestige than out-of-school, partly because formal is much more professionalized but also because its symbols of accomplishment — its certificates, diplomas and degrees — are popularly believed to have special value in the marketplace and social structure. Still, out-of-school education, curiously enough, is often more highly valued than formal education by its immediate consumers in terms of its actual substance and what it actually does for them. Lacking the appeal of prestigious symbols and being for the most part a voluntary affair, it is to win and hold its clients on the basis of its actual substance.

This means, of course, that out-of-school education programs are perennially exposed to a much harsher consumer test than is usually the case with formal education. If, for example, a farmer training center or functional literacy program seems boring or irrelevant to most of its intended beneficiaries, they can send it into oblivion simply by staying away in droves. This no doubt (along with lack of adequate and sustained resources and leadership) helps to explain the high dropout and mortality rate among out-of-school education programs. (One wonders what would happen to the rate of innovation of formal educational institutions if they depended for their survival on satisfying their customers that what they were teaching them was of direct relevance and critical value to their future lives!)

These few considerations — and there could be many others — may suffice to make it clear that planning out-of-school education on a comprehensive scale would present difficulties far greater even than those entailed in planning formal education. Right at the outset there would be the problem of achieving a reasonable concensus among the diversified sponsoring organizations about how to look at the whole field, and then of getting them to pull together in more or less the same direction. Even to obtain a reasonably comprehensive snapshot picture of what is already going on would present substantial difficulties, not to mention the necessity of projecting an agreed picture of future needs and devising an integrated act of plans and a workable division of responsibility for meeting these future needs.

Then there would be the formidable problem of financing these plans — a problem not unfamiliar to formal education, but for out-of-school education the support must be extracted from a great many sources.

Again, the problem of teacher supply is even stickier than with formal education, for the 'teachers' of out-of-school education range from a relatively small number of highly trained and experienced civil servants to much larger numbers of relatively untrained volunteers. This is potentially one of the great strengths of out-of-school education for it can tap a great range of human resources not generally available to the formal system, often at very low cost. But the fact remains that actually mobilizing this potential talent, orienting and organizing it, putting it to good use and sustaining its enthusiasm and efforts is undoubtedly even more difficult than recruiting an adequate supply of certified teachers under a set salary scale, then keeping them on the job.

Perhaps the practical answer to these formidable difficulties is for a nation not to aspire too quickly to achieving *comprehensive* planning of out-of-school education. Better to approach it in smaller, more feasible steps. After all, considerable good has come from efforts to plan formal educational planning, even though they have fallen far short of being really comprehensive.

This does not rule out the feasibility and value of trying to conceptualize the field of out-of-school education in the broadest perspective, or of seeking basic planning principles that could have wide application throughout the field, or of attempting a general assessment of what is now going on and what main gaps should be filled in the future. These broad-visioned efforts are needed. But it does not follow that a fully comprehensive plan of action covering every type of out-of-school education is mandatory for progress. Quite the contrary, it seems evident that an imaginative planning effort applied to selected key areas of out-of-school education could pay large dividends and is certainly the most promising place to begin. Let us consider, then, some steps by which this more selective approach could be applied.

Logical Steps in Planning Out-of-School Education

There is a familiar and understandable tendency among educational experts, particularly those away from home, to prescribe solutions for other people's education needs in terms of existing educational models with which they are most familiar and competent. Occasionally this approach succeeds, but often it flounders or fails altogether, for the simple reason that the imported model was never designed to fit the particular needs and circumstances of the situation in question.

The clear lesson of past experience in this regard is that the planning of out-of-school educational activity (or of any formal one, for that matter) should not begin with a preconceived notion of what educational model will best serve the need. It should begin instead with a serious diagnosis of the particular context to discover what the need really is.

Step One: Diagnosis of the Particular Area

The starting point is to determine the salient characteristics of the particular locality and its people. If it is a rural area, for example, what is its state of development and its natural potential for further development? What are the educational strengths of the population at present and their various other strengths? Given these natural and human resources, what general pattern of agricultural and rural development would appear to be feasible and sensible for this area in the short run and the longer run, not only as judged by outside experts but by the local inhabitants themselves? What other sorts of local programs and actions are already planned or underway in this direction — such as land reform, improved irrigation and transport, credit facilities, increased supplies of new seeds, fertilizers, insecticides, and so forth? What are the status and prospects of formal education?

Obviously an educational planner cannot answer these questions by himself; he will need to get all the help he can from other specialists and planners. But before he can prescribe intelligently he must first understand the potentialities of the particular area.

Step Two: Defining Priority Learning Clienteles, Needs and Objectives

Having obtained such a general appreciation, the next step is to determine — even if very crudely — what the local populace will need in the way of new skills and knowledge to develop the potential of their area and themselves. If it is basically a static and low potential situation, then the opportunities for out-of-school education to make a real difference may be very limited. But if it is a changing situation they may be considerable. If, for example, the water supply is to be drastically transformed by a new irrigation project, the chances are that the traditional practices of local farmers will also have to be drastically transformed to take advantage of the new situation. But as experience has shown repeatedly, this calls for considerable out-of-school education, properly directed and timed.

For effective planning of out-of-school education, the population will have to be divided into various functional subgroups, each with its particular development roles and learning needs. The same educational program cannot fit them all; there must be a series of coordinated programs, each with its own well-tailored objectives. The small subsistence farmer will need something different than the larger commercial farmers; tomorrow's farmers (today's teenagers) will need a somewhat different educational diet than today's active farmers. The managers of local cooperatives, the blacksmiths, the small local builders, and other 'specialists' will each have their special learning needs (and possibly some common needs as well, such as functional literacy). It will be important for girls and mothers to obtain, among other things, new knowledge and skills pertaining to household management, childrearing, health, nutrition, and family planning.

None of these learning needs are very real, of course, unless the potential learners themselves see and feel them as real needs and are motivated to fill them. Thus the process of identifying priority needs and learning objectives must involve the 'consumers' themselves; otherwise the whole effort may result in waste and frustration.

Some priorities will also have to be set (as painful as this may be) because all of the different potential learning groups and objectives cannot be well served all at once. The problem is to strike a good balance between immediate and future benefits and to try to get the sequence of things in the most productive order.

Step Three: Design of Appropriate Educational 'Delivery Systems'

Only after the various learning groups and objectives have been clearly identified and defined and a feasible set of priorities has been established does it make sense to consider what kinds of educational arrangements would best serve them, taking into account the practical resource limitations and other constraints. The selection of the best 'delivery system' should not be made simply by choosing from among existing prototypes. The best approach is to design one on the spot, specifically tailored to fit the particular conditions, much as an architect might design a building to fit a particular site. This, in other words, is a *micro* planning job, one with many factors – pedagogical, psychological and socio-logical – which a more global educational planner might be inclined to ignore.

This is not to say, of course, that important lessons cannot be borrowed from the experience of other countries – or other parts of the same country – in designing an educational solution for a particular situation. Indeed a creative job of educational design will very likely borrow a number of components from here and there and combine them in a fresh way, along with some new elements.

The point to be emphasized is that the design process suggested here is quite the opposite of simply importing an existing model – lock, stock and bar-rel – on the unexamined assumption that it worked so well somewhere else that it will work equally well anywhere. This is not planning but simplistic imitation.

Step Four: Implementation and Continuous Evaluation and Adaptation

There is not the time here to delve into the many problems involved in converting a plan into action. But past experience suggests a few simple imperatives worth bearing in mind.

First, plenty of time should be allowed for advance planning and preparation. The compulsion to rush into action prematurely for the sake of the record produces more failures than successes.

Second, provision should be made from the outset for continuous evaluation of performance as a necessary means for steadily improving performance. This requires a clear initial definition of objectives, spelled out in operationally meaningful terms, along with an equally clear definition of the criteria and types of evidence to be used in assessing progress (or the lack of it). Provision must also be made to accumulate such evidence systematically.

In all candor we must serve warning at this point against the zealous 'evaluation expert' who may produce an intellectually elegant evaluation scheme that will soon collapse under its own weight. A few well chosen 'critical indicators' that are feasible to apply will be far more useful, even though they leave many interesting questions unanswered. But getting the *right* critical indicators is essential, and would be a big step forward from common practice.

A third imperative is to provide for the flexible adaptation of the initial program to changing circumstances and to the lessons of experience. We are tempted here to observe that nothing fails like success, when initial success results in a rigid adherence to the initial formula in the face of changing conditions, induced in part by the initial success itself. We can take it almost as an iron law that out-of-school education programs sustain their vigor and effectiveness only if they adapt quickly and readily to changes in their clienteles and in their social and economic environment.

In the interest of brevity, the foregoing steps in planning have been stated in a more dogmatic way than is actually intended. Moreover, stated in this form, they may seem like a prosaic glimpse at the obvious. Yet even a cursory review of many types of past out-of-school education programs in many different places suggests that a great many have been seriously handicapped or have failed outright precisely because the steps suggested above were not followed.

The Productivity of Out-of-School Education

We come finally to the important question of how and under what conditions out-of-school education can contribute most to the welfare of individuals and, more broadly, to general social and economic development.

Our first suggestion is that there is nothing to be gained by great debates over whether education in general is a 'good investment' in development or in particular whether out-of-school or formal education is the more productive and should enjoy priority. Posed in this form the questions are senseless and cannot be rationally answered.

Experience clearly shows that education, whether formal or out-of-school, can in some circumstances create individual and social benefits far in excess of the costs involved, and in other circumstances can be a total waste or, worse still, can produce negative benefits. Much depends, obviously, on whether it is the right education for the particular learners at the particular place and time. It depends further on whether this education is provided with reasonable efficiency in terms of the use of available resources.

What is apparently not so obvious, however, judging from the record of decisions made and actions taken, is that the ultimate benefits flowing from a given educational program also depend heavily on what else is going on in the same geographic area that affects development and induces change. This is perhaps even more the case with out-of-school education, than formal for a higher proportion of the participants are likely to remain in the same area. The point is that the process of change and development in any given area calls for a combination of development inputs and forces, of which education is only one — though a very essential and potent one.

To illustrate, a major effort to teach modern farming techniques in a static, isolated rural area where no other dynamic forces are in motion — such as improved irrigation, new supplies of seeds, fertilizers, insecticides, better transport and marketing facilities, and credit availability — can readily prove abortive. By the same token, a major effort to train out-of-school adolescents in various skills for which there is not prospective local market can also prove to be a wasted investment. On the other hand, the same educational efforts in an area of reasonable development potential, where other positive steps are being taken to strengthen agricultural inputs and the rural infrastructure, can be highly productive and can raise the productivity of the complementary efforts as well.

This is simply to say — and here the lessons of hard experience have upset widely held doctrines of only a decade ago — that education all by itself is unlikely to precipitate a dynamic process of development in an otherwise static situation. Education, formal and out-of-school, is most productive when joined with complimentary forces and factors of development — it cannot be a bargain basement substitute for these other factors.

In planning out-of-school education, therefore, it becomes highly important to look around and determine what other positive development steps are being planned or are already in motion in the same geographic area, and then to design the educational effort in such a way as to achieve maximum mutual reinforcement. Which is to say that out-of-school education should be not only related to broader national development goals and plans but closely integrated to the fullest extent possible with *local* development schemes.

A further word should be added concerning the linkage and integration of out-of-school and formal education to the advantage of both. Here we must take note of the view held in some quarters that out-of-school education is a potentially dangerous competitor of formal education, which may somehow do formal education out of needed funds, and the related view that out-of-school education is merely a fringe benefit that should be provided for only after the full needs of formal education have been met. These views, we submit, reflect a very myopic outlook. A broader and more valid one would see the two as partners, indispensible to one another.

In this context it is important to note that out-of-school education plays three different roles in relation to formal education. First it can be complementary, as when rural secondary students, for example, participate simultaneously in a young farmers' club out of school, or attend a mobile training program to pick up practical skills not available through the school curriculum. Second, out-of-school education can be an important successor and follow-up to formal education, as when an on-the-job training program builds on the foundations of general education acquired in school (or when a doctor or teacher or administrator keeps from becoming obsolete by following new developments in his field through out-of-school means). Third, especially where there are severe restrictions on the supply of formal education due to resource limitations, — as threatens to be the case, unhappily, for years to come in the rural areas of many developing countries — out-of-school education may be a viable (even if not perfect) substitute for formal education, especially if it can be provided at low cost and supported substantially by sources not equally available to formal education. In all three situations, out-of-school education is helping education, not jeopardizing it.

In turn the quality and effectiveness of out-of-school education is heavily dependent on the kinds of support and reinforcement it receives from the formal education system. An agricultural extension program, for example, depends greatly on how well the agricultural colleges and universities prepare its staff and supply it with usable research results that can be conveyed to practising farmers. Similarly, community development programs of health, nutrition, homemaking, and the like depend heavily for their effectiveness on what sort of backstopping they get from the formal schools and higher institutions. The point is too obvious to require elaboration, though the record is unfortunately replete with examples of noncollaboration.

The main conclusion to be drawn for planners and policy-makers is that the respective contributions of formal and out-of-school education to national development depends in no small measure on how well the two work as partners within an enlarged conception of the nation's overall educational system (not simply the 'formal' system), and on how well both are planned in relation to the realistic social and economic development needs of the nation and of individuals.

The dilemma still remains, however, of how formal and out-of-school education are to be jointly planned and wedded. Who is to take the lead, particularly with out-of-school education. The Ministry of Education has its hands more than full trying to expand, nourish and improve the formal system, while out-of-school education remains an orphan with no place to call home.

How this problem of administrative structure, responsibility, and leadership is resolved in each country — if indeed it is resolved at all — will be a determinant of whether out-of-school education pushes vigorously ahead in coming years, or simply stagnates. This is a matter on which educational planning experts can be of little help. It is a matter for enlightened statesmanship at the highest levels, in every nation.

Notes

1. For a discussion of the evolution and future needs of educational planning see: P.H. Coombs, *What is Educational Planning?* Booklet no. 1, Fundamentals of Educational Planning, IIEP/Unesco, Paris, 1970.

13 Economic Evaluations of Nonformal Education

EINAR HARDIN

Educational programs have existed for many years outside of the regular, graded school system in the United States. Under the impact of concern with problems of unemployment, poverty, and race and minority group relations, and as symbolized by the adoption of a national manpower policy, these nonformal education programs have greatly expanded in numbers and scope during the last two decades.[1] This expansion has been accompanied by sustained activity to evaluate systematically the effectiveness of new and old programs. This chapter sets forth the results of economic evaluations of three types of nonformal education in the United States, and it offers some thoughts on the relevance of methods and results to nonformal education in poor countries.[2]

Institutional Retraining of Manpower

Holding no patent on an international "first," the United States commenced a decade ago a large program of occupational training for adult workers, usually unemployed or seriously underemployed, in vocational schools and other training facilities not owned and operated by employers. This so-called institutional program, sponsored by the federal government under the Manpower Development and Training Act of 1962 (MDTA) and the Area Redevelopment Act of 1961 (ARA) or by state governments, has been evaluated in West Virginia, Tennessee, Massachusetts, Connecticut, and Michigan.[3]

The West Virginia study by the Somers group covered ARA and state courses largely designed for semiskilled manufacturing and service occupations: riveters, welders, machine tool operators, auto repair men, construction workers, nurse's aides, and clerical workers.[4] The courses took place in an economically depressed area with an economic base of manufacturing, mining, and some agriculture, and with an unemployment rate ranging from 6.0 to 23.5 percent depending on year and locality. Average class length was 3.2 months for men and 2.2 months for women in the study but with only a small number of classroom hours per week. Several reports were prepared which differ in criteria of evaluation and in details of coverage and statistical method and which, accordingly, give somewhat differing results.

Three reports contain estimates of the social economic benefits from training,

159

measured as the increase in annual earnings attributable to training. Cain & Stromsdorfer found first-year annual economic benefits of training of $1,008 per man and $192 per woman, with an average of $736 per graduate.[5] Stromsdorfer found annual benefits of $828 per male and $336 per female graduate. Gibbard & Somers classified the sample not only by sex but also by age[6] and years of formal schooling and estimated training gains in annual before-tax earnings ranging from a high of about $1,200 to a low of approximately zero depending on subgroup, but the subgroups were often too small for reliable analysis.[7]

Cain & Stromsdorfer calculated the total social economic costs of training as $918 per male and $527 per female graduate. However, these costs included two types of transfer payments — welfare payments and training and subsistence allowances — which should be disregarded in a social economic analysis fundamentally concerned with impact on national product. The adjusted costs consisting of pretax earnings lost while in training and of the direct instructional and administrative costs were somewhat lower: $789 per male trainee and $401 per female trainee.

Thus the annual economic benefits from training as calculated by Cain and Stromsdorfer were 128 percent of total social economic costs (as revised by me) in training of men and 48 percent in training of women. Based on the Stromsdorfer results they were 105 percent for men and 84 percent for women. For each sex and according to each study the initial investment of society was recovered in two years or less.

If benefits lasted for ten years but were discounted at 10 percent per year, the benefit cost ratio was between 6.5:1 and 7.9:1 in training of men and between 3.0:1 and 5.2:1 in training of women. The benefit-cost ratios were naturally higher, by 50 to 60 percent, if one accepts the Cain & Stromsdorfer assumption that the annual benefits continued until retirement, 36 years later for men and 26 years later for women, and even higher if one uses lower discount rates. These results represent very handsome economic rates of return on society's investment in training.[8]

The Gibbard & Somers study and the Stromsdorfer study show that a very favorable employment impact, ranging from 10 to 15 weeks per graduate, was a major explanation of the benefits from training. The related study of Tennessee retraining by Solie showed an average employment gain of 6.5 weeks, an average unemployment reduction of 4.1 weeks, and consequently a 2.4 weeks average increase in labor force participation.[9] The implication that the gains in earnings resulted more from increased employment than from increased earnings while employed was also supported by the Borus (1964) study of retraining in Connecticut.[10]

The Michigan study by Hardin & Borus covered MDTA and ARA courses for a broad range of occupations, including may of those studied in the West Virginia project.[11] Each designed for a single occupation the courses took place during the early 1960s in a number of Michigan communities, the economic base of which included auto production and other durable and nondurable manufacturing, government and private services, trade, agriculture, and mining in varying proportions. Some labor markets were chronically depressed, some suffered from a recession which heavily affected durable goods production, some had a relatively high level of economic activity, and the unemployment rate before each class ranged from 2.9 to 19.1 percent.

The Hardin & Borus study differed from the West Virginia studies in several ways. First, it evaluated retraining on three basic criteria: social economic (national product), private economic (disposable income), and government budget (government cash outlays and receipts). Second, it put heavy stress on ascertaining any relationship of economic benefits and costs to the characteristics of courses, trainees, and local labor markets. Third, as part of its concern with differential impact, it analyzed the relation of the length and quality of training to the magnitude of economic effects.

The most striking finding was that short training courses, ranging from 60 to 200 hours per enrollee, had very favorable economic effects. Before-tax annual earnings rose by $976, and the social economic cost of training (instructional and administrative costs, reduced before-tax earnings during training, and trainee expenses) amounted to only $346 per entrant into short training. Since annual economic benefits to society were almost three times as large as total social economic cost, the economic returns were magnificient. This is also indicated by the benefit-cost ratio, which amounted to 17.3:1 for a ten-year service life and a ten percent discount rate.

The economic returns from short training varied with the demographic characteristics of trainees. In particular, when course length was held constant, more years of formal education meant lower socioeconomic returns.[12] However, since the benefit-cost ratios for short training were all far above unity, ranging from 9:1 to 30:1 depending on subgroup, it was very profitable for society to retrain disadvantaged as well as advantaged groups in short courses.

The economic benefits for the individual trainees were also very substantial in short courses. Largely because of special allowances, the trainees did not lose any disposable income during the course, and on the average they gained $743 of annual disposable income aftr the course. All subgroups of short training featured an attractive economic reward and a remarkable absence of investment barriers.

Short courses were not only very beneficial to national product and to the disposable income of trainees but also to the cash position of the government. Government outlays of cash — increased transfer payments and reduced tax collections during class and outlays on instruction and administration — amounted to $404 per trainee. Annual gains of cash after training, composed of reduced unemployment benefits and welfare payments and increased tax receipts, were $275 per trainee, or about 68 percent of total government cash expended. Thus short training had the additional virtue of not only being self-liquidating but actually generating a substantial cash surplus starting not more than two years after the end of training.

In contrast, medium and long training, represented by classes designed for 201-1,920 hours per enrollee, gave dismal economic results. The social economic benefits were negative or approximately zero. The social economic cost was substantial, ranging from $885 to $3,293 per trainee depending on class length. No demographic subgroup was found in which society obtained positive annual benefits exceeding 15 percent of total cost from medium and long training. The private economic benefits, measured in disposable income, were also mostly dismal. Only whites with less than twelve years of formal education obtained significant rewards for enrolling. Blacks lost disposable income both during and after training, the latter effect being attributable in part to a sharp reduction in welfare payments. Medium and long training also worsened the cash position of the government, the average annual gains being less than 1 percent of the total outlays.

These evaluations from the Michigan study carry important policy implications. If the economic goal of retraining is to raise national product as well as the disposable income of trainees without burdens on the cash position of the government, the United States should continue and, indeed, expand its short training program, and at least some of the additional resources should be obtained from the medium and long program. A transfer of resources from the medium and long to the short courses would add greatly to national product, turn private losses into private gains, make the program self-liquidating and cash-generating, and enable the government to aid a significantly larger proportion of the target population with a given total effort.

Since the social cost was much higher in medium and long than in short classes and since only a minority of MDTA-ARA trainees in Michigan and in the nation was in short courses, a complete transfer of resources would lead to a manyfold increase in short-training enrollment. The training facilities could no doubt adapt to this redistribution of effort after appropriate notice. It is less certain that the labor markets for which short courses were designed, or could be designed, would be able to absorb the great increase in trainees. Thus the impressive benefit-cost ratio for short training might perhaps decline noticeably. Compulsive caution in making policy recommendations, not a fear that the government will move with excessive speed, prompts me to add that the transfer of efforts from medium and long training should be accompanied by monitoring the labor market success of persons trained in short classes.

On-the-Job Training

Private and public employers have long trained their employees in job skills, mostly at the work place or at least on establishment premises. Looking for an alternative to institutional occupational training such as studied in West Virginia and Michigan, the federal government has attempted in recent years to encourage private employers to arrange programs for their low-skill employees and also to train new employees without any definite commitment of long-term employment. In a sense the federal government has sought to purchase training from private employers.

Few economic evaluations of these forms of on-the-job (OJT) training appear to have been published. The study by Scott of the Bureau of Indian Affairs (BIA) training program in Oklahoma is an exception.[13]

Nine employers who in the period 1960-66 signed contracts with the Oklahoma BIA for on-the-job training of Indians were covered in the study. Fearing that there exists an important systematic difference in motivation between trainees and control groups of the kinds used in the West Virginia and Michigan studies, Scott rejected the control group approach and based his benefit calculations on adjusted before-after differences in earnings and other relevant variables for a sample of Indians who all entered OJT programs. The average adjusted before-after change in annual earnings was found to be $1,970 after taxes. Since Scott assumed that no earnings were lost during training and since the Indians were apparently not eligible for any transfer payments, no private benefit cost ratio could be calculated. However, the net present value accruing to trainees, given a 10 percent discount rate, ranged from $7,500 to $19,000 depending on assumed service life.

The impact on before-tax earnings was used as a measure of annual social economic benefits. The BIA administrative costs and the BIA subsidies to contracting employers were the two components of social economic cost. The end results were an annual benefit of $2,034 per trainee, a total social economic cost of $1,010 per trainee, and a benefit-cost ratio ranging from 7.6:1 to 19.5:1 given a 10 percent discount rate and five or thirty-five years of service life.

Unfortunately, there may be less content in the Scott findings than meets the eye. Changes in economic activity and general wage levels, spontaneous decisions to enter or leave the labor force, and regression toward the mean all affect the behavior of annual earnings over the course of time. The effect of these forces was likely to be an increase in annual earnings and, hence, an overstatement of the economic gains from the BIA program. Furthermore, there are indications that some employers first hired Indians and then ascertained whether subsidies would be paid, so that some members of the sample would have been hired and retrained even without the BIA program. Finally, the contractual training period for which subsidies were paid greatly exceeded the actual learning time according to trainee opinions, and skills were acquired more by learning from doing than by systematic training. One may wonder how much of the subsidies represented compensation to employers for increased cost of training and how much was a simple windfall gain.

The Neighborhood Youth Corps Program

The Economic Opportunity Act of 1964, with the task of mobilizing human and financial resources to combat poverty, established the Neighborhood Youth Corps (NYC), which has now grown to be one of the largest federal manpower training programs in the United States. By creating useful work experience opportunities for unemployed youth it seeks to make enrollees more employable or to enable them to resume or continue their formal education. The out-of-school program of the NYC serves primarily the school dropouts.

An economic evaluation of one part of the NYC program was made by Borus, Brennan, and Rosen.[14] The study covered NYC programs in five cities in Indiana, two of which added remedial education to work experience projects. Most of the jobs were with government agencies, but some were with nonprofit private organizations or community organizations. The enrollees worked as aides, assistants, or helpers to regular full-time employees, and they could normally choose from a range of work stations. Entrants could choose to remain in the program for short or long periods of time.

The annual benefits from the NYC out-of-school program were defined in terms of impact on earnings after end of participation.[15] Social economic benefit-cost ratios for men, based on a ten-year service life and a 10 percent discount rate, ranged from 1.8:1 to 7.4:1 depending on years of formal education and on assumptions concerning forgone earnings during participation, about which no data were available. For training of women the ratios ranged from zero to 2.1:1. These findings suggest that there were substantial economic net benefits, at least in terms of current earnings, from arranging NYC out-of-school programs for men, especially those who dropped out in the early years of high school, but that little was gained from such programs for women.

Implications for Poor Nations

What do these evaluation efforts in the United States[16] mean for nonformal education in the poor nations? First, if American experiences are directly transferable, the poor nations can make substantial economic gains by commencing selected programs of nonformal education. Substantial contributions can be made to national product, the economic well-being of the recipients of such education can be noticeably improved, investment in people can be spread broadly in the population instead of being concentrated on a small group, and — under a reasonably efficient tax collection system — nonformal education may put no permanent strain upon the government budget. Programs having such desirable economic effects in a rich nation deserve the most careful attention of poor countries.

Second, substantial progress has been made in devising methods for the economic evaluation of nonformal education programs. Many of these methods are sound and can be applied elsewhere with little modification.

Third, there remain many issues and problems to resolve before economic evaluation of human resource programs in the United States becomes a fully valid and well-established routine activity.[17] Certainly there does not exist a very big box of tested and true tools ready to be shipped abroad with instructions for assembly and use.

Something can be learned both from successes and failures in evaluation methods. The remainder of this chapter offers thoughts about some aspects of evaluation procedure to which poor countries might want to give special attention.

Relating Evaluation to Policy

The economic evaluation capabilities of any nation, rich or poor, are too limited to deserve being engaged on problems the resolution of which will not be influenced by evaluation findings. Consultation with planners and decision-makers before evaluations commence may help evaluators ask questions about program efforts which bear on an opportunity for choice instead of assessing the merits and demerits of a practical necessity. It may help them choose economic criteria of evaluation which are likely to have policy significance instead of merely reflecting their personal preferences.

The nature of organizational arrangements which are most conducive to appropriate interrelations between economic evaluation and policy-making will differ from nation to nation according to the structure of government organization, the availability of specialized talent, the need for access to data which cannot be released to nongovernmental users, and the general feasibility of research in government agencies. Evaluation work may be subcontracted to independent groups or institutes, perhaps located in universities; it may be carried out in a central policy planning agency; or it may be conducted in staff units of individual operating ministries or agencies. Most nations may be well served by a policy to make evaluation reports available to all interested persons and to solicit or at least facilitate comments and appraisals from scientific and other groups.

Need for Differentiated Estimates

Any elaborate or large nonformal education program is unlikely to have the same economic effects in all its components, on all its target groups, and in all its environmental settings. One task of an evaluator is to look for variations in effects, to estimate their magnitudes, and generally to provide information for assessing the economic desirability of a within-program transfer of resources. The value of such information is generally high, and its extra cost is relatively modest. Special attention should be given to three differentiating factors.

1. The relationship between size of treatment effect and length or intensity of

treatment has great significance for policy in a nation where available resources do not suffice to give everyone a thorough education. A politically and ethically valuable broad distribution of the benefits of nonformal education is possible without loss of aggregate output, if the benefit-cost ratio is independent of the length of education. If the ratio rises with increased length of education, a given aggregate of educational resources will tend to be concentrated for the use of fewer persons.

2. The nature of the relationship between the extent of formal schooling and the benefits from nonformal education may influence the income distribution effects of nonformal education programs and the impact of nonformal education programs upon investment requirements in formal education. At the present time, the empirical evidence as to substitutability between formal and nonformal education is quite mixed, even after one disregards the fact that instructors and administrators in many nonformal education programs may require much formal education in order to do their jobs well.

3. The economic environment may influence the optimal timing and location of nonformal education activities. Although earnings of semiskilled and unskilled workers (the main targets of manpower training programs) are naturally high in periods and labor markets with general economic prosperity, it does not follow that training will necessarily raise earnings more in prosperity than recession or in tight rather than loose labor markets. Until more findings are available, it remains difficult to specify the general economic conditions under which nonformal education has its most favorable economic effects.

Field Survey Requirements

Detailed data on earnings and employment are usually crucial raw materials for economic evaluations. Government data may have limited coverage, lack important details, vary conceptually and in actual accuracy, exist only in local or area files, and be closed to evaluators on ground of confidentiality. Elaborate field surveys, with personal interviews or mailing of questionnaires, usually become necessary.

The skills required for effective field surveys differ from those needed in statistical analysis and economic interpretation. In the United States many economic evaluators have learned sampling methods; construction of interview schedules and mail questionnaires; selection, training, and supervision of interviewers and other field representatives; and data editing and coding. Developing nations should try to develop general-purpose national field survey institutes, possibly within census bureaus and central statistical offices, and relieve the economic evaluators of the direct burden of field operations. Better data, lower cost of data collection, and quicker reporting of results are among the potential benefits of such a rearrangement.

Observation Units

The predominant approach in economic evaluations of human resource programs to date is to use the individual person as the unit of observation. Although quite correct when the concern is with private economic benefits and costs, this approach may become misleading when the evaluator is also concerned with the impact on nonparticipants and on the whole labor market. The trainees of a successful program may displace other persons into unemployment, or they may fill shortages that would otherwise have persisted and in doing so may vacate jobs subsequently filled readily by the unemployed. The trainee earnings and employment gains exceed the community gains in the first case and fall short of it in the second case; the discrepancies are at times called displacement and vacuum effects. Broadening the unit of observation to encompass the whole local labor market where the educational activity takes place may help allow for displacement and vacuum effects, since the person whom the trainee displaces and the job he vacates are both likely to be located in that labor market.

However, the local labor market approach also entails problems. First, program enrollment is normally very small compared with market size, and extraneous variations in employment and earnings may overshadow program effects. Second, when routine reports to government agencies are not available, assessment of market changes requires expensive sample surveys. Third, the labor-market approach may still have to be accompanied by a treatment-group approach, since an evaluation of the private economic benefits and costs remains a desirable part even of an economic evaluation which assigns highest priority to national product effects.

Control Group Design

The measurement of program effects requires knowledge both about the treatment group and a group fully comparable except for not being treated. Finding such a fully comparable control group is a major problem. Most evaluations of training rely either on qualified, interested nontrainees or on persons representative of the target population. In either case there are usually systematic between-group differences that affect the variable of concern to evaluation, and statistical methods are employed to remove their effects, before the treatment effect is calculated. As economic evaluations and basic research accumulate, we gain increased ability to choose appropriate control groups, to identify and measure important control variables, and to incorporate the control variables in appropriate mathematical forms. However, because we cannot expect to reach a reasonably complete understanding of these matters in the foreseeable future, absence of control group biases cannot be guaranteed, unless potential recipients of treatment are assigned by random methods into an experimental (treatment) group and a statistically equivalent control group.

The principle of randomization has long been recognized as essential in agricultural research and field trials. While more difficult to implement, it is equally essential in studies of human population, including economic evaluations of nonformal education. In the absence of strict experimental control one risks rejecting, on erroneous assertions of incomparability, those correct results which are opposite to existing beliefs while accepting those results which, although possibly quite false, conform with one's expectations. Economic evaluation work then becomes an expensive exercise in defense of preconceived notions.

International Cooperation

Economic evaluation work on nonformal education and other human resource programs is currently dominated by the rich nations. Their methods and results may not be wholly appropriate to poor nations. A rapid exchange of information across national boundaries may help accelerate the testing and development of methods and findings.

The creation of one or more international institutes for program evaluation may help promote such an exchange of information. These institutes may be assigned additional functions. They may become data-processing centers with appropriate computing equipment and statistical advisory staffs. They may arrange seminars and create in-service training opportunities for economic evaluation staffs. They may help coordinate cross-national experimental studies of nonformal education programs.

One may hope that international cooperation in evaluation work will commence and expand so that poor and rich nations alike will not go through a long process of isolated trial and error but speedily put their intellectual resources to productive use.

Notes

1. For descriptions of U.S. manpower programs see the *Manpower Report of the President*. Washington, D.C.: U.S. Government Printing Office, annually.

2. A handy guide to the growing literature on economic evaluations of formal and nonformal education has been prepared by Wood & Campbell, 1970.

3. For a detailed comparison of these studies see Hardin, "Benefit-Cost Analyses of Occupational Training Programs: A Comparison of Recent Studies." in Somers & Wood (eds.) *Cost-Benefit Analysis of Manpower Policies*. Kingston, Ont.: Industrial Relations Centre, Queen's University, 1969, pp. 97-118.

4. Somers, Gerald G. (ed.) *Retraining the Unemployed*. Madison: University of Wisconsin Press, 1968.

5. Cain, Glen W. and Stromsdorfer, Ernst W. "An Economic Evaluation of Government Retraining Programs in West Virginia." in Somers (1968), Ch. 9, pp. 299-335.

6. Stromsdorfer, Ernst W. "Determinants of Economic Success in Retraining the Unemployed: The West Virginia Experience." *Journal of Human Resources,* Vol. 3, No. 2, Spring 1968, pp. 139-158.

7. Gibbard, Harold A. and Somers, Gerald G. "Government Retraining of the Unemployed in West Virginia." in Somers (1968), Ch. 2, pp. 17-124.

8. Cain & Stromsdorfer also calculated private economic benefits and costs of training and found highly favorable private economic returns on the training of men. Among the benefits, they included not only the training effects on after-tax earnings and transfer payments but also the impact on voluntary leisure, valued at the weekly earnings on the last job before the person left the labor force voluntarily.

9. Solie, Richard J. "An Evaluation of the Effects of Retraining in Tennessee." in Somers (1968), Ch. 6, pp. 193-211.

10. The Borus study has attracted widespread attention by reporting socioeconomic benefit-cost ratios which range from 73.3:1 to 137.3:1, depending on circumstances. It embodies a set of assumptions that differ from those of many other studies and entail unresolved methodological issues. Ribich (1968), have attempted to reconcile his results with other evaluations and offer revised benefit-cost ratios in the order of 6:1 to 15:1. Retraining in Massachusetts was analyzed on a very narrow data base by Page (1964), who reported a socioeconomic benefit-cost ratio of about 6.2:1, which Ribich and Hardin independently adjusted to the neighborhood of 4:1.

11. Hardin, Einar and Borus, Michael E. *The Economic Benefits and Costs of Retraining.* Lexington, Mass.: D.C. Heath & Co., 1971.

12. Very few trainees had fewer than eight years of formal education, and mean schooling was eleven years at class start. Extrapolation of the relationship to education ending far below the eight-grade level would be hazardous.

13. Scott, Loren C. "The Economic Effectiveness of On-the-Job Training: The Experience of the Bureau of Indian Affairs in Oklahoma." *Industrial and Labor Relations Review,* Vol. 23, No. 2, January 1970, pp. 220-36.

14. Borus, Michael E., Brennan, John P., and Rosen, Sidney. "A Benefit-Cost Analysis of the Neighborhood Youth Corps: The Out-of-School Program in Indiana." *Journal of Human Resources,* Vol. 5, No. 2, Spring 1970, pp. 139-59.

15. This choice was consistent with one goal of the NYC program – increased employability. The degree to which the other goal, resuming or continuing formal education, was attained by the program was not analyzed, and those members of the initial sample who were known to have obtained additional education or training were eliminated from both experimental and control groups.

16. For practical reasons my survey of evaluation efforts was confined to the United States, and only a limited number of these evaluations were actually discussed. However, evaluation work is also done in Canada, European countries, and other nations. There is a need to take stock of all results obtained and methods employed.

17. See Cain & Hollister (1969), Hardin (1969), and Somers & Wood (1969).

Part 5
Comparative Programs

Introduction to Part 5

Several authors of previous chapters emphasized the need to take stock of existing nonformal education programs as the first step in planning. Such stock-taking serves two functions: (1) for the country taking stock, it establishes a base line from which to start planning new programs and improving and coordinating existing ones, and (2) for other nations such surveys provide data, ideas, and experiences from which they can draw in planning their own programs.

If planning is to begin with a firm foundation, those responsible for it must be aware of the organizations, skills, and other resources available. Important as financial resources are, human resources, too, play a crucial role in every development program. And no amount of capital can adequately substitute for the skills, knowledge, and aspirations of participants. But these are less readily identifiable without some sort of stock-taking.

Planning can make use of other's experience both as a source of new ideas and as a means of avoiding past mistakes. One nation's stock taking may thus assist another in better meeting its needs. Such studies are least useful when they are mere program descriptions. They should also include some evaluation, backed by hard data where possible, and they should try to determine key factors of success or failure. In making such studies the possibilities and advantages of comparative studies should not be over looked. For example, by studying similar programs in different countries a comparative study can provide a perspective which makes it easier to identify the links between the program and its environment.

The array of nonformal education programs already in existence is vast, and without some vantage point from which to survey the scene the collection of programs may remain only a "heterogeneous conglomeration." The chapters in this concluding section look at a variety of programs from different points of view and with different purposes. The selection makes no attempt to be exhaustive or systematic in its coverage; other vantage points are possible and more program examples can be cited. For example, the *World Yearbook of Education* for 1968 provides a perspective not fully covered here; it examines education within industry using both historical and case studies. Callaway in chapter 2 provided still another perspective – programs divided by age of participants, and Paulston in chapter 6 gave examples of programs for youths.

Paik in chapter 14 classifies a whole range of programs using the scheme presented earlier by Harbison. Besides presenting an overview of the nonformal education programs in Korea, he also raises a series of questions that should be asked in any stock-taking. These are the questions that move the inquiry beyond cataloging to include an analysis and evaluation of the programs in their relation to developmental goals.

Chapter 15 describes what Paulston calls the "shadow school system" in Peru. These skill-oriented educational programs are all short term, achievement-oriented, and located close to the place of application. They are also flexible, a quality much needed but lacking in the formal schools. The programs he examines are classified by their location: industry, military, and trade union. The contrast between vocational education as conducted in the schools and as carried out in other locations illustrates, as Grandstaff pointed out in chapter 4, the importance of the fit between the potential of an educational agency and the needs of the group served.

Further examples of national training schemes are presented in a comparative framework by Harbison and Seltzer in chapter 16. Their presentation allows prospective "borrowers" or adapters to examine one type of program operating under alternative forms of organization and implementation. And it gives some information on comparative costs. Evaluations of the effectiveness and efficiency of the programs in meeting their goals are lacking at present, but they would enhance the usefulness of comparative studies, as well as make it possible to improve existing programs.

In final chapter 17, Griffin discusses a University of Kentucky regional development program; he reminds us that the problems discussed in these chapters are not unique to the less developed countries. The formal school system in developed countries is over burdened and not well attuned to the needs of all those it serves. Nonformal education is not intended to be the poor country's cheap substitute for schooling; it is a real alternative. The choice between formal and nonformal education should be made in terms of effectiveness as well as cost.

Griffin's description of the Kentucky program also calls our attention to the importance of regional analysis in stock-taking and program-planning. National aggregates can obscure regional differences in both resources and needs. While such differences have not always been acknowledged in national plans, they are most important at the operational level.

Finally this chapter illustrates the need for establishing links between formal and nonformal education, and the need for coordinating what might otherwise be piecemeal attempts to meet specific problems. A coordinated program can result in regional development rather than in patches of progress.

14

Nonformal Education in Korea: Programs and Prospects

HYUN KI PAIK

The purposes of this chapter are (1) to present some aspects of nonformal education programs in Korea, (2) to compare these programs with various components of formal education, (3) to evaluate in part the effectiveness of these programs and identify the gaps presently existing in them and (4) to make recommendations for long-term planning and needed changes.

Nonformal education may be defined as the process of generating knowledge and skill outside the formal educational system. It is perhaps one of the most "unsystematic of all systems," but here we will try to organize a wide range of activities and programs under this rubric so that meaningful comparisons can be made.

Using the classification that Professor Harbison[1] developed, we have grouped all nonformal education under four categories: (1) programs and activities designed to upgrade the skill and knowledge of members of the labor force, (2) programs and activities that seek to provide necessary skill and knowledge for initial entry into the labor force, (3) programs and activities not specifically connected with a particular occupation, but aim at further cultivation of the social and cultural aspects of citizens, and (4) those activities and programs that cannot be clearly classified under any of the other categories.

Within the foregoing categories further subclassification is possible. The subcategories below include most of the nonformal education activities in Korea.

1. The upgrading of skill and knowledge: (a) vocational training programs of the Office of Labor Affairs such as public vocational training institutes, in-plant training programs and programs of rural vocational training centers, (b) programs of the Central Vocational Training Institute, (c) Rural Development and Guidance Services of the Office of Rural Development such as the activities of farmer training centers, the training program for rural guidance workers, 4-H agriculture and farm machinery training and other farmer training programs being carried out during the winter, and (d) government officials' training programs, etc.

2. Initial entry-skill programs: (a) youth brigades, (b) vocational training in the military, (c) private vocational institutes, and (d) nonformal education programs of the Ministry of Education, (such as higher trade schools and higher civic schools), as alternatives to, or extensions of, formal education in primary and middle schools of Korea.

3. Cultivation of social and cultural aspects: (a) family planning training programs, (b) programs and activities of cultural centers, (c) adult education programs, (d) student enlightenment campaign, (e) citizenship education and community development, (f) micro-library programs, (g) Peace Corps programs, (h) Korean Association of Voluntary Agencies, and (i) other voluntary agencies.

4. Miscellaneous: (a) participant training programs and (b) a wide range of political education efforts, etc.

It is impossible in this chapter to present intricate details of the programs listed above; many of these details were given in two previous papers.[2]

There are several significant observations that should be made about the general functions of nonformal education efforts in Korea. First, it is difficult to assess the achievements of most programs without further study. At present input-output or utility estimates are more difficult to generate than they are in conventional educational ventures. Second, in spite of the many agencies and organizations, both public and private, engaged in the nonformal education program, a large part of the population is still unreached by systematic nonformal education. Some 49.2 percent of the middle school age group, 72.9 percent of the high school age group, and more than 90 percent of the college and university age group have no access to any kind of formal schooling. Many thousands of out-of-school youth and adults still do not get the benefits from existing programs, while others are not being given the kind of nonformal education they ought to have in order to increase their opportunities for employment and personal fulfillment.

These problems notwithstanding, the plan of action initiated is impressive. Two kinds of correspondence course programs are under consideration to deal with the problems involved in reaching those who fail to go on to colleges and universities, as well as youth and adults who have not received the benefits of formal education above elementary school. The number of youth without access to middle school and above was estimated at 1.7 million in the years between 1966 and 1971. Adults between the ages of 18-33 who had no access to or left middle school were estimated to be approximately 4 million by the 1966 census.

With the foregoing, this chapter now attempts to interpret the available information about nonformal education in Korea by raising a series of questions.

What Is the Evidence of the Actual Benefits of Particular Programs, both to the Individual Concerned and to National Development?

We have some reliable evidence to indicate the effectiveness of some of the programs, especially under the first category. The programs seem to provide measurable benefits to the individual and to the society of which he is a member.

In a study recently completed by the Manpower Development Research Institute, it was found that the individual who has had six months of training by a public vocational training institute has increased considerably his lifelong earning capability as compared to the individual who has not received such training.[3] During the period of the study there were some 19,054 trainees enrolled in about forty different public vocational training institutes. Among them 600 graduates of the middle schools receiving training were sampled. It was estimated that the 600 graduates attained a rate of return 15 percent higher than that of individuals of the same age group without institutional training.[4]

While it is difficult to establish cause-effect relationships, the findings of the study suggest a cost-benefit effectiveness of this program. Another study[5] conducted in 1965 and using a stratified random sample disclosed that those farmers who participated in so-called rural guidance activities, when compared with those who did not, had a higher rice income and yield.[6]

Moreover, in a case study of Farmer Training Centers of the Office of Rural Development (ORD) in Korea,[7] carried out for last two months by the Central Education Research Institute, we have found through interviews with trainees and rural guidance workers both direct and indirect benefits from these programs. Direct benefits expressed by trainees and rural guidance workers are that farmers with the training course ranging from one to two weeks (1) have become familiar with the proper and timely usage of various pesticides, (2) have acquired skill in using farming machines, mist machines, and air pumps for irrigation as well as the skills to repair those instruments, and (3) that training programs in "side jobs" available in rural areas have led to the expansion of home industry and thus brought increased income.

The indirect benefits mentioned by those trainees are: (1) graduates have come to have the desire to seek and apply more effective and better ways of farming; (2) acquiring the skill of handling farming machines, pesticides and fertilizer has given trainees confidence in dealing with them, and (3) they have come to have the enthusiasm for desirable improvements in farming and to feel the necessity of a closer relationship with rural guidance groups in order to realize personal objectives.

Economic benefits of the Farmer Training Centers Program are yet to be determined, for the study is still under progress, but the effects of the programs seem to be beneficial not only to individual farmers but to rural communities.

Additionally, campaigns conducted by radio, Student Enlightenment for Rural Community Development, and the Peace Corps Program in their activities in Korean schools and nonformal educational agencies are some examples of actual benefits to social and national development. Although the effectiveness of these programs has not yet been assessed, it is a widely believed that eventually they will bring benefits to the country.

At this point in the development of Korea, evaluation of the programs and of their instructional effectiveness has been focused primarily on formal education. While such studies as those referred to above are not plentiful, they do suggest the likelihood of significant benefits to society. Certainly more systematic research on the outcomes and values of nonformal education are needed.

What Critical Factors (Either Present or Missing) Account for the Relative Success of Some Programs and the Lack of Success of Others?[8]

Some of the important contributing factors to the success or failure of programs are able leadership, good initial planning and clear definition of objectives, enthusiasm of participants in programs, good staff and organizational arrangements, along with adequate provision for relevant instructional materials and equipment, and adequate financial resources. Above all, however, first consideration should be given to financial resources.

Any kind of nonformal education program must have adequate financial resources to survive and grow. However, for the most part, nonformal education programs do not have the same support base as do formal education programs. In adddition to that limiting factor, the distribution of available resources among the various programs is not functionally appropriate. Some programs are in a position to gain more support than others. For example, the programs of the Central Vocational Training Institute and family-planning training programs which relate to economic development plans seem to draw, comparatively speaking, adequate funds to support their operation. But programs run by local cultural centers, adult education classes and programs relating to the cultivation of social-cultural qualities of man can hardly survive under the present financial conditions, let alone expend their operations to include more participants.

While the unequal distribution of existing resources creates immediate problems for the institutions concerned, more serious problems are the attitudes of various funding agencies about the distribution of the funds. If the present attitudes prevail, many of these institutions in the long run will not be able to expand their functions or even to continue to provide quality services. Hopefully, through either friendly persuasion and/or legislative engineering, some of the attitudes prevailing among the leaders of these funding agencies will change, thus making it possible to identify and support the quality programs in each of the four categories.

Responsible leaders in the government, industry, and farm cooperatives have generally shown strong interest in contributing to the growth of nonformal education programs. It is expected that more people in positions of authority will support future plans for comprehensive programs in this domain. This would be consistent with their support of development projects such as rural electrification, expansion of the telecommunication system, and development of a complete network of superhighways.

What Do these Programs Cost per Learner and per Family
Unit (Both Public and Private Costs), and How Might These
Costs Compare with Comparable Formal Education?

It is well known that the exact cost of formal education is difficult to calculate. With nonformal education, however, the cost of the programs is virtually impossible to establish because there are so many different programs with a multitude of purposes, as well as diverse sources of income and different ways of budgeting and record keeping. Given these constraints, we still observe some situations wherein the general cost of nonformal education is much less prohibitive than that of formal education. For example, the programs sponsored by the Office of Labor Affairs cost approximately $25 per trainee per year.[9] In formal education the cost has been estimated to be $125 per pupil per year (middle school). In other words, the cost-ratio of formal education to nonformal education is 5 to 1. If we compare the benefits of the programs with the costs, there is no doubt that certain programs of nonformal education are by far more functional and provide a higher return than programs of formal education. To take another example, family planning programs also cost approximately $25,[10] yet the benefit to society is virtually inestimable.

To What Extent Do These Nonformal Programs Find
Themselves in Direct Financial Competition with Formal
Education or, on the Contrary, Draw Upon Noncompeting
Sources for Support?

This question is difficult to answer because (1) some of the sources of the funds allocated to certain nonformal education institutions are held private or are submerged in the present budgeting system, (2) the amounts budgeted for each activity are not easily ascertainable, and (3) the sources of funds are not discrete enough to make meaningful comparisons. For example, should one use only two categories of sources — private and public? Should this be the case, the competition for funds within each of the two sectors could not be fairly represented.

Let us assume for example that administrative agencies within the government at the ministerial level represent different sources of funds. Let us now estimate the extent to which formal and nonformal educational institutions compete for funds from the same agency. It can be said that a large part of category operations are supported by the Ministry of Education, thus placing these operations in direct competition with formal education. In category 1 the competition for funds within the framework of presumed ministerial differentiation is not as severe as in category 2. For example, three of the most important nonformal education agencies — public vocational training institutes, in-plant training programs, and rural vocational training centers — draw their funds fully or in part from the Office of Labor Affairs, and thus do not compete with formal education activities which are supported largely by the Ministry of Education.

Within category 3 it is difficult to establish whether or not there is competition for funds with the corresponding bureaus in formal education. Some programs operate under highly competitive bases; for example, adult education classes, micro-library programs, and the student enlightenment campaign all draw funds from the Ministry of Education. Other programs, such as family-planning training programs and programs of local cultural centers operate under noncompetitive bases; they draw funds from private sources and from ministries other than the Ministry of Education. It can be said with some confidence that nonformal education programs depending upon the Ministry of Education for support operate in a highly competitive sphere. On the other hand, the programs which draw heavily from outside the Ministry of Education operate with little or no competition with formal education programs. Of course competition with other ongoing noneducational fields is inescapable, but this is not our concern for the moment.

With regard to private sources that come primarily from individual donors, the competition is not evident at first glance. However, institutions that depend upon private citizens for their support are indirectly in competition with the public institutions that depend on citizens for their support through taxes.

In the same context, parents who send their children to the private schools have to pay twice in order that their children receive a proper education. In that sense, the system resembles that of the United States where all citizens are taxed to support the public school system and yet many of them also contribute an equal and, often, a greater amount than their local taxes in order to send their children to the parochial schools.

What Instructional Systems Seem to Have Been Particularly Effective? What Innovations Have Been Tried? and with What Results?

While there has been a proliferation of programs in nonformal education, systematic evaluation of these programs has been minimal. However, some programs have shown positive results and can provide some bases to assess their effectiveness. One such program is the family-planning training provided for nurses, midwives and other paramedical personnel under the auspices of the Planned Parenthood Federation of Korea. This program has been in operation since 1961 and has been found to be relatively effective in training sizeable numbers of individuals to furnish advice on the use of birth control devices.

In 1969 programmed instruction[11] was used to help participants acquire knowledge and understanding of various aspects of family planning. While the exact effectiveness of such programs cannot be ascertained yet, it is interesting to note that such instructional innovation has been introduced through nonformal education.

The mobile unit program for providing rural and agricultural guidance services has been quite effective. This program has used some of the most advanced audio-visual techniques, suggesting the readiness of nonformal education to introduce instructional innovation.

Occupying a highly prominent place among the farming population has been a morning radio program offered by the Office of Rural Development and transmitted to the public by the Korean Broadcasting System. It has been estimated that this daily program reaches approximately 2.4 million farmers in the rice production areas. When the program was introduced some ten years ago, the educational radio broadcast was regarded as an instructional innovation.

Lastly, there has been a variety of nonformal education programs offered through correspondence courses. Such programs as those conducted by the Central Vocational Training Institute with the cooperation of the Office of Labor Affairs have a relatively long history. In 1970, alone, they reached some three thousand individuals and offered programs in such specialized areas as fitting, welding, sheet metal work, diesel engine repair and electricity.

To sum up, although systematic evaluation still remains to be done by the Central Education Research Institute, the programs cited above have been relatively effective and have met with success in pioneering new instructional approaches for learning.

As a matter of fact, some instructional innovations which have been for a long time advocated by such educational leaders as John Dewey, Jerome Bruner, Benjamin Bloom, and others have been introduced primarily through nonformal education. A case in point is the program offered by the 4-H Club which operates under the principle of "learning by doing," i.e., attempts to combine theory with actual work in the field.

What Does All This Suggest for the Future? How Might Larger and Better Programs Be Designed and Implemented that Would Spread Useful Learning More Widely and Rapidly among the People of Korea? What Would This Require in the Way of Resources? How Might Outside Assistance Agencies Best Help?

The status of nonformal education in Korea has been established and compared in some aspects with formal education. While the assessment work has been based on rather limited data, several propositions emerged: (1) nonformal education programs provide important benefits to society, especially when they are functionally related to socioeconomic development, and (2) one of the critical factors for the survival and continuation of any program is the amount and source of support. If competition for the limited resources is high, then available funds are not widespread among the public and private agencies. In such a case it is very difficult to guarantee the successful performance of the nonformal educational programs.

It will be advisable in the future to diversify the sources of income of both formal and nonformal educational programs. Also, new sources of income should be tapped. For example, the so-called special accounts set up by various ministries such as the agriculture development account, the industrial development account, and the economic development account should be expanded and should be more widely used to develop nonformal educational programs. Another funding source would be the many foreign voluntary agencies operating in Korea under the name of *Korean Association of Voluntary Agencies.* There are seventy-seven such agencies. These voluntary organizations, concerned as they are with education in Korea, could shift their present program emphasis to launching and demonstrating new types of nonformal education.

As we have seen over the past decade, there has been a psychological reconditioning of the Korean people to accept the programs offered by nonformal educational agencies. However, the effort in this direction needs to be constantly reenforced so that training, both in the technical and sociocultural domains, can keep up with technological and social change. To provide this continued reenforcement, special incentives may have to be introduced. These incentives may be in the form of making the programs legitimate and giving rewards for work well done. Providing licenses, special bonuses, government citation and/or offering a salary while trainees are enrolled in the program are additional incentives to induce a high level of participation.

It is premature to make definitive claims for the effectiveness of many of the nonformal education programs. However, the evidence that we have in Korea suggests that programs are no less effective than formal educational programs for training personnel in the acquisition of certain skills and knowledge. We have also found that instructional innovations, such as programmed learning, "Rural Guidance Works for the Air," the mobile unit program, and special correspondence courses have been introduced into Korea through nonformal education. This suggests that Korean people are no less receptive to instructional innovation through nonformal education than through formal education. It is possible that nonformal education programs may have much greater potential to introduce experimental instructional methods than formal educational programs since the former are more diversified in nature, more flexible and less rigid than the latter.

In view of this potential, it is highly advisable not only to expand the existing programs of nonformal education, but to keep up the innovative spirit by introducing new instructional systems such as multimedia instruction, educational television, closed-circuit television, and Brunerian-oriented programs stressing the development of creative and cognitive processes in the individual.

Along with these instructional innovations, there should be a systematic and well-coordinated effort to evaluate the effectiveness of various programs in accordance with principles of accountability. This evaluation can also provide feedback to the people responsible for program operation so that appropriate improvements may be made as needed.

There is a great proliferation of programs and activities within the nonformal education domain. There is also a great deal of overlap between nonformal and formal education programs. Some activities that properly belong to formal education are duplicated by nonformal and vice versa. And there are gaps in the services offered. These conditions make it difficult for decision-makers to provide intelligent remedies. In view of this, it is recommended that a plan be devised to coordinate all the programs of nonformal education and to provide communication lines with formal education. This type of coordination may be based on the model devised by the Office of Rural Development in Korea, which brought together the work of vocational agricultural high schools and rural agricultural guidance programs.

We are at a critical juncture in Korean education development. While there is a great deal of ferment about education in general, very little attention has been given to nonformal education in particular. Before it is too late, we need to initiate a number of studies whose results may be used by educators for intelligent allocation of resources.

Notes

1. F. Harbison, "Developing the Potential of Non-Formal Education," SEADAG, 1970, p. 13 (mimeo).

2. *An Inventory of Non-Formal Education in Korea and the Working Paper on Non-Formal Education,* This survey covers all of the principal existing programs and illustrates their purposes and clienteles served, etc.

3. Manpower Development Research Institute, *The Profitability of Investment in Manpower Development in Korea* (Ministry of Science and Technology, Seoul, Korea, 1971), p. 153.

4. Both groups — those who received the vocational training and those who did not — were graduates of middle school. Their rate of return is the ratio of wages earned to total cost of training.

5. J.H. Lee, "Economic Value of Korean Farmers' Education: Their Productivity and Earnings," unpublished Master's Thesis, Cornell University, 1969.

6. At this point, it is very difficult to establish that participation in this type of agricultural activity increases agricultural productivities. The same study indicates that there is also high correlation between amount of formal education and productivity.

7. *A Case Study of Farmer Training Centers of the ORD* has been carried out by the writer and staff of CERI at the request of Dr. Philip Coombs,

vice-president of ICED. For this case study, two of ten provincial farmer-training centers and 5 of 111 city and county farmer-training centers were sampled.

8. While the subject of advantage and disadvantage of nonformal education is not within the scope of this chapter, it is too compelling to resist. Many factors make such programs easier to implement but harder to evaluate; hence difficult to attract institutional authorities with funds. Timing and scheduling are much easier. Learner motivation is frequently well established. Formative evaluation is essential but terminal summative efforts almost impossible. Many school regulations are avoided since regular school populations are seldom involved. Last, but not least, utility is of paramount importance, yet only inputs are measurable; outputs are diffused into many social benefits.

9. As estimated by the vocational training section of Office of Labor Affairs, Republic of Korea.

10. See Population Council's report made by George Worth.

11. Ibid.

15 The "Shadow School System" in Peru

ROLLAND G. PAULSTON

Peru's formal, articulated school system begins in preschool, or *transición,* and culminates in the universities. This chapter examines Peru's nonformal, or second school system — the varied assortment of short-term, skills-oriented educational programs offered by industry, by the military, by the government, or by voluntary organizations. They are, for example, not planned or coordinated in any systematic or comprehensive manner. Little knowledge exists about their number and functions, nor do we know much about their total contribution to the development of human resources needed for modernization. We do know, however, that because of growing demand for new skills and the serious limitation and deficiencies of formal education, Peruvian nonformal education activities play an increasingly vital role in bringing about the requisite new behavioral capabilities — i.e., work skills, communication skills, as well as new attitudes and understandings, essential for modernization and nation-building. The rationale for nonformal educational programs in poor countries is both compensatory and complimentary in nature. It seeks, as Coombs recently observed, the dual objectives of supplementing the formal school system and compensating as much as possible for its inadequacies.

A developing country . . . must use nonformal education not only to build upon the previous formal education of a small fraction of its citizens, but more especially to raise the economics and social level of the vast majority of its citizens who never acquired literacy. The priority for such countries at present must go to *work-oriented* literacy and training programmes, which have an early impact on individual and national economic development.[1]

Peru provides an excellent example of a developing country where the combination of rapid, if uneven, modernization combined with an inflexible archaic formal school system has given rise to an impressive array of nonformal educational programs. Before we examine a number of the most representative of these programs, it may be helpful to first briefly summarize some of the major obstacles to qualitative and substantive change in the orientation, organization, and content of the formal school system.

Perhaps the most enduring obstacle of the creation of a more developmently

185

oriented formal education is the continuation of the "aristocratic" model in society and in the schools. This is a basic problem throughout much of the ex-colonial Third World where imported school models such as the lycée and grammar school once served a small elite. With independence, the democratic revolution, and the explosion of demand for schooling, these "gentle-man-forming" institutions – the lycées, the grammar schools, etc. – once attended only by children of the upper classes, have become, without major changes in curriculum and orientation, schools for the masses. Predictably, one result, as a Brazilian sociologist has put it, has been that the "democratization of education in his country has meant spreading throughout Brazilian society the aristocratic school of the past."[2] In Peru, as in all of Latin America except Cuba, the traditional disdain for "practical work," for problem-solving, for any activity involving manual labor, is inculcated and reinforced by the high culture-oriented curriculum and teachers, and by the archaic value system undergirding formal schooling. Lipset claims that the core problem obstructing change in Latin American formal educational systems is simply that:

Education has remained impermeable to economic, social and political revivalist influences. Misunderstanding and contempt of popular education has subsisted, and the excessive prestige enjoyed by the humanistic culture of the old upper class as patrons of a corresponding type of anti-experimental book-learning has been perpetuated. The school continues to be an isolated institution divorced from man's conditions of existence and specializing in the transmission of bookish techniques, potted knowledge and routine intellectual concepts. Formal education, in a word, is guarded from any impact that would adjust it to the constructive social functions which it should properly carry out in a society aiming at homogeneity and expansion.[3]

In Peru, moreover, this problem has been greatly compounded by the prevalent beliefs that the country's three major cultural groups, i.e., the "Indian," the "civilized Indian," and the "nonIndian," form a value hierarchy with indigenous culture at the bottom and the Hispanic or national culture at the top. As race is largely defined in cultural terms, Peruvians increasingly seek to change their race, or *raza*, by changing their culture – and formal schooling is the traditional means to this end. All formal schooling is powerfully shaped by the near-universal desire to learn the behaviors associated with the "aristocratic" model which represents an idealization of the quintessence of non-Indian or European culture. Thus the schools in large measure become the accepted vehicle for culture change and for certifying students attempting to move up the cultural hierarchy. The disdain for physical work, for practical knowledge, and the lack of concern for community inculcated in students striving for "cultural mobility" are clearly dysfunctional in terms of national development.

In marked contrast, nonformal educational programs are offered to youth and adults for the most part as a short-term basis and seek to teach new skills and behavioral capabilities. They are characteristically achievement-oriented in that new learning is frequently quickly rewarded by a wage increase, a promotion, or some other form of tangible gain. Program content is often dictated by the needs of workers, farmers, and adults to learn new skills and information or to upgrade existing competencies. Such programs, in sharp contrast to formal schools, are innovative, flexible, and responsive to the needs of employers, workers, and development in general.

Something of the content and utility of nonformal education programs in Peru might be best demonstrated by looking at a number of specific case studies in industry, in the military, in unions, and in a variety of other public and private settings.

Education and Industry

Education and training programs in Peruvian industry demonstrate how nonformal education can help to compensate for the inadequancies of the formal educational system, in this case, at the public secondary technical schools.[4] These schools prepare students at the skilled-worker or low- to middle-level technician categories, and are plagued by a number of serious problems. Out of a total of 473 technical schools, the 134 industrial training schools alone, for example, graduated over thirty-thousand students in 1969. Yet is is estimated that less than 11 percent of these students take employment in their areas of preparation. Factors contributing to this situation are several. The economy and job market are restricted by the fact that considerably less than 40 percent of Peru's population have an annual cash income permitting them to purchase goods and services. Moreover, industry and industrial employment is almost exclusively found in the coastal region (some 79 percent), and of this over three-fourths is concentrated in Lima. Due to lack of suitable training and education — over 83 percent of manufacturing industry workers have not completed primary school — the work force is characterized by low-skill levels and inefficiency. The serious oversupply of unskilled labor vis-a-vis a continuing shortage of skilled workers is indicated in table 15-1.

Table 15-1. Supply and Demand for Industrial Manpower in 1965

Work Category	% Needed	% Employed
Professional	5	1.5
Technicians	10	2.5
Executives and clerical	18	16.0
Skilled workers	33	18.0
Semiskilled workers	29	26.0
Unskilled workers	5	36.0
	100	100.0

Source: SENATI, 1966.

Periodic attempts to improve formal instruction in the secondary technical schools have met with little or no success. Facilities and equipment are scarce or absent. The curriculum and staff manifest a cultural orientation quite in keeping with the desires of many students to use technical school training as a base to move into more prestigious nonmanual employment, especially in the professions. Industrial employers complain that job applicants from these schools are poorly prepared in language and mathematics, that they are ignorant of industrial processes and concepts, and that they have, as secondary school graduates, an inflated opinion of their worth and status.

In response to a growing demand for skilled labor, Peruvian industrialists banded together in 1961 to create their own nonformal education subsystem called SENATI.[5] Following the example of several other Latin American countries, SENATI is a semiprivate organization which seeks "to contribute to human, social, and economic promotion and welfare of workers in manufacturing industry through technical training of apprentices and advanced instruction for the workers themselves."

By taking a practical approach to a serious national problem, SENATI's highly innovative, practical approach is unique among Peruvian organizations. Moreover SENATI is not subsidized by the government but solely supported by a 1 percent payroll tax collected from approximately two thousand Peruvian industrial firms employing fifteen or more workers. A large number of European nations as well as international organizations, such as UNESCO, ILO, and others, have donated equipment, technical assistance, scholarships, and funds for the main training center near Lima and the proposed regional center at Chiclayo in the north and Arequipa in the south.[6]

In marked contrast with technical education programs in the formal school system, the educational offerings at SENATI have a marked practical bias and are closely aligned with existing industrial technological levels and needs. All member firms (i.e. those paying the payroll tax) are entitled to a systematic study of their skilled manpower training needs. If so requested, SENATI personnel will first study an employer's total work needs, assess and classify the various skills required, and then determine existing skills in his work force. Following this diagnostic appraisal, a plan is offered in which the skill needs of each worker are evaluated and proposals are offered as to how needed training might be best provided at the employer's plant or at the National Center. All employees who enroll for apprenticeship training at the SENATI center are required, in addition, to spend half-time studying general educational subjects. Through agreement with the Ministry of Education, these studies may be credited toward completion of formal primary or secondary school programs. SENATI also offers apprenticeship training to boys between 14 and 18 years of age who are sponsored by employers in the manufacturing industry and who pay a half-wage during the twelve-month course.

Something of the quantitative and qualitative contributions of SENATI's three training programs are indicated in the following inventory of accomplishments.

1. In the on-the-job worker and supervisor improvement program, over ten thousand persons had received technical training by early 1969. Regardless of the technical specialty studied, these students spent one-half of their class time in general education courses.

2. In the general education program, basic studies were offered in Spanish, mathematics, social sciences, drafting, blueprint reading, and basic physical sciences. In cooperation with the Ministry of Education, many of these courses are taught by public school teachers in ministry schools. Other classes may be taught by SENATI teachers at industrial plants or at the National Center. There seems to be fairly general agreement that these courses have had a positive effect on work efficiency, in developing a better understanding of worker's rights and duties, and on enlarging employee capacity for learning and adapting to new developments. The general education program has reached more than ten thousand participants. Of this impressive total, 65 percent studying at the primary level and 35 percent at the secondary level have passed their examinations and received their school certificates.

3. The apprenticeship program began in 1966 and the first class of 377 completed the preapprenticeship and basic cycles (i.e., three and nine months respectively) in 1967; the second and third classes of 530 and 500 respectively, in September of 1968 and 1969. In this as in all SENATI programs much effort is devoted to inculcating positive work habits as well as high levels of competence in industrial skills. A variety of excellent teaching materials are provided free of charge as are cafeteria meals, bus service, and other student amenities. Instruction is of a very high level and apprentices are well prepared to enter a variety of specialized six-month programs (i.e., in machine operation, watch repair, welding, forging, auto-motor mechanics, metal work, electricity, carpentry, etc.) following the basic cycle.

Although SENATI suffers from a shortage of income and from high operating costs — per pupil costs are, for example, more than double the very high per student cost of formal technical vocational education — the program has been strikingly innovative and successful in achieving its objectives. Plans are even underway to add special courses for employers and expose them as well to new perspectives on work responsibilities, to productivity needs, and to the importance of counseling and training as means toward these typically non-Peruvian goals.

With success, SENATI has recently become increasingly well known and appreciated both in Peru and abroad. Discussions were begun in late 1969, for example, with the Minister of Education and an ILO representative to better coordinate Peru's formal and nonformal technical education problems. One distinct possibility is that the third-year public school students might transfer to SENATI for two years of intensive, modern, and efficient apprenticeship training prior to entering industry. Thus students could conceivably graduate from secondary school with a Ministry of Education certificate and still obtain the high quality training necessary for them to become a skilled, valuable worker in industry.

On the international level, SENATI continues to receive encouraging support. Moreover, studies by the Organization of American States are currently underway to examine the possibility of converting SENATI to a truly intercontinental institution where technical school instructors from other Latin American countries could study, specialize, and, in general, benefit from the SENATI program.

Education in the Military

Where SENATI primarily serves a *compensatory* function with regard to formal schooling, nonformal education and training programs in the Peruvian military are in large part directed at the individuals who have been beyond the reach of the formal schools.[7] Since about 1962, the Peruvian military, with persistent U.S. urging and assistance, has created a wide variety of educational programs essentially for Indian and *cholo* conscripts. These programs, in large part aimed at imparting skills and knowledge to be used after completion of military service, also seek to raise literacy and basic education levels, to teach nonmilitary vocational skills, and to further national identification, political socialization, and cultural assimilation.

The Peruvian armed forces, although small in size (the thirty thousand man army is far larger than either the navy or air force), has traditionally been deeply involved in national politics. More often than not, the military have ruled the country and have been, until recently, staunch defenders of the *status quo*. With increased members of *non-blanco* officers moving up the ranks and into positions of authority, however, the military has recently taken a more progressive attitude toward the need for fundamental socio-economic reforms and toward the proper role of the military in gaining these objectives. One manifestation of this encouraging trend has been the increasing concern of the military to contribute more directly to national development; and military educational programs and other "civic action" programs should be seen in this light.

In Peru, military service is, in theory, obligatory for all males between 18 and 50. Secondary school and college students, however, are exempt, as they receive compulsory military training at school. As a result, conscripts come largely from the lower classes of the urban population and from the rural *campesino* peasant groups. Conscripts from these marginal social groups are, by and large, illiterate, unskilled, and without much patriotic feeling. They represent, moreover, less than 5 percent of all Peruvian youth supposedly eligible for the two-year compulsory military service.

Because between 60 and 80 percent of the five to six thousand recruits inducted yearly are illiterate — many speak only Quechua or Aymara — the literacy program to teach reading, writing, and speaking in Spanish is started early and given top priority. In 1961 alone, for example, the army spent over $227,000 to provide teachers, facilities, classrooms, etc., for this program.

The army's vocational training program, in contrast, is designed to teach various civilian trades to selected conscripts during their final three months of military service. Five centers — one each at Lima, Cuzco, Piura, Arequipa, and Iquitos — offer instruction in some twelve different trades including electricity, plumbing, welding, weaving, automotive repair, blacksmithing, furniture upholstering, construction, etc. At the same time, soldier-students also receive instruction in labor law and management, in civic and community relations, and in small business management. A public relations unit attached to each center is charged with liaison to industry, and helps to place students following graduation. Efforts are also made to encourage graduates to join government resettlement schemes located along highway developments in the tropical eastern Andean area. The cost of this program to the government in 1964 exceeded $563,000. In addition, USAID contributed services and equipment valued at about $400,000 between 1962 and 1964. By the end of 1966, over nine thousand young men had completed the course and entered the economy as semiskilled workers. Many of these graduates are self-employed and own their own modest shops. Efforts are underway to double this output, and also to regionalize course content when possible so as to make training more useful and relevant to local needs and employment possibilities.

A third related army training program in agriculture is offered to selected conscripts during their last six months of military service. Instruction covers operation and maintenance of farm equipment, animal husbandry including work with poultry and cattle, the preparation of dairy and meat products, crop-control practices, and the growing of fruits and vegetables. Training focuses on small-farm operation but includes instruction in the creation and operation of farm cooperatives as well. Training is offered to approximately 200 students annually at a number of military farms on the coast and in the *sierra*. As in the vocational training programs, a limited number of lower-class civilian youths are also enrolled in these programs that slant preparation toward self-employment. In 1965, the first year of operation, the army spent over $186,000 on the program for operating staff, faculty, and facilities, and both Israel and the United States contributed technical assistance and equipment.

A fourth (discontinued) program sought to prepare conscripts upon discharge to teach civilian adult illiterates. Promising conscripts chosen on the basis of "character, intelligence, teaching aptitude, and leadership potential" received a one-month teacher-training course while still in the army. Upon discharge, each instructor was given a literacy-teaching kit, i.e., ten reading texts, ten flash-card sets, and ten course-completion certificates. Each instructor was required to pledge that he would teach at least ten people in his village to read and write Spanish within one year. Results of this program defy measurement, but seem to have been insignificant when one considers the size of Peru's illiterate population

— i.e., over four million youths and adults. Between 1964 and 1966, 6371 conscripts were prepared as literacy teachers. Once discharged, all contact with this group ended, and the results of their work is unknown.

An overall evaluation of nonformal educational activities in the military might conclude that they are expensive, strongly influenced by U.S. assistance, and that they show more promise than performance. The need to teach literacy and vocational skills to working class and *campesino* conscripts is certainly apparent, but results are difficult to measure.

Perhaps the most valuable contribution of educational programs in the military, as in SENATI, are to give disadvantaged working class youth new skills in a straightforward, practical manner that does little to imbue them with the "aristocratic" value model that continues to dominate rural schooling and is incompatible with manual and practical work.

Education in Unions

In contrast to SENATI and military training activities, nonformal educational programs for adults in trade unions do not supplement or compensate offerings of formal schools. Rather, they are offered along with labor-sponsored social projects in housing, in cooperatives, in credit, and other fields to strengthen the trade union movement. In concert with U.S. labor interest, Peruvian trade unions since 1963 have sought to prepare union members to (1) represent the organized economic and social interests of workers; (2) to manage union affairs and activities; and (3) to further responsible relationships with both management and the government in collective-bargaining activities and national development programs.

Beginning in 1962, the American Institute for Free Labor Development, or AIFLD (AFL/CIO), contracted with the Ministry of Labor to assist Peru's half million trade unionists in the nationwide Peruvian Confederation of Workers (CTP). Courses have been offered on a regular basis since that time at the Peruvian Labor Studies Center in Lima and in the United States. About 300 trade unionists annually participate in full-time courses at the center, the stated purpose of which is "to prepare trade union leaders to direct their organization democratically along lines of enlightened self-interest and to participate responsibly with government and industry in the country s'development."[8]

From 1963 through 1968, emphasis has been on direct leadership training of union leaders and workers and on assisting middle-income worker housing. Beginning in 1969, the program shifted to creating educational facilities and programs in major urban, mining, and industrialized farming (i.e., sugar and cotton) unions, and to training rural *campesino* leaders. Additional emphasis has been placed on training blue-collar rather than white-collar workers and on building housing for lower- rather than middle-income union members. In addition, the Lima Center's training programs have been duplicated in a new

Arequipa branch with the twofold objective of "strengthening the existing weak unions and reducing the Communist influence."[9] During late 1967 and early 1968, 550 workers were trained at the new Arequipa branch center, while in Lima 8,777 members completed training programs offered from 1963 to 1968. During 1969/70, Peruvian unions are scheduled to take full charge of all night courses and train some 2,000 workers, while AIFLD will train more specialized instructors.

Peru's "shadow-school system" also includes a plethora of educational programs in governmental ministries that defy description in their range and diversity. The Ministry of Agriculture sponsors a variety of farm extension and land reform courses; the Ministry of Labor and Communities offers periodic instruction in literacy, in creating cooperatives, in community development techniques, as well as in survey research methodology and data processing. The Air and Navy Ministries mount a number of training programs that, although less ambitious than the army's educational efforts, are impressive nevertheless. The Ministry of Education also offers courses in literacy, adult, and community education outside the formal school system. Unfortunately, little is known even by educational planners — about these myriad short training courses that spring up to meet specific manpower needs and as quickly fade away.

The human resource development situation in contemporary Peru is such, however, that a greater understanding of nonformal inputs and outputs is imperative. As the formal system becomes increasingly dysfunctional for modernization, and as the Revolutionary Government implements ever more far-reaching reforms, the nonformal system must, as Coombs puts it, "carry the extra burden." It must prepare *campesinos* for rural land reform, industrial workers for cooperative management of the large costal sugar and cotton plantations, for educational reforms, etc. And even more difficult, it must by deed and example demostrate that for a country seeking rapid development, the "aristocratic" model is inferior to the "achievement" model, an awareness that is, unfortunately, only faintly implicit in the deeds and pronouncements of the current nationalistic revolutionaries. To do all this and more, nonformal education must be given better resources, better coordination with formal programs, and a large measure of critical and systematic examination. If it is to function more efficiently, nonformal education must be better understood not only in Peru, but wherever the phenomenon occurs. In sum:

Intensified research is urgently needed to develop appropriate planning and evaluation techniques for nonformal education. All countries will be well advised to maintain a running inventory of such activities and to create mechanisms for assessing, planning, and harmonizing their far-flung nonformal education programmers.[10]

Unfortunately, this vital research need has yet to be understood in revolutionary Peru or anywhere else, for that matter.

Notes

1. P.H. Coombs, *The World Education Crisis – A Systems Analysis* (Paris: UNESCO, 1967), p. 178.

2. F. Fernandes, "Pattern and Rate of Development in Latin America," in *Social Aspects of Economic Development in Latin America,* Vol. 1, De Vries and Echavarria, eds. (Paris: UNESCO, 1963), pp. 1967.

3. Cited in S. Lipset and A. Solari (eds.), *Elites in Latin America* (New York: Oxford University Press, 1967), p. 19.

4. Materials used to prepare this section include: K. Beaumont. "SENATI: Peru's Answer to Shortage of Skilled Labor," *Overseas Development,* January 1968; R.L. Garrison, *A Survey of SENATI,* TCCU, 1968; SENATI *Boletin de la direccion nacional;* numerous writings of Dr. Fernando Romero, SENATI Director from 1962 to 1968.

5. *Servicio Nacional de Aprendizafe y Trabajo Industrial* (National Apprenticeship and Industrial Labor Service). Cognate nonformal training programs in other countires include: SENAI in Brazil, 1942, SENA in Columbia, 1956, and INCE in Venezuela, 1958. CNAOP in Argentina, 1944, is a related program but it has taken an academic rather than an apprenticeship bent.

6. Countries aiding the SENATI project include: Great Britain, Holland, Denmark, Switzerland, Belgium, Germany, Austria, Spain, and Japan. The United States has supplied twelve peace corps technical instructors.

7. Materials used in this section include: D. Gates, *An Exploratory Study of the Role of Armed Forces in Education,* RAC, 1968; and various USAID/PERU materials.

8. *USIS, Cooperation for Progress,* Lima, 1966, p. 7.

9. *USAID, Project Budget Submissions, FY 1970,* September, 1968, p. 85.

10. Coombs, *World Education,* p. 178.

16 National Training Schemes

FREDERICK HARBISON AND
GEORGE SELTZER

A central issue in educational human resource planning is the extent to which responsibility for the development of specific skills can be placed upon employing institutions. The planner is faced with questions such as these: What kinds of skills are best developed off the job or at the work place? Who should bear the costs of such skill training? How will the required funds be raised? What kind of organizational machinery is required to deliver the appropriate training services?

Many countries in Asia are deeply concerned about these questions. Some already have established through legislation various kinds of training programs. Others are investigating possibilities for the future. Indeed, the role of employing institutions in training and skill building is a high priority item on the agenda of national planning in almost all of the newly developing countries.

This chapter sketches briefly three approaches. The first is the Latin American type program which is now well established in Brazil, Chile, Peru, Colombia, and Venezuela and is being extended to most other countries in the area. The chapter describes the program in Colombia (SENA) which has been in operation for fourteen years. The second is the approach of the Industrial Training Act of 1964 in the United Kingdom. The third is a modification of the UK program which is being initiated in Kenya.

In all three cases training is financed through levies on employing institutions. All three aim through taxation and incentives of various kinds to place the main burden of specified training costs on the shoulders of employing institutions. All three, in effect, establish a "system of training" quite separate from and beyond the system of formal education. Each is described very briefly, and the critical problem areas in their operation are identified. A short concluding summary highlights some of the more important comparisons and contrasts.

The National Apprenticeship Service in Colombia

The National Apprenticeship Service (SENA) is the largest, the most extensive, and the best financed training organization in Colombia, and probably in all of Latin America. It organizes and operates a vast array of training programs for workers in industry, commerce, and agriculture.

195

Financial Base. SENA draws its final support from tax of 2 percent on salaries and wages paid by both public and private enterprises with capital exceeding 50,000 pesos or employing at least ten workers, and from a tax of 0.5 percent on salaries and wages paid by the central government and the territorial departments and municipalities.

Scale of Operations. By any measure, SENA is a "big operation" in Colombia. Its total projected expenditures for 1971 are close to 500 million pesos. This is a sum equivalent to about one-eighth of total public expenditures on all education, about a third of expenditures for secondary education, and a little less than half of expenditures for higher education. SENA, moreover, has an assured growth of income based upon payroll taxes.

As a semiautonomous organization within the Ministry of Labor, SENA budgets and controls its own programs and is relatively free from control or interference by other government bodies. The government ministries, and particularly the Ministry of Education, look with envy on the autonomous status and assured financial resources of SENA.

Importance. The SENA Experience is important for these reasons:

1. It has been in operation for some fourteen years and thus has accumulated great experience in training.

2. It is a strong and powerful organization with a far-flung constituency of employers, unions, government officials and politicians. Its permanent role in Colombia is assured.

3. Other newly developing countries in Africa and Asia are now planning to establish "SENA-type" organizations, and thus they can benefit from greater knowledge of, and contact with SENA.

4. SENA commands vast financial resources and dominantes middle-level training in the modern sector. The effectiveness of the use of these resources is a critical factor in national development of Colombia.

Range of Activities. SENA provides a wide range of training services in industry, commerce, and agriculture. These include classes in its own training centers (there are over 100 of these), training within enterprises, mobile training units in both rural and urban areas, and consulting assistance to enterprises. These activities are described in some detail in the SENA *Five Year Plan* (1970-74).

According to the 1971 plan, SENA will have a total of 337,000 persons in all training programs. The grand total of trainee-hours is estimated at 68,391,500. Thus the average class time in training per student is about 200 hours. A breakdown by major categories is as follows:

Formal Apprenticeship Training (3-year program)	No. of Students	Trainee Hours
Agriculture, etc.	8,324	8,579,712
Commerce	9,539	9,903,784
Industry	11,398	10,215,920
Total	29,261	28,699,416
Training of Adults		
Agriculture, etc.	20,848	3,725,028
Commerce	74,501	9,859,745
Industry	59,044	9,464,947
Rural basic training	87,795	9,896,082
Urban basic training	65,818	7,746,282
Total	308,001	39,692,084
Grand Total	337,262	68,391,500

Formal apprenticeship training thus involves about 9 percent of the trainees but nearly 42 percent of training hours, whereas rural and urban basic training, largely for the unemployed and underemployed, accounts for nearly 45 percent of trainees but only about 22 percent of total training hours.

One must remember that within these broad categories there is a very wide range of training programs, from foreman and supervisory training to short courses for semiskilled industrial, agricultural, and commercial workers. In 1971 SENA will operate more than 1000 classes. Consulting and technical assistance will be given to about 1,200 enterprises. This a a rapidly expanding activity. In 1969 it involved only 250 enterprises; by 1974 is expected to reach 2,200.

Excluding the basic-training programs for the unemployed, which have been initiated only during the last year, most of the SENA trainees are employed in public or private enterprises, but most of the actual training, probably more than 80 percent, takes place off the job in the SENA training centers.

SENA develops its program in response to requests by enterprises and government agencies. It also is guided by regional manpower surveys that it undertakes itself. Its training programs are thus constantly changing. Some of the more significant new programs are vocational training in the military and the mobile units, which provide basic training in simple skills for those seeking employment in the modern sector. In general, the entire SENA operation is geared to the needs of the modern sector. In effect, SENA is the servant of its constituency, the enterprises both public and private whose payrolls are taxed to support its activities.

Some Problem Areas. Some of the more important problem areas in the SENA operation are these:

1. **Relevancy of Training to Employment.** One criticism of SENA is that it has trained some persons for whom there were no jobs, and that it has failed to provide training where shortages exist. There is evidence that some SENA-trained workers are unable to find employment. And some employers complain that the quality of training is poor in some areas. For the most part, however, employers, unions, and workers are reasonably well satisfied with the relevance as well as the quality of the training. SENA maintains very close contacts with industry; it is under obligation to provide training to meet the specific needs of employers; it employs competent teachers and pays them well; and its human resources division makes continuous assessments of manpower requirements. But SENA does need a better system for evaluating the effectiveness of its various training programs. The experience of persons completing courses is seldom traced, and the payoffs of training in terms of increased wages and salaries are not measured. The human resources division, however, has made some "opinion surveys" of course completers, but these provide little "hard data." Perhaps the most crucial area for follow-up evaluation is the impact of the newly initiated rural and urban basic skill development programs for the unemployed.

2. **High Cost.** SENA has been criticized widely for the very high cost of many of its training programs. For example, the unit costs for apprenticeship training probably exceed those for many categories of university students. Even the shorter courses for semiskilled workers have higher per student costs (in terms of instruction hours) than many kinds of secondary education.

    The high costs of SENA training may be the result of several factors: rapid expansion of the whole program; the necessity to provide a very large number of specialized courses to meet specific training requirements; the quality of training provided; the relatively high salaries paid to instructors; the high cost of plant and equipment in very modern and elaborate training centers; and rather high costs for instructional materials and administration. Another basic reason for high costs is probably the easy availability of financial resources provided by the tax on payrolls.

    SENA is aware of the need to reduce the cost of training as well as to increase greatly the numbers of workers being trained. It has been making detailed studies of unit costs. It is attempting to reduce costs and expand services by increasing class sizes, shortening training periods, introducing new teaching technologies, and improving administration and control. It is quite possible that, with expansion during the seventies, unit costs may be reduced substantially. This is an area of high-priority concern.

3. **Coordination with the Educational System.** In reality SENA is a massive, far-reaching organized system of training which is separate from the formal system of education. In some respects the two systems are complementary,

but there is also much duplication and overlapping of their activities. For example, the vocational school, the new multipurpose secondary schools (INEM schools) and the projected junior colleges of polytechnic institutions (all under the jurisdiction of the Ministry of Education) are involved in the development of the same kind of skills as SENA. Presumably, SENA concentrates on training employed manpower, whereas the formal education system is primarily concerned with preemployment education and training, but the lines of demarcation are not at all clear.

Many of the established ministries, particularly education, would like to tap SENA's financial resources to help finance some of the activities of the junior colleges and the multilateral secondary schools. Some have suggested that SENA funds should be used for training outside of the modern sector. Up to now, however, SENA has resisted all attempts to share its payroll tax income with other organizations. It has maintained its exclusive prerogative to manage and spend all of its own resources.

The great danger is that the new secondary and polytechnics will duplicate the facilities, machinery and even teaching personnel of SENA. There is much talk about joint use of facilities and teaching personnel as well as coordination of activities, but concrete programs for effective integration at the local level are at best only in the initial stage of development. Here is an area where objective investigation and hard-headed negotiations are urgently needed.

It is generally agreed that SENA needs to develop a better system of measuring the effectiveness of its programs, particularly by following or "tracing" the work and earnings experience of those who have completed the various programs. In a broader perspective, there is need for rationalization and much better integration between SENA and the formal education system which at the moment itself is undergoing great change. There is great concern in Colombia about this problem, and the time is ripe for more objective investigation in depth.

A final observation may be in order. During the last decade SENA has received technical assistance from several international agencies and a great many advanced countries. It has had virtually no assistance from, or contact with, the United States. Yet in terms of effectiveness of training programs for its constituency, SENA probably has a better record of operation than that of U.S. programs, such as MDTA, Job Corps, Neighborhood Youth Coprs, and other manpower development projects. The SENA experience is certainly more relevant to the problems of other developing countries than is the experience of the United States. It would be appropriate, therefore, to explore some areas of collaboration and partnership between SENA and other countries in Asia and Africa which are in the process of establishing employer-financed training systems.

The United Kingdom: Industrial Training Act, 1964

Purposes. The Industrial Training Act of 1964 sets out a comprehensive public policy for skill acquisition in the United Kingdom. Its objectives are:

1. To ensure an adequate supply of qualified employees
2. To improve the quality of training
3. To distribute more equitably the costs of training among employers

Basic View. The act is predicated upon the view that employers acting within industrial groupings are the key to the formulation of training needs and the provision of training programs. It does not impose a direct obligation to train; rather, it provides the basis for financial penalties and incentives to encourage employers to undertake, expand, or improve training programs.

Industry-by-Industry Approach. The act takes an industry-by-industry approach. Its implementation is centered in the Industrial Training Boards established by the secretary of state for manpower. The respective boards are vested with the obligation to impose periodic levies (taxes) and the task of making training grants (rebates). The levies, when approved by the secretary of state, have the force of a "statutory instrument" and provide the bulk of funds deployed by the act. The grants, also subject to the approval of the secretary, provide the mechanism for industry-wide training standards. The basic thrust of the act is to center the impetus and locus for training decisions within industry groups rather than leaving these to the individual firm.

Central Training Council. The act provides for a central training council to serve in an advisory capacity to the secretary of state for manpower. The council's membership is broadly based and is made up of employers, trade unionists, representatives from nationalized industries, chairmen of industrial training boards, educationists, and others with a special interest in industrial training. The council's role is clearly advisory. It provides an overview and educational function through its examination of training issues. Its memoranda have drawn attention to training guidelines, the training of trainers, release time as a necessary component, commercial and clerical training, programmed instruction, management development, computer staff, training standards for common occupations, etc.

The Industrial Training Boards. By the end of March, 1970, the secretary of state had designated twenty-eight industrial training boards. These were estimated to cover some 15 million employees or between 85 and 90 percent of those to whom the act is potentially applicable. The act is not confined to manufacturing, but also includes agriculture, wholesale-retail trade, and other services.

The boards vary widely in the homogeneity of their constituency (i.e., in terms of product market, occupational mix, mechanization, etc.) and the number of firms and employees within their scope. Thus, for example, in 1970 the Carpet Board included 281 establishments with 45,000 employees, whereas the Engineering Board covered 27,800 establishments with more than 3,500,000 employees. Indeed, the Engineering Board accounted for more than 20 percent of employment covered by all twenty-eight boards.

The majority of each board is made up by equal numbers of employer and trade union representatives. A number of members drawn from education constitute the remainder of the membership. The act does not stipulate the precise membership size or the industrial scope of a board. These are determined by the secretary of state. General board policies are voted upon by its entire membership. However, only employer and union representatives vote on issues pertaining to levies.

Board Initiative and Industrial Self-Government. Once established, the Boards — as is intended — have the initiative. The terms and conditions of levies and grants, however, are subject to approval by the secretary of state. Morever, should a board fail to act or submit satisfactory proposals within a reasonable period, the secretary has the authority to dissolve and create a new one. This power is not intended to be utilized in a coercive manner but is in reserve as an ultimate sanction. Collaboration, negotiation, and consensus between government and industry sum up the spirit of the act. A large measure of differentiated, industrial self-regulation is the chosen instrument in the United Kingdom for determining training needs, formulating programs, and providing the financing.

Board Levies. Accordingly, considerable variation in levy base and rate, on the one hand, and grant basis and amount, on the other, is manifest from Board to Board. The initial five years have been characterized by cautious steps and experimentation in these matters.

Boards typically (twenty-two of twenty-six making levies at the end of 1969) use a percentage of total payroll as the base for levy. Some use a per capita assessment; a few, Construction and Civil Air Transport, for example, have switched from one base to the other. In the fiscal year ending March 1969, the percentage of levy ranged from 0.035 in Electricity Supply to 2.5 in Engineering; the Iron and Steel Board imposed the highest per capita assessment at £ 23 10s.

Increasingly, boards have provided exclusion from levy for very small employers and have evolved in the direction of multirate structures to take account of interfirm variations in size, degree of skilled labor utilization, extent of process integration, end-product, etc. Moreover, the levy rates within industries reflect upward and downward variation from one assessment period to the next and indicate a tendency to "fine tuning" in terms of the total funds to be raised as well as the share to be paid by each firm. The boards have been careful not to build large reserves.

For the fiscal year ending March 31, 1969, the boards collected about £ 130 million in levies. This approximated the outlays for training grants to employers. About another £ 10 million was disbursed by the Boards – almost £ 4 million for administrative costs and more than £ 6 million for advisory and direct training services. While the system operated in a deficit position during that period, many individual Boards recorded surpluses. The excess of expenditures over receipts was financed by charges against funds raised in previous years, by charges on future receipts, and by government grants or loans.

Government Grants to Boards. The act allows the secretary of state to make grants or loans to boards up to a limit of £ 50 million. From 1964 to March 31, 1970, the Department of Employment expended a total of £ 12.3 million under this provision. The levies by the boards, however, are expected to – and do – cover the greater proportion of their expenses; the government grants are designed to facilitate initial organization and to encourage selected board activities. The following types of grants are indicative: 100 percent reimbursement of administrative expenses incurred during a board's initial twelve months; 50 percent reimbursement of the training of training officers and instructors during the first eighteen months of a board's establishment, and 25 percent of such outlays thereafter during the first three years of the board's existence; partial support (i.e., subject to negotiation) for industrial training in selected sandwich courses; 25 percent running expenses (exclusive of trainee wages) for additional off-the-job training places and annual per capita grants (£ 100) for each new on-the-job trainee; etc. The government grant schemes are not static; in the future they may give less attention to board start-up time and direct more to selected issues affecting the numbers, quality, occupational mix, and geographic location of training.

Board Grants and Services. Diversity and evolution likewise denote the grant schemes and training recommendations of the respective Industrial Training Boards. The redistribution of training costs between firms is central in the process of grant setting. Along with this consideration, boards have reflected their concern with numbers trained and the quality of training. Boards have given particular support to apprenticeship training – especially, the need for off-the-job training, release for further education, and reduction in the years required. Increasing emphasis has been assigned to management development and training. The training needs of the full range of the occupational spectrum have been encompassed. And by March 1970 almost all of the boards (twenty-four) were making grants for the training of union shop stewards.

In addition to grant support, the boards provide various central services to their member firms. These include: training advisors to assist individual firms in their programs (more than 800 were employed by the boards in 1970), nonresidential centers for off-the-job training (e.g., engineering, ship-building, hotel and catering), residential training centers (e.g., construction, road transport, water supply), standardized training materials and procedural guides.

Evaluative Comments. Various pros and cons have surfaced regarding the working of the act. The following are indicative of the criticisms:

1. The act is faulty in concept in that its frame is an "industry" whereas individuals, occupations, and geography provide more appropriate terms of reference for training, and yet these tend to be ignored or subordinated.

2. The act provides little or no additional funds for industrial training but merely reallocates training outlays within industry. The "poaching" of trained workers by nontraining firms lacks justification.

3. The act yields a short-run time horizon. This is evidenced by the "fine-tuning" of levies and grants on a year-to-year basis.

4. The act places undue reliance upon the industrial sector for initiative in the programming of training. This is not to say that effective training can be carried on without collaboration of employers, but the leadership role is centered in Industrial Training Boards, and these are more likely to respond to current shortages and cost reallocation than to anticipate impending needs.

5. The act institutionalizes and bureaucratizes what has to be a dynamic activity. It gives emphasis to training per se as an approach to dealing with manpower needs and subordinates consideration of alternatives — e.g., job redesign, production scheduling, etc. It may encourage training for the sake of training.

On the positive side, it is noted:

1. The act has heightened awareness of the economics of training and has forced explicit consideration of training by top management. In the short run, this has vastly increased knowledge of training needs, approaches, and costs; in the long run, it may evolve into more effective manpower planning generally.

2. The act has jarred the simple "sitting by Nelly" emphasis of the past with explicit attention to off-the-job training.

3. The act has stimulated group training among smaller companies (some 500 programs).

4. The act has provided impetus for pervasive reconsideration of length of training period, content of training, training methodology, adequacy of trainers/facilities, etc.

5. The act has added awareness of the linkage between industrial training and further education (growth of "day-release," "block-release," and "sandwich" programs.

The ultimate consequences of the act are difficult to perceive at this point in view of the brevity of the period since its inception and its continuing evolution. It could, as its critics indicate, result in a highly bureaucratized set of arrangements which simply level off and redistribute costs. Or it may evolve into a system that brings into working balance the role of the industrial sector and government policy.

Kenya: Industrial Training Act, 1970

The Kenyan Industrial Training Act of 1970 is the first in Africa which establishes a comprehensive framework (i.e., beyond apprenticeship) for systematically linking the private sector with public policy for manpower training.

Initial Stage. The Kenyan Act was passed by Parliament in December and received final presidential authorization in late January 1971. It, therefore, is in the start-up phase of its implementation. Extended comment regarding its operations must necessarily be deferred.

Purposes. The act, in the form of a series of amendments to a more limited vocational training statute, stipulates the following:

1. It shall ensure an adequate supply of properly trained manpower at all levels of industry
2. It shall secure the greatest possible improvement in the quality and efficiency of vocational training
3. It shall share the cost of training as evenly as possible between firms

Employer Support. The act was forged with the active support of the Kenyan Federation of Employers. The membership of the latter operates in a context denoted by:

1. Pervasive skill shortages
2. Reported high turnover and "Piracy" of experienced employees
3. A policy for "Kenyanization" of employment

Patterned on UK Model. In Broad outline, the Kenyan approach to industrial training is closely modeled after that of the United Kingdom. Its basic frame of reference, too, is an industry-by-industry basis. Like the United Kingdom program, the Kenyan uses economic penalties/rewards and gives an employer the option of maintaining training activities or contributing to the cost of employers within his industry who meet training standards. And, as in the case of the United Kingdom, the text of the Kenyan Act does not set out specific levy/grant terms but provides organizational machinery to work these out.

Machinery. The Kenyan Act provides for the establishment of a National Industrial Training Council. The act stipulates that the council shall be comprised by a chairman and "not less" than twelve representatives drawn equally from employers, employees, and "other interests." The minister of labour appoints the council's membership and holds ultimate authority for the imposition of industry levies, and the making of training grants. The council, in turn, is authorized to establish tripartite industry training committees and to direct these to submit levy proposals. Council approval of a training committee's levy proposal is a requisite condition for its transmittal to the minister of labour. Thus, unlike the advisory role of the UK Central Training Committee, the Kenyan National Council is assigned a direct role in the levy-grant decision process with the industry training committees explicitly subordinate to it.

Further differences between the UK and Kenyan policies will undoubtedly emerge in practice. This is already indicated with respect to the development of training levies. The Kenyan policy is being implemented with explicit concern for any negative impact on the level of employment. As a result, the respective industry levies are being tailored – at least in the initial phases – upon such bases as value added, percentage of prime contracts, or percentage of physical production. Taxes on payroll – or employment – per se are to be avoided.

Concluding Comments. Kenyan manpower planners anticipate a close working relationship between specific industry training programs and various educational facilities of both a formal and nonformal nature. Thus heightened usage is expected of the National Industrial Training Centre, the Management Training and Advisory Centre, the Kenya Polytechnic, the Mombassa Technical Institute, etc.

Whether or not the Kenyan Act will make a significant contribution to trained manpower, or will get mired in the redistribution of costs between employers remains to be seen. A lack of adequate information about training needs, limited training resources, and sparse training facilities pose major problems.

Comparisons and Contrasts

The outstanding feature of the three approaches may now be summarized.

Scope of Training Activity. SENA is the most comprehensive program. It services agriculture, commerce, and the military as well as industry. It provides a wide variety of courses for unskilled and semiskilled workers as well as intensive apprenticeship programs for master craftsmen. It also provides short courses for unemployed youth and others seeking entry jobs in the economy. The UK and Kenya programs offer services to workers already employed in industry. Relatively more of the training is provided within the work place than in off-site training centers as such. SENA is administered as a nationwide enterprise. The UK and Kenya plans are directly linked to individual industries.

Financial Support. SENA is supported mainly by a 2 percent statutory tax on payrolls of all enterprises *both* public and private employing 10 or more persons. No rebates or grants are given to employers who have their own training programs. The UK and Kenya plans are based upon levies which are differentiated among industries and which may vary from year to year. They also give grants to employers operating their own programs.

The main thrust of SENA's across-the-board payroll tax is to generate extensive financial resources for broad training purposes. The emphasis of the levies in the UK and Kenya Programs is more on redistribution of training costs between employers.

Relationships to Formal Education. All three programs are managed autonomously from the formal education system. In some instances, the training provided duplicated that offered in the formal vocational schools. In all cases the impetus for policy and program, and, perhaps, effective control is centered for all practical purposes in employer and union groups rather than in ministries of education or labour.

Costs. As yet there have been no really definitive studies of unit training costs in any of the programs. There are indications that SENA's costs are excessively high, but efforts are being made to lower them through more efficient management and use of resources.

In the case of the UK sizeable and continuing administrative and service costs are being incurred by the industry training boards. It is too early to say what the costs are likely to be in Kenya.

Relation of Training to Employment. In all three cases, major emphasis is given to training workers who are already employed. The instruction provided is therfore closely related to specific jobs. As originally constituted, none of the three programs aimed to train the unemployed or those seeking employment for the first time. But, because of mounting unemployment and consequent political pressures in Colombia, SENA has recently instituted programs for out-of-work youth in both rural and urban areas. The effectiveness of these programs in reducing unemployment is doubtful. Other nations introducing national training programs might well examine this experience.

Exchange of Information on National Training Programs

Because of the rapid introduction of national training schemes in the newly developing countries, information on legislation and operating experience should be made available.

The ILO is probably the most appropriate organization to undertake the task. SENA and similar organizations in other Latin American countries are able and willing to provide information and receive study missions from other countries. National training schemes should indeed be given serious study by countries pressing forward with rural and industrial development programs.

17 A Land Grant University's Program in Appalachia

WILLIS H. GRIFFIN

For more than fifty years the Cooperative Extension Service of the University of Kentucky has provided county agricultural, home demonstration, and 4-H agents to carry out nonformal educational programs. This effort brought the results of research and knowledge from campus to farm throughout Kentucky; it identified important problems of rural Kentucky and referred them back to the teaching and research programs on campus. Through this system of integrating teaching, research and extension, the university has made its contribution to the revolution in agriculture in the United States.

During recent decades several factors have brought about a reorientation in the extension program of the university. First, an "embarrassment of riches" has caused many people to question the current appropriateness of priority traditionally given to services for productive farmers. Second, the realization has grown that a focus on agriculture is either wrong or too narrow for many areas of rural Kentucky, particularly those areas in which topography and soil fertility place limitations on the extent to which the search for a better life is to be found primarily in agriculture. Third, critical problems of urban areas have come on the scene and are crying for attention. Fourth, socially conscious and activist students and professors are calling for a university role in combating poverty and social problems wherever they may be found. Fifth, there is a growing interest in the contributions to be made through extension and nonformal education activities by segments of the university formerly concerned mainly with research and on-campus teaching. These include medicine, architecture, education, sociology, art, business administration, political science, engineering and dentistry, to name a few. Finally, faculty and students are beginning to realize that education should include carefully planned experience for students out in the community where they learn to deal with social and economic problems.

In response to these influences several steps have been taken: (1) an administrative position has been created under the president to provide university-wide coordination of extension; (2) individual colleges have named associate deans for extension and continuing education; and (3) individual colleges have initiated new efforts to serve communities in the state through extension and nonformal education activities. These factors are particularly influential in the university's involvements in Appalachia — an area comprising approximately one-fifth of the territory of the state of Kentucky.

Appalachia: An Underdeveloped Area

The Appalachian Mountains reach from the northernmost state of Maine to Georgia and Alabama in the southernmost tier of states. Much of the area has severe economic and social problems, and that portion of Appalachia which fails in Kentucky is part of one of the most economically depressed areas of the United States.

The people of this area are of European ancestry — largely English, Irish and Scottish; they are desendents of persons incarcerated in the crowded prisons of Britain during the seventeenth and eighteenth centuries — orphans, debtors, and minor criminals. They were released to come to the southern Atlantic coast of what is now the United States to work on the labor-hungry and expanding tobacco plantations. The British Parliament was happy to get rid of them. Their transportation costs were advanced by the plantation owners in the New World, and they were indentured for seven years to repay these costs. Some of these people, particularly children, were "kidnapped" by gangs and put abroad ship to travel to a strange land to take up a new life. A few of them moved up through plantation life and became owners and planters themselves. The majority ran away to the West or left plantation life when their bonds expired and became "backwoodsmen" on the eastern edges of the Appalachian mountains.

The land of eastern Kentucky into which the settlers came was rich in natural resources not fully known at the time, chiefly timber and coal. During the first half of the nineteenth century, the mountaineers earned an income by cutting timber and floating it down rivers to sawmills. Following the Civil War the need for timber and coal burgeoned. At first, land speculators from outside Kentucky came into the mountains and purchased rich timber lands from the ignorant owners for a fraction of their worth; later industrial corporation representatives came in and purchased mineral rights for small sums which provided ready but temporary cash for the mountaineers. Railroads were built into the region to take out the wealth which by 1910 was owned largely by outsiders. During periods of intensive need for timber and coal, jobs were plentiful, new villages were developed and the way of life dependent on the land was altered. After the majority of the timber was removed and when coal was in low demand, the mountaineers fell back on their own resources and on the land from which they had become alienated. Their existence came to depend on forces beyond their control and their fortunes rose and fell with the industrial fortunes of the nation.

The 1960 and 1970 censuses show a number of significant facts about the situation in Appalachia and changes that are occurring. For many decades there has been a population exodus from the area to nearby urban centers; those who moved out included the young and the more enterprising. During the ten-year period ending in 1960 this exodus continued. The state as a whole lost 15 percent of its people between the ages of twenty and twenty-four; the Cumberland Plateau lost more than twice that number. During the same period the number of people eighty-five years or older increased 62 percent. Births in eastern Kentucky continue to be high; the 1960 census reveals that the mountain area produced nearly twice as many children as did the stable and more wealthy areas of the state. Per capita income was one-half that of the rest of the state and one-third that of the nation as a whole. Unemployment was four times the national average. The average educational level was approximately seventh grade and illiteracy was approximately 20 percent.

The 1970 census reveals a sharp decrease in the overall population decline in Kentucky Appalachia. Births declined markedly and deaths increased, but out-migration decreased enough to more than offset the other factors. Perhaps the university programs to be described in this chapter made some contribution to encouraging people to remain in eastern Kentucky during the past ten years; undoubtedly other factors, many of them economic, played a large part.

Because of a lack of educational opportunities, most of those migrating to the cities take low-paying jobs and live in slum areas among the hundreds of neighbor families who have preceded them. After a few years of earning and saving, many return to Appalachia, pulled back by family ties that are strong and by a nostalgia for their home area which life in the cities has not seriously challenged.

Although the above stretch provides only a glimpse of the history and current situation of the area the following items will serve as a general summary of conditions:

1. Communities are isolated from each other by the mountainous terrain separating populated valleys and by attitudes of independence, suspicion, and familism, making community spirit and cooperation on common problems rarities.

2. Social customs, cultural values, and psychological outlooks tend to discourage communication and contact with people outside the area.

3. Numerous factors discourage local initiative and inhibit productive efforts: a population heavy at the older and younger ends, a large percentage of untrained or untrainable persons, overdependence on extractive industries which remove the natural resources and return little to the area, excessive participation in welfare with unrealistic expectation of benefits, and fatalism and pessimism regarding the future.

4. Citizens in general are reluctant to take community responsibility or to exercise political power in support of change.

5. There is a prevailing shortage of those competencies and facilities necessary for development — planning and management, skills, establishments for processing raw materials locally, construction skills and equipment, and abilities and procedures for group cooperation.

Two schools of thought predominate regarding the economic and social plight of Appalachia. One suggests that the answer is to be found in bringing industry into the area to provide the economic base for development. The other relies on helping people to leave and find their fortune elsewhere. Regardless of the strategies employed to bring change and progress, one does not need to emphasize the challenge of the area to both formal and nonformal education.

The Eastern Kentucky Resource Development Project

The land grant model of higher education is among the better known innovations in American higher education. It has made a unique contribution to the development of agriculture and rural life through an integration of teaching, research, and extension. But changes are currently occurring, particularly in the extension services of land grant institutions, as higher education is motivated to reorient its efforts to meet social problems other than those found on farms. This reorientation is evident in the University of Kentucky contribution to development in Appalachia through extension and nonformal education programs.

This survey of efforts begins with the Eastern Kentucky Resource Development Project initiated in 1961; it characterizes the reorientation of the Cooperative Extension Services of the University's College of Agriculture. The 1968 report of this project reviewed the discouraging Appalachian situation and then stated:

"On the other hand a small group of leaders, both within Eastern Kentucky and at the University of Kentucky, recognized a potential for social and economic development of the area. There were natural resources and human resources—both underdeveloped. There were educational, financial, social, and political institutions which could be caused to function more effectively for progress within the area. Also, there were possible new organizational and programming arrangements through which the people might move faster and more directly toward solving their common problems with programs of overall development. It was upon the basis of such hypothetical concepts that the EKRDP was born.

The objectives and methods stated for the project indicate the extent to which this effort differed from, and went beyond, the traditional services of the county agricultural agent and the home demonstration agent. The objectives and methods were to:

1. Utilize the skills of a coordinated team of specialists employed by the University of Kentucky and located in the area
2. Search out and develop pockets of opportunity for development within the thirty-county depressed area
3. Stimulate local citizen groups and agency workers to participate in the development process

4. Enlist the cooperation of other agencies and organizations interested in and/or operating in the area

5. Involve the appropriate technical competencies of the total university

6. Develop a modified Cooperative Extension Service program to complement the EKRDP

7. Test methods in resource development which may be useful in establishing state and national policies pertaining to depressed areas

8. Make use of a state advisory committee broadly representative of (the colleges and departments of) the University of Kentucky

A selection of the accomplishments of this project will serve to indicate the kinds and extent of nonformal education methods and activities used:

1. Seminars were organized by specialists in business management involving more than five hundred businessmen in five trading centers. The seminars were structured around problems identified in discussions with the managers of business practices. In addition to a focus on specific problems, the seminars attempted to change attitudes such as the prevailing one that the appearance of a business should be that of unkept disarray to keep from scaring away the trade of the poor people.

2. A program was organized for the promotion of tourism in eastern Kentucky. Specialists in tourism helped to organize five tourism committees, advised on the preparation of brochures, radio and television programs, newspaper articles, and other means of promoting tourism. Training programs were organized for food service operators and other services related to tourism. Campaigns were organized to clean up and upgrade the area to make it more attractive. Nonformal education and training activities were aimed at reestablishing pride in the mountain area as well as enhancing those skills needed for successful tourism.

3. An industrial development specialist counseled existing industrial development corporations in eastern Kentucky to improve procedures for acquiring new industrial sites and bringing new industry into the area. During the period the number of such corporations grew from nine to thirty-seven. Workshops were held for development leaders, counseling was provided for local government officials on their development roles, information was provided for financial institutions on outside sources of funding for development projects, and task forces were organized to conduct informational meetings throughout the area.

4. An effort to build awareness of the needs and opportunities for vocational education was organized by a specialist in adult education. In recognition that many people lacked the education necessary to be trainable in vocational skills, basic adult education programs were organized. The communications media, talks and demostrations before civic clubs were used to promote the program. Vocational school facilities and labor-training programs more than doubled in several years of such effort.

5. A public affairs educational program was organized for the purpose of opening up and giving thoughtful consideration to the fundamental issues affecting development in eastern Kentucky. These issues included out-migration, planning and zoning, forms of local government, cultural heritage of the mountains, health and education, and many others. This program contributed to an upgraded intellectual and informational level in community dialogue on controversial issues as well as to an increased quantity of such discussion.

6. Demonstration techniques were used in a number of projects as means of building interest in various innovations. A food specialist demonstrated the preparation and use of dried milk much needed in the diet of mountain children. Methods of winterizing homes were demonstrated with a resulting crash effort to make use of government grants for such purposes. Forestry specialists demonstrated the use of local timber for handicraft products which led to the establishment of wood utilization centers.

7. Numerous committees and organizations were created across village lines for purposes of mobilizing cooperative effort to solve problems and to provide training on how community problems can be attacked through such efforts. Community pride, increased expectancies from government services, increased harmony among previously feuding families, greater initiative and cooperation were some of the results in the building of improved human resources.

8. In hard-core poverty areas not reached effectively by other programs, teams of subprofessional development workers were given special training and assigned to selected individual valley communities to carry on community development projects; these personnel were supported by the professional resources of the University of Kentucky who were called upon as needed. As illustrated in the above summary of selected activities, EKRDP made use of numerous nonformal educational devices, but the principle ones were the involvement of people from the mountain area in resource development projects and the use of local leadership personnel wherever possible. Not only were the people of the area given the opportunity of gaining knowledge and skills contributory to individual, community, and area development, but specialists from the University of Kentucky also gained new insights into the problems of the mountains and new skills in working with mountaineers. Professors from many parts of the university participated — political science, physical education, law, medicine, sociology, engineering, business and economics, pharmacy, and others.

The Mountain Program of the College of Architecture

The program of the EKRDP was an attempt to adapt the traditional extention program in agriculture and rural home improvement to the particular conditions existing in a depressed, mountain area. It involved many elements of the university as well as people and agencies in the mountain area, but it did not particularly involve regular students and the university campus. The Mountain Program of the College of Architecture, in contrast, was initiated largely by architecture students assisted and encouraged by faculty members. An informal report on the parent organization states:

The Mountain Institute, Inc. is the result of efforts through a number of years among professional students to relate their formal, technical training to the problems and challenges of East Kentucky. The objectives of participants in the Mountain Institute, Inc. are to provide ways for improving professional services in East Kentucky and other rural areas by bringing about changes in academic curricula, arranging for interprofessional and interdisciplinary involvement in on-going community development projects, and encouraging students and residents of rural areas to pursue higher education for the growth of themselves and their communities.

For several decades professional colleges of architecture have placed architecture training in the broader context of community planning, taking into account the many social and human factors that influence the kind of living and working structures architects design. In recent years a number of prominent colleges of architecture have come imbued with a social conscience and a particular concern for the application of architectural skills to the problems of living among the poor, in cities and in rural areas. Several years ago some University of Kentucky architecture students, with encouragement and assistance from faculty members, volunteered to join with similar-minded students from other universities on a summer project in Appalachia. Through other development agencies in the area, they located communities interested in improving recreation facilities for their youth. With the assistance of community leaders and young people of the communities, the architecture students designed and built community recreation centers and helped to initiate activities to use them. During this project the students had occasion to become involved in the lives of mountain people, to talk with them about community planning, and to learn of the many factors that must be taken into account in planning improvements in the physical facilities of such communities. On the other hand, they were able to contribute extensively to the understanding of community leaders and others about the possibilities of community improvement through planning.

Since these summer projects several years ago plans have matured to include this type of community experience for academic credit in the training program for architects, and plans are now under discussion to include students from other professional areas and disciplines in a continuing program of service to Appalachian and other areas of the state.

Two other projects carried out very recently will further illustrate the potentials of this nonformal education complement to formal studies.

Project One. In a particular county of eastern Kentucky a group of architecture students learned that the county judge (the chief administrative officer of a county in Kentucky) was actively interested in the problems of a small valley village. The topography of the village is such that there is no area for expansion without cutting down a piece of mountain or filling in a swampy area along the stream running through the village. The students attended village council meetings over a period of time during which this problem and others were discussed. When their interest and their area of study became known, they were gradually drawn into discussions on village planning possibilities. It became known that the state highway department was contracting with a large firm to build a nearby connection with the mountain parkway and the students suggested that the dirt and rock that would be cut away in building the road through the mountainous terrain would provide the answer to the problem of filling the swamp and enlarging the village area. They worked with the village council and representatives of the road-building firm to draw up a contract to move the material from the road site to the village. The students joined village officials in presenting the proposed contract to state highway officials in the state capitol. Unfortunately, the proposal was turned down; the reason being, it is assumed, that the county judge is of an opposing political party to the one in charge of state government at the moment. It is likely that the project will be approved in time, or one similar to it, if the political situation changes with the next election. It is obvious that the architecture students learned much from the experience, both in terms of community planning and in terms of political forces and processes. The community and its leaders benefited as well from the relationship with the students and from working together on the project plan, even though it has not yet been successfully implemented.

Project Two. In another mountain community, architecture and other university students became acquainted with several progressive residents of the area including the publisher of the local weekly newspaper and his wife, and a civic-minded coal mine operator. The publisher and his wife provided housing and hospitality for faculty members and students who spent short periods of time in the area. Eventually a faculty member was stationed in the community to supervise the voluntary community development work of student groups. Someone suggested that local school children would be interested in making films of the mountain area for use in schools, public gatherings and service clubs in other communities. The architecture students, the publisher and his wife, and the coal mine operator all cooperated in planning a project that included designing and building a simple film workshop, involving local students in learning how to make films, and in the actual production of several films on the community. From the project the school children came to understand aspects of their home community about which they had been only partially informed, came to have greater pride in their community, and learned something about the process of group cooperation to accomplish a set of objectives.

A Team Approach to Learning Community Medicine

The University of Kentucky Medical Center was initiated in 1960 with the establishment of the College of Medicine and has grown to include five colleges including medicine, nursing, and dentistry, the latest being the College of Allied Health Professions. The Medical Center was established to serve a research and training function primarily for the eastern third of the state; many students are drawn from Appalachia and return there to practice medicine. During its short history the center has taken leadership in innovation in medical education on a number of fronts. One of the most outstanding areas of innovation is found in the Department of Community Medicine, which gained national and inter-national recognition.

In recent years medical education has been pulled in two directions. One is toward greater and greater specialization and the solution of medical problems through increasingly sophisticated scientific research in the laboratory. The other is in the direction of solving the enormous health problems facing local, national, and world communities. The Department of Community Medicine has accepted the challenge of this second area and the answers it has devised include a rich input of nonformal learning experience out in the communities of Appalachia as well as in other parts of the state and in other countries. This department attempts to serve three increasingly recognized needs in the training of health professionals, whether they be pharmacists, dentists, physical therapists, nutritionists, nurses or physicians; these three needs are: acceptance of the concept of comprehensive health care, professional responsibility beyond the individual patient to include the family, the community, and the society around them, and the team approach to health service. Related to these needs is one of the overall teaching goals of the Medical Center — educating medical students for their social and community responsibilities.

The social and community orientation of the program is accomplished in several ways, but the central focus for it is provided by a community clerkship (field) experience, often carried out in Appalachian communities. It has been found that the community clerkship is more beneficial when it is carried out on a team basis, each team including students from several of the health professions. A brief description of a particular team experience will illustrate the nonformal learning techniques involved in these medical clerkships.

In this case an eastern Kentucky urban center of sixteen thousand population was chosen for the team study. This city is located in the corner of one county and spills over into two other counties, thus providing a regional setting. The team of students included a senior medical student, a postgraduate student in clinical nutrition and one in social work, a student in dental hygiene and one in physical therapy. As part of his more advanced responsibility, the team captain — the senior in medicine — made an advance three-week study of the community. As a base for this study the student was attached to the office of a local physician with whom he interacted on a daily basis as data on the community was collected. He studied the historical background of the community, its demographic characteristics, economic bases, out-migration patterns, stage of technological development, family child-raising and food practices, community organization, major institutions, existing health units and agencies, extent of community-wide cooperation on such problems as health needs, and other factors that gave him a picture of the multitude of physical, biological, social, economic, and cultural characteristics of the community. Using this data he developed a general plan for the team to use in studying the total health situation, following the World Health Organization guide for studies of local health situations.

Prior to their field experience the team members studied formally the theoretical considerations of community health, surveyed the literature, and consulted university faculty. (Many of those consulted were to backstop the team in their field experience.) The team was also given a briefing on the community by its captain, and the community medicine faculty instructed the group on the process of making a field study. Each student developed an individual plan which related to the overall community survey presented by the team captain and to his individual specialty; the plan included additional analysis of the community, carefully coordinated with the plan of other students so as not to duplicate effort and to avoid repreated contacts with the same community leader or health officer. The physical therapist focused on knowledge and attitudes towards physical therapy service of the physicians of the community; the clinical nutritionist studied obesity in high school girls; the social worker investigated the role of the medical social worker as seen by other health personnel; and the dental hygienist evaluated knowledge of her profession among high school seniors. In addition each student studied one family in detail, focusing on a particular individual in that family and his particular medical problem. Each student also did an epidemiological study of the community.

During the field clerkship the students met together each evening to share their findings and to discuss their implications. Each student has an opportunity to submit his findings to the critical analysis of other students. After one week in the community the team met again with the faculty; this was repeated near the end of the second week, and again at the end of the field experience back at the Medical Center. Each student was required to give a report of his study, integrating it with information gathered by other students, presenting it to a peer-faculty group. The presentations were videotaped for further analysis and for teaching use.

In evaluating this nonformal learning experience students pointed to such benefits as a greater understanding of the rule of different health professions, the needs for different specialties in a total community health system, the opportunity gained to see a community whole, a sense of the need for comprehensive health care, how different health services in a community relate to particular health needs, the importance for a medical practitioner to take into account social, economic, government, and other factors in his work, and skills gained in studying a community and its health needs.

Technical Assistance to Small Business

One of the activities reported above under the Eastern Kentucky Resource Development Project was supeirvsed by a professor of the College of Business and Economics and was concerned with management education for small business operators in the mountain area. His experience in working with EKRDP led to the establishment of a continuing program of technical assistance to small business which focuses on the management problems responsible for a large percentage of business failures and lack of profit in small business in eastern Kentucky. This program makes use of a particular approach to nonformal education by placing program officers throughout the state who act as change agents, backed up by resource persons from the faculty of the College of Business and Economics and other parts of the university.

"Small business" is defined by this program as including (1) small manufacturing establishments that produce a product for regional or local consumption, (2) small wholesale operations, and (3) retail operations that sell directly to consumers. Failures among small businesses are historically due to a lack of qualifications by the owner to operate a business, lack of training in management, improper pricing and disadvantageous buying practices, poor selling and promotion programs, and inadequate record systems. In the mountain areas of eastern Kentucky two problems are outstanding: poor management and scarce supply of capital. Regarding the latter point, the banks in eastern Kentucky are accustomed to dealing with the coal companies and other large enterprises, and they have developed little experience in working with small business on several assumptions:

1. That the success of small business operations is important to development in depressed areas and that the potential for their development exists in such areas as Appalachia
2. That the reasons for lack of success in small business must be understood within the total social, economic, and cultural milieu of the area in question
3. That consultants, advisors or educators intending to work with the managers of small business in underdeveloped areas must establish credibility with them, must gain access and acceptability with them, must gain access and acceptability in the community, and must work slowly and indirectly until direct assistance is openly requested
4. That links must be built between the small business and a number of local and state agencies whose support is necessary for success — banks, other businesses and industries, government agencies, etc.

Because of these factors, the change agent model has been accepted in the selection and training of the program officers placed in the various regions. The change agent sees himself as an analyst of the total situation, as an advisor who suggests alternative answers to problems, who occasionally advocates particular solutions, who innovates solutions more responsive to local conditions when needed, and who helps to link the small businessman to other agencies whose assistance and cooperation are needed. The program officer plays these roles selectively and in combination and on occasion brings in other program officers or faculty members from the university to assist. The challenge is to mix the necessary knowledge, skills, motivations and rewards appropriate for each client at a given moment. A selected number of graduate students in business management have contributed to the program and learned from participating with other staff and faculty members.

This program is judged successful in that it is assisting individual businesses to solve some of their problems; it is building among community leaders and businessmen a greater awareness of the concepts, meanings, and requisites of economic growth; it is building connections between depressed communities and agencies of the area and the state to the advantage of the communities, and it is contributing to a greater sense of reality and actual expertise regarding the problems of development in Appalachia among faculty, staff, and students at the University of Kentucky.

University Year in Action — A New Problem

The Center for Developmental Change, a university-wide unit, was established six years ago with responsibility to promote and coordinate teaching, research, publications, and training on problems of planned social change and development — domestic and international. The center has planned and initiated several projects involving Appalachia, including evaluation of anti-poverty programs in one county, demographic research on out-migration, and training of family planning workers.

Recently, in recognition of increased interest in voluntary service in American society, CDC established a committee to explore the question and recommend to the president of the university ways in which preparation for voluntary action and service could be more systematically integrated into the total university program. Soon after this committee began its work, the president of the United States announced the merger of the Peace Corps, Volunteers in Service to America, and several other nationwide volunteer movements into a single agency called ACTION. There followed an invitation to colleges and universities to submit proposals for planning grants for a program called "University Year in Action." Under this program students would spend a year in voluntary service with poverty agencies and the service would be recognized for a full year of academic credit. Another university-wide committee was established by CDC which made use of the work of the first committee and, in cooperation with formal faculty groups and academic administrators, prepared a formal proposal to ACTION.

Support for this new program has been such that it is likely to be initiated with or without funding from ACTION. The next logical step is to follow-up the several programs described above that involve students in community experience as part of their academic programs – combining formal and nonformal learning activities. University Year in Action will bring about coordination between the two modes of learning for those who choose this alternative to the traditional program of undergraduate studies.

Summary and Analysis

The above programs illustrate what can be done through nonformal education to link the formal education responsibilities of a university to the nonformal education potentials as they relate to underdeveloped areas. As indicated at the outset, this survey is not intended to picture a matured or comprehensive program. It does indicate, however, a direction and a set of purposes and expectancies that constitute one of the frontiers of higher education in the United States; perhaps ideas and possibilities are suggested for institutions of higher education in developing countries.

A number of considerations require further thought and planning:

1. To what extent and toward what ends should involvement in the solution of development problems become an expected role of higher education?

2. A number of the activities described above are financed by special foundation or government grants; can financial support for such programs be integrated into the regular budgeting of universities?

3. What kind, amount, and sequence of community experience in voluntary services and nonformal education activities are appropriate for what kind and level of students?

4. What should be the role in these activities for units of a university that do not normally become involved in community affairs; how should those potential roles relate to the desire of many units for cooperative, interdisciplinary programs?

5. In what ways should the nonformal education programs of institutions of higher education relate to those of other agencies in society?

6. How can nonformal education programs of a university be best coordinated within the institution?

7. Who should be responsible for coordinating all educational efforts for community development, those of formal agencies and the many nonformal agencies?

8. Serious consideration of these and other questions may lead to a variety of alternative and more productive contributions of education to development.

About the Contributors

C. Arnold Anderson, Professor of Education and Sociology, Comparative Education Center, University of Chicago.

Cole S. Brembeck, Director, Institute for International Studies in Education, Michigan State University.

Archibald Callaway, Institute for Commonwealth Studies, Oxford University.

Philip H. Coombs, Vice Chairman, International Council for Educational Development.

John Dettoni, Research Associate, Institute for International Studies in Education, Michigan State University.

Marvin Grandstaff, Associate Professor, Secondary Education and Curriculum, Michigan State University.

Willis H. Griffin, Director, Office for International Programs, University of Kentucky.

James F. Guyot, Associate Professor, Department of Political Science, Columbia University.

Frederick H. Harbison, Professor of Economics, Woodrow Wilson School, Princeton University.

Einar Hardin, Professor and Associate Director, Labor and Industrial Relations, Michigan State University.

John F. Hilliard, Director, Office of Education and Human Resources, Bureau of Technical Assistance, Agency for International Development, Department of State, Washington, D.C.

Alex Inkeles, Margaret Jacks Professor of Sociology and Education, School of Education, Stanford University.

Lois McKinney, Research Associate, Institute for International Studies in Education, Michigan State University.

Hyun Ki Paik, Director, Central Education Research Institute, Seoul, Korea.

Rolland G. Paulston, Professor, International and Development Education, School of Education, University of Pittsburgh.

George Seltzer, Professor of Economics and Industrial Relations, University of Minnesota.

Timothy J. Thompson, Research Associate, Institue for International Studies in Education, Michigan State University.

Frederick Waisanen, Professor of Sociology, Michigan State University.

Ted Ward, Professor, Secondary Education and Curriculum, Michigan State University.